VIRTUAL HISTORY

Virtual History examines many of the most popular historical videogames released over the last decade and explores their portrayal of history.

The book looks at the motives and perspectives of game designers and marketers, as well as the societal expectations addressed, through contingency and determinism, economics, the environment, culture, ethnicity, gender, and violence. Approaching videogames as a compelling art form that can simultaneously inform and mislead, the book considers the historical accuracy of videogames, while also exploring how they depict the underlying processes of history and highlighting their strengths as tools for understanding history. The first survey of the historical content and approach of popular videogames designed with students in mind, it argues that games can depict history and engage players with it in a useful way, encouraging the reader to consider the games they play from a different perspective.

Supported by examples and screenshots that contextualize the discussion, *Virtual History* is a useful resource for students of media and world history as well as those focusing on the portrayal of history through the medium of videogames.

A. Martin Wainwright is Professor and History Department Chair at the University of Akron, Ohio. He has authored two books on Britain and India's interactions during the nineteenth and twentieth centuries. He teaches courses on global history and the portrayal of history in videogames.

VIRTUAL HISTORY

How Videogames Portray the Past

A. Martin Wainwright

Routledge
Taylor & Francis Group

LONDON AND NEW YORK

First published 2019
by Routledge
2 Park Square, Milton Park, Abingdon, Oxon OX14 4RN

and by Routledge
52 Vanderbilt Avenue, New York, NY 10017

Routledge is an imprint of the Taylor & Francis Group, an informa business

© 2019 A. Martin Wainwright

British Library Cataloguing-in-Publication Data
A catalogue record for this book is available from the British Library

Library of Congress Cataloging-in-Publication Data
Names: Wainwright, A. Martin, author.
Title: Virtual history : how videogames portray the past / A. Martin
Wainwright.
Description: Abingdon, Oxon ; New York, NY : Routledge, 2019. |
Includes index. |
Identifiers: LCCN 2019005290 (print) | LCCN 2019009466 (ebook) |
ISBN 9781315157351 (Ebook) | ISBN 9781138069084 (hardback : alk.
paper) | ISBN 9781138069091 (pbk. : alk. paper)Subjects:
LCSH: Video games–Social aspects. | Video games–Design. | History in
popular culture.
Classification: LCC GV1469.34.S52 (ebook) | LCC GV1469.34.S52
W35 2019 (print) | DDC 794.8–dc23
LC record available at https://lccn.loc.gov/2019005290

ISBN: 978-1-138-06908-4 (hbk)
ISBN: 978-1-138-06909-1 (pbk)
ISBN: 978-1-315-15735-1 (ebk)

Typeset in Bembo
by Swales & Willis, Exeter, Devon, UK

To Elizabeth and Alexandra

CONTENTS

IMAGES AND TABLES

Images

Tables

ACKNOWLEDGMENTS

Although the ideas in this book are mine, I'm grateful to many for their help and input. The inspiration for this book emerged from my course on historical video-games, and many students, too numerous to name, shaped my thinking through their classroom presentations and lively discussions. I'm particularly grateful to Brittany Amiet, Nathaniel Bassett, Daniel Hovatter, and Thomas Weyant, former students who continued to discuss videogames and theory with me after their graduation. My thanks also go out to Collin Kuhn and Valentina Ziccardi for hours of animated dis-cussions about videogames that informed my work while paradoxically distracting me from it. The staff of Bierce Library, particularly Don Appleby, have also supported my work. Colleagues have helped greatly, especially Kevin Kern, Michael Levin, Gina Martino, Stephen Harp, and Gregory Wilson, in commenting on part or all of my manuscript. My thanks also go out to Josh Gellman and Eliott Bryant for commenting on this project and embracing it as a somewhat unusual introduction to my family. I also want to thank my nephews, William and Thomas Wainwright, for informing me regarding details of various games I discuss in this book. As ever, I greatly appreci-ate the moral support of my mother, Betty Wainwright, during this whole process, as well as my in-laws, Jim and Judy West. Most important, I'm especially grateful to my daughters, Alexandra and Elizabeth Wainwright, and my wife, Christine Wainwright, for reading and discussing my work – and for "understanding" that all my time spent playing videogames was actually "research."

Finally, I must acknowledge the contribution of my father, Arthur Wain-wright, who commented on my manuscript at the copy-editing stage, but did not live to see the book in print. An accomplished scholar and professor, he has been a constant source of valuable advice and inspiration throughout my life and career. Indeed, by introducing me to much of Western civilization during my formative years, he had a major influence over the development of my interest in history to begin with. Moreover, as a partner with me, my brother, and friends in playing historical board games when I was a teenager, he helped lay the foundation for my interest in the intersection of games and history that ultimately led to this book. I shall feel his absence keenly, but his influence in my life and career will carry on.

INTRODUCTION

History in the videogame age

Introduction

In November 2010, *Harry Potter and the Deathly Hallows: Part I*, the seventh installment of the Harry Potter film franchise, opened in theaters across much of the Western world. As expected, it was one of the best-selling movies ever, grossing $154.3 million across the United States and the United Kingdom. In the former it had the sixth-biggest, and in the latter the third-biggest, weekend opening of any movie until that date. However, it was not the best-selling entertainment title of the year, nor even the month. That record went to *Call of Duty: Black Ops*, which grossed $360 million within twenty-four hours of its release. In fact, within that day, *Black Ops* became the best-selling entertainment title ever up to that time ("Black Ops Annihilates Record"). At $50 per copy, *Black Ops* was four to five times as expensive as the *Deathly Hallows*'s first installment, so the movie sold more tickets than the game sold units during their initial releases. On the other hand, *Black Ops* takes many times longer to play than *Deathly Hallows* does to watch, so the total amount of time consumers spent with the videogame probably outweighed the amount that they spent with the film. However one interprets the data, the press noted the comparison as an indication that videogames now rivaled movies as major forms of entertainment. The age of the videogame had clearly arrived.

Less important to the press was the fact that *Black Ops* takes place in a historical context, the Cold War during the early 1960s. This venue was fairly novel. Most first-person shooters (FPSs) such as the *Call of Duty* and *Medal of Honor* series occurred either in contemporary settings or during World War II. FPSs and other action-adventure games are by far the most popular games with historical themes, but certainly not the only ones. In fact, a large number of popular commercial titles have historical settings or purport in some way to simulate aspects of history.

They include the FPSs mentioned above, third-person action-adventures such as the *Assassin's Creed* series, strategy games such as the *Sid Meier's Civilization* series, and games combining strategic and tactical elements such as the *Total War* series. All of the above franchises have sales totaling in the millions of dollars and large fan bases. Consumers of these products spend hundreds of hours a year playing them. Although no studies attempt to quantify the extent to which these games influence players' perceptions of history, they surely have some effect.

As a history professor, I know these games inform my students, because they have told me so. Whether it's learning about the Ottoman Empire in *Empire: Total War*, understanding the principles of *Blitzkrieg* through *Hearts of Iron*, or appreciating Renaissance architecture by playing *Assassin's Creed II*, students in my classes have witnessed to the importance of these games either in reinforcing their interest in history or sparking it in the first place. Moreover, their first exposure to many historical themes comes through videogames. Not surprisingly, educators and historians now recognize that historical videogames, that is, videogames that deal with historical themes, are a major and growing source of historical information to the public at large.

It is this larger public, particularly students at the senior secondary school and undergraduate university level, who are the target audience for this book. Since many students, and casual observers of history, now encounter the past through these games, and since videogames are such compelling means of discovering the past, it is worth examining how well they do it. This is not the first time that historians have asked this question of a modern medium. They have been doing it for decades with popular films. Many of the methods that scholars use to analyze cinematic portrayals of history also apply to videogames. However, games provide an extra dimension to the historical narratives of film or the written word, because games allow the player to participate in the portrayal of history, and even shape its virtual development. This level of interactivity makes videogames a particularly powerful form of entertainment, but also an important medium to address when learning about the past in more formal settings, such as classrooms and scholarly books.

As with film, however, the history that videogames portrays depends on a variety of factors, such as the decisions of the design teams, limitations of the programs, and target audience. This book examines many of the most popular historical videogames released over the last decade and assesses how well they portray history. It looks at the motives and perspectives of the game designers and marketers. It also compares the games to what historians and other scholars have written regarding the themes they cover.

While it's important to identify the extent to which videogames get the details of history correct, it's even more essential to understand how these games depict the underlying processes of history. For history is much more than names, dates, and strings of events. It is the interpretation of the significance of events and the relationship of causes and effects that make history continue to be such a dynamic and controversial discipline of study. Our understanding of the past influences our behavior in the present. For instance, a modern American president who identifies a current international crisis as similar to that of the Vietnam War in the 1960s might behave differently depending on how he or she interprets the United States' involvement in that conflict. A president who believes that fighting the Viet Cong insurgency against the South Vietnamese government was a waste of human lives and taxpayer dollars may be less willing to intervene in a similar crisis today than a president who believes that the United States could have won the war if only it had been willing to use overwhelming force. Similarly, modern politicians who believe that deficit spending ended the Great Depression are more likely to favor direct government intervention in modern economic crises than are politicians who believe that market forces would have created economic growth during the 1930s and 1940s if the government had simply left them alone. It's, therefore, easy to imagine videogames depicting the Vietnam War or the Great Depression angering one political camp or the other, depending on how they encourage players to solve the strategic and economic problems of those historical scenarios. In other words, the way a game designer interprets history plays no small role in determining how the player wins the game.

Similar examples could apply for any number of issues in the past that continue to be sensitive in the present and are the subject of videogames. How, for instance, should game designers portray the interaction of Christians and Muslims in the Middle Ages or the Renaissance? How do games deal with the momentous events that Christopher Columbus's voyage inaugurated? Historians rarely differ over what actually happened, but they do argue over what is most important to emphasize. Inasmuch as game designers make choices about what to emphasize in their creations, they work to predetermine the player's view of historical events and their likely consequences just as historians do.

How this book is organized

This book examines these issues and many more in a way that is accessible to audiences who aren't professional historians. Rather, it focuses on how professional historians and other scholars analyze the past, by introducing us to major historical themes that videogames touch on. This practice is called "historiography," and it is usually the topic that undergraduate history students dread the most. However, when we apply historiography to the study of historical videogames it is far from boring. On the contrary, it helps us understand what videogame designers get wrong, what they get right, and where they intentionally or unintentionally take sides. Videogames can be a powerful tool for understanding history, but we have to appreciate how they present it in order to make effective use of them.

In order to do so, this book begins by considering general issues that frame the portrayal of history in videogames. Chapter 1 covers the major issues that this book considers throughout, starting with what history is and how our understanding of history has changed and continues to change. It also considers the reasons that people design and market historical videogames, and the reaction of players to the history these games present. Chapter 2 focuses on the strengths and limitations inherent in games as a medium for exploring history. The requirements of computers to calculate everything, including intangibles such as cultural practices, and the simple fact that gamers may already know much of what occurred in the past, limit the ability of videogames to truly recreate history.

The remainder of the book focuses on six major themes. After raising an introductory example or issue, each chapter discusses the scholarship surrounding the theme. Attention may also focus on current issues surrounding the theme as it applies to videogames. For instance, the chapter on gender discusses the Gamergate controversy. Finally, each chapter analyzes how videogames depict (or fail to) the themes of the chapter. In some cases, doing so requires further breaking the analysis down into distinct sections dealing with sub-themes. Where necessary these sections provide further historiographical information to limit or expand the general observations made earlier in the chapter.

The first theme, discussed in Chapter 3, is contingency and determinism. This theme is the most basic philosophical issue underlying the study of history. Are humans free agents who can change history through their actions, or are they automata going through motions predestined by social, genetic, or environmental forces beyond their control? The ability to allow players to explore the counterfactual alternatives implicit in any cause-and-effect relationship makes videogames unusually powerful tools for learning history, and sets them apart from earlier media, in which the audience usually can't influence the development of the story.

Another old theme in historical scholarship is economics, the focus of Chapter 4. For more than two centuries, economists have used evidence from the past to explain how the economy works in the present and predict how it will behave in the future. This chapter follows the role of economics in history and discusses how videogames portray economic issues in their reconstructions of the past.

Environmental history, the subject of Chapter 5, is a much newer area of study. This chapter discusses the application of science to historians' understanding of what happened in the past, particularly regarding the exchange of plants, animals, and diseases across the world, and the role of the environment in shaping social and political developments. This chapter examines the extent to which videogames incorporate these processes.

Chapter 6 focuses on cultural and ethnic bias. This issue has been a major feature of historical scholarship over the past forty years. It has informed our understanding of relationships between peoples of different lands, particularly when one country dominated another. It has also helped us understand how people define their own ethnic and national allegiances. This chapter assesses the extent to which videogames are sensitive to this issue. It also deals with videogames' portrayal of religion, a particularly sensitive aspect of culture, which many producers have chosen to ignore, but others have handled in innovative ways.

Another aspect of society that historians tended to ignore until relatively recently is gender, the topic of Chapter 7. Nevertheless, it is now a significant issue in most historical scholarship. Gender, as a topic, covers much more than the history of women, which it has largely supplanted in most universities. Rather, it deals with traditionally masculine and feminine qualities and identities as products of their cultural and social settings. Gender therefore permeates all of history even when it involves only men. Similarly, videogames have come under intense scrutiny as products of predominantly masculine mindsets. This chapter examines how the resulting biases have shaped these games' depiction of history. It also discusses ways in which designers have attempted, or could attempt, to overcome such biases.

Besides gender bias, the most frequent charge levelled against videogames is that they contain violent content, which encourages similarly violent behavior among their players. Chapter 8 examines the ways in which videogames depict violence in history. In contrast to popular assumptions regarding violence, this chapter suggests that, if anything, videogames sugarcoat the brutality of the past in order to avoid offending consumers. Because a major theme of this chapter is videogames' coverage of war, it also analyzes the accuracy of videogames' depiction of combat, comparing it to what we know about the experience of soldiers in battle, their motives for fighting, and their interaction with civilian populations.

What this book covers

Just as historical videogames work under certain constraints, so does this book. Hundreds of games have some connection or reference to history and it's clearly impossible to examine them all. For instance, one can argue that games set in J. R. R. Tolkien's fantasy world of Middle Earth bear some relation to history, because they tap on Medieval European themes and cultural influences. Moreover, Tolkien's works are themselves a response to the mechanized, violent world of the early to mid-twentieth century, and their popularity among readers arises from escapist, heroic, and nostalgic impulses in mid- to late twentieth-century Western societies. Some of the most popular games on the market, among them *World of Warcraft* and the *Elder Scroll* series, have fantasy settings that tap on Medieval European themes. Even the tactical and strategic *Total War* series, which has previously stuck solely to themes set in the real world's past (albeit with the potential for counterfactual developments), has recently released two titles set in the Warhammer fantasy world. None of these worlds purports to depict the actual past, and all of them involve supernatural elements as a core feature of their universes.

If some games far removed from reality deal with the past, so do others firmly set in the present. Series such as *Tomb Raider* and *Uncharted* involve Indiana Jones-style adventures that focus on ancient artifacts and refer to historic people and past events. The central characters and action all occur in the present, but the focuses of their efforts usually refer to the past. These games can teach players a lot about history as the main characters comment on what they encounter.

Finally, some games occur in future settings, and often have a backstory set in something that refers to our past. For instance, the *Fallout* series occurs in a dystopian future but refers to a timeline that broke from ours during the Cold War. Artifacts from this historical period litter *Fallout*'s devastated landscape. The same is less true of *Civilization: Beyond Earth*, which begins with humans settling another planet after devastating Earth. Its reference to history is apparent more in how the mechanics of the game can serve as a model of how to depict the evolution of societies, whether at the technological or ethical levels.

This book refers to these types of games when they illustrate some aspect of history more effectively than games set in the past. However, the focus of this book is games whose main setting is the past. These include action games occurring in a virtual reconstruction of the past and strategy games encouraging players to manipulate the past. Plenty of games fit these categories. Among them are franchises, such *Assassin's Creed, Call of Duty, Civilization, Europa Universalis* (and related Paradox series), and *Total War*, that have lasted, in some cases, for decades. Although this book refers to several single-release games and independent small franchises, its focus is on the large, popular franchises for several reasons. First, because these games are popular, more readers have played them than many single titles published by independent design teams. It is therefore easier for players to relate to this book's analysis of them than it is for games they are less likely to have played. Second, because these games belong to series published over many years, it's possible to track changes in their content that have sometimes been responses to critiques from players and even historians. A recurring theme of this book is that games in these franchises have become, with occasional exceptions, more nuanced in their approaches to history with releases of successive titles. Finally, some of these series contain so many games that they simply provide a plethora of good illustrations of what this book explains. *Assassin's Creed, Civilization*, and *Total War* in particular provide a wide variety of examples from various historical settings, to explain the functioning of history in videogames. They also happen to be among the most popular series in their respective genres.

Although this book examines the development of series over time, it focuses on franchises that are still producing games. The assumption is that most players are less interested in games that are "out of date" whether conceptually or graphically, and that they are more likely to play older games if they form a part of an ongoing series. *Age of Empires*, for instance, does not receive as much attention as it would have ten years ago. Important exceptions, such as *Oregon Trail*, exist when they have clearly had an impact on a generation's understanding of history, and when they provide examples of an issue in the development of historical videogames that more recent titles don't.

Finally, this book focuses on games for the most part produced and marketed in Europe, North America, and Australia. This admittedly cultural limitation is not because games produced elsewhere don't deserve attention. Rather, it is because any attempt to deal with the vast and complex gaming market in East Asia, for instance, deserves a book in itself. While the Western and East Asian markets certainly overlap, they involve enough distinct characteristics that doing justice to the latter requires more space than this book allows.

Just as space considerations limit the number of games and examples discussed, so these concerns also limit the presentation of historiography. Rather than presenting a laundry list of the many historians who have recently published on a particular theme, this book focuses on a handful of major scholars who have shaped our understanding of history. This book, therefore, provides an introduction to historiography more suitable to lay readers and undergraduates first encountering major historical debates rather than postgraduates immersed in theoretical analysis of these themes. Where this book focuses on an old theme in historical writing, such as the role of great men versus economic forces, it may begin its summary of the historiography long before our time. In such cases, however, this book also explains how subsequent historians refined or abandoned earlier scholars' views. Where branches of historical inquiry only came into existence much more recently, such as gender and environmental history, then the major scholars involved may be much more recent. However, professional historians should understand that these introductions to the scholarship surrounding a particular theme are not comprehensive. Rather, they outline some of the most important debates surrounding a theme.

The citation of works discussed in historiographical summaries receives special treatment. When knowing the date of a work's original publication is important for understanding its role in the development of historical analysis, the text mentions that date. However, in such cases the "Works cited" section lists an accessible version of the work, often available on line. If a work's original publication was not in English, the text uses the English title and the "Works cited" section refers to an English translation. Direct quotes from works discussed in their historiographical contexts come from the version in the "Works cited" section.

While each chapter deals with a distinct major theme, many issues cut across these themes, so the chapters frequently reference one another, building on knowledge gained earlier in the book. Equally important is an overarching theme, the ways in which videogame developers have to adapt (many might argue distort) history in order to present a product that is playable and marketable.

Finally, this book does not set out solely to criticize videogames' presentation of history. It is far too easy to poke holes in creative works set in the past, whether novels, films, or games, and doing so often fails to recognize the constraints under which these entertainment media operate. When this book highlights inaccuracies, it does so mainly to illustrate a problem that game developers encounter in depicting a larger historical theme. In many cases, this book's analysis goes on to show how these problems arise from the type of constraints mentioned above. However, this book often highlights ways in which videogames engage players, spark their interest, and encourage them to think analytically about the past. In doing so, it attempts to give readers a better appreciation of what they are playing and the history it portrays.

Works cited

Age of Empires (games series), Ensemble Studios/Microsoft Studies, 1997–2016.

Assassin's Creed (game series), Ubisoft, 2007–18.

Assassin's Creed II, Ubisoft Montreal, 2009.

"Black Ops Annihilates Record Harry Potter Weekend." *Computer and Video Games*, 22 November 2010. http://www.computerandvideogames.com/277090/news/black-ops-annihilates-record-harry-potter-weekend/

Call of Duty (game series), Infinity Ward/ Treyarch, 2003–18.

Call of Duty: Black Ops, Treyarch, 2010.

The Elder Scrolls (game series), Bethesda Game Studios, 1994–2018.

Empire: Total War, Creative Assembly, 2009.

Europa Universalis (game series), Paradox Development Studio, 2013.

Fallout (game series), Interplay Entertainment/Bethesda Game Studios, 1997–2017.

Hearts of Iron (game series), Paradox Development Studio, 2002–18.

Medal of Honor (game series), 2015, Inc./Dreamworks Interactive/EA, 1999–2012.

The Oregon Trail (game series), MECC, 1971–2011.

Sid Meier's Civilization (game series), Microprose/Firaxis Games, 1991–2018.

Sid Meier's Civilization: Beyond Earth, Firaxis Games, 2014.

Tomb Raider (game series), Core Design/Eidos, 1996–2015.

Total War (game series), Creative Assembly, 2000–18.

Uncharted (game series), Naughty Dog, 2007–17.

World of Warcraft, Blizzard Entertainment, 2004.

1

HISTORIANS, CONSUMERS, AND THE VIDEOGAME INDUSTRY

Introduction

No one is born a historian. Every person who develops an interest in history does so for a reason. For me, there were several: relatives of previous generations reminiscing about the two world wars and the Great Depression; movies portraying people in colorful clothing and settings undergoing experiences that seemed very different, yet somehow similar, to mine; and tabletop games, mainly about war and diplomatic relations, that I played with friends and relatives as a teenager. Today many people become interested in history through videogames. They buy a game because of the action or strategic challenges it promises, one that only incidentally has a historical setting. As they play the game, they immerse themselves in the setting and want to discover more about it. This response, which may be barely conscious at the time, is in fact part of a complex set of interactions involving gamers, who buy and play the games; designers, who usually develop the concept behind the games and bring them to completion; and corporate managers, who market the games. Often missing from this relationship but increasingly engaging with it are historians, whose research and writing society often regards as the benchmark of "real" history in contrast to videogames, which are "merely" entertainment. Yet the relationship between the history that historians write and teach and the history that videogames present is far more complex than simply a relationship between serious scholarship and dumbed-down or distorted ideas about the past.

This chapter explores these relationships, between consumers, designers, marketers, and historians. In doing so, it examines their motives for engaging in the production of history, whether as scholarship or entertainment. It also considers the overlap between designer and consumer inherent in this interactive medium. These relationships are often characterized by tension caused by differing motives for producing what some scholars argue are, for better or worse, historical works. However, these relationships also involve surprising levels of cooperation, not only between designers and marketers, but also between both these groups on the one hand and the consumers who play their products on the other. Understanding videogames' production and consumption, and the extent to which this process compares and contrasts with the production of historical scholarship, enables us to better understand and appreciate videogames' portrayals of history in subsequent chapters.

The meaning and presentation of history

In order to understand how well videogames depict history, we must first agree on what history is and whether videogames can present it at all. Historian John Lukacs points out an obvious problem with the term "history": it "has a double meaning. It is the past, but it is also the study and the description of the past" (1). Historians have increasingly disagreed over what precisely constitutes history. For professional historians, history is not simply what occurred in the past; it is also the interpretation of those occurrences. Many historians shy away from using the term "history" to describe the actual past. For instance, theoretical historian Alan Munslow asserts: "'the past' and 'history' are separate entities or categories" (9). He has good reason to do so. No account of the past, however exhaustive, can include *everything* that occurred. The historian's job is, therefore, to decide what is worth attention and what is not, and to explain its significance, either as an illustration of what the past was, or as an explanation of why things turned out the way they did. These are interpretive acts. What one person considers significant, another might not, and vice versa. This process, of choosing what to focus on and why, and then interpreting the evidence, is what separates the discipline of "history" from the actual past.

For millennia, history was usually a matter of community memory. Most people were illiterate and relied on oral tradition to learn what had occurred in the past. The elderly might remember (or think they remembered) details of family life and the greater societal events that influenced them. They also passed on tales they had heard from their grandparents. Such oral traditions were biased in their origins (reflecting one community's perspective), and suffered from embellishments over time. Occasionally, men of wealth and prestige (rarely women and the poor) would write accounts of great events and the people (usually leaders) involved in them. A disturbing amount of our detailed knowledge of the politics of ancient Greece and Rome comes from a mere handful of "historians" who wrote accounts from personal memory or hearsay. As a result, much of what we know of these details from the ancient past is more of a guess, taking into account the inherent biases of the sources, since few of them have much corroborating evidence. For instance, Herodotus, the fifth-century-BCE "father of history's" estimate of the size of the Persian army in its wars against the Greek city-states is widely considered a gross exaggeration.

Rarely did ancient, Medieval, or even early modern histories cite their sources, leaving no way to check the veracity of their assertions.

In the nineteenth century, however, history became an academic discipline in its own right, with dedicated faculties of historians at universities across Europe and North America. These professional historians developed the "historical method," protocols for researching and writing history. This method involves assessing the accuracy of sources from the past – by determining authorship, context, and potential bias. The original authors of the sources rarely created them with the intent of historians using them later on. Rather, they generated them in the context of events at the time. Indeed, the more the author designed a source to send a message to the future, the more suspect its interpretation of events. For instance, a secret memorandum authored by Winston Churchill during World War II, intended only for the eyes of senior cabinet members or generals, is more likely to express what the prime minister really thought at the time than are the assertions he made years later in his six-volume memoir, *The Second World War*. The two sources represent the difference between how frank one might be when speaking with a close confidant as opposed to a large public gathering. Historians assess the usefulness of such sources in piecing together what they believe are the most likely explanations of what occurred and why. Having identified what is important, historians rarely simply narrate past events. Rather, they make an "argument" about how the events they are describing are significant or relate to one another. Like the decision regarding the significance of past events, the argument about their relationship to one another is also an interpretive act. Other historians may look at the same evidence and disagree on what it tells us about the nature of past society or the connections between events. Rather than thinking of history as a novel, relating a story that happens to be true, it's better to think of it as a court case, with different parties presenting different interpretations of what occurred.[1]

Although the rigor with which modern professional historians vet their sources and present their arguments is greater than that of historians writing before the last two centuries, many of their motives for studying history remained the same. John Tosh identifies four "long standing and influential aspirations of historians" (2; for the discussion below, see 2–16). Although he describes aspirations fulfilled through the written word, some of them also apply to the motivations behind videogame designers in creating games with historical themes, and videogame consumers in buying them.

The first aspiration is curiosity to find out what happened. Most modern historians would not pursue their subject if they were not passionately interested in it, so this reason remains a powerful one, even for historians who also have other reasons for pursuing their research. If a gamer is buying a game partly because it is set during a particular period of history, then he or she is probably buying the game for similar reasons. Many people are drawn to the past out of a desire to understand where they and their families came from or simply out of the type of escapism associated with reading a historical novel. Professional historians must exercise their imaginations to appreciate the perspectives and circumstances of people living in the past. However, they do so by adhering to rigorous standards of evidence and logic.

The second aspiration is to demonstrate how history is progressing toward an end. This attitude toward history – also called "teleological" – was popular in the nineteenth and early twentieth centuries. It appeared in the writings of British and American historians, justifying imperialism and "manifest destiny." It was also central to Karl Marx's prediction of the inevitability of a classless society. Teleology is still alive in the insistence of many Americans that their country is "exceptional" and therefore not bound to the supposed trajectories of rise and decline experienced by all other societies. However, the two world wars, the Great Depression, and the Holocaust, among other developments, shook historians' faith in progress. Academics, therefore, no longer favor this approach, although notions of inevitable progress remain popular among the general public, particularly in the United States.

The third aspiration is to support political and ideological agenda. Popular narratives and shared memories of the past often serve to justify a community's reasons for existence and to bolster a sense of unity. Doing so has been particularly important over the last couple of centuries as fairly static members of village communities, in which most people knew one another personally, have transformed into more mobile citizens of nation-states, "imagined communities" (Anderson), in which each individual knows only a small fraction of the fellow members of their larger societies. Narratives of shared societal experiences and common aspirations, often taught through universally mandated education, help to instill primary loyalty to the nation-state, diminishing communal violence and preventing civil war. Unfortunately, such narratives often insist on national superiority over rival nation-states or minority groups within one's own society, therefore justifying oppression at home and warfare abroad.

The final aspiration is to enable us to use past experience to inform our own choices today. Politicians often invoke the past to argue for a particular social, economic, or foreign policy. Avoiding a recurrence of the events leading to the two world wars or the Great Depression are topics that often arise in public forums. While many historians believe we can learn from the past, however, they tend to approach the topic with greater nuance. The past never truly repeats itself, since the circumstances surrounding our existence constantly change. Learning about the past, however, can give us a better appreciation of how we arrived at our current set of circumstances. It can help to diminish the abuse of history for political and ideological ends. It can also encourage us to appreciate the behavior and attitudes of people in other parts of the world, and in other cultural and ethnic groups, who hold different perceptions of the past from our own.

Whatever their aspirations, however, until the mid-twentieth century, professional historians used the same two media, the printed word and the lecture, to disseminate their knowledge. However, changes over the last half-century of scholarship in the humanities and social sciences have resulted in two processes that allow us to regard portrayals of the past delivered outside the classroom or the scholarly publication as legitimate venues for encountering history.

First, particularly during the 1960s and 1970s, historians shifted their focus away from the activities of the social elite to those of people wielding less-formal power. In this process, historians initially focused on the working class. However, the shift toward the powerless also gave rise to a whole set of fields cutting across social science and humanities disciplines that dealt with specific disempowered groups, such as people of color, immigrants, women, and the lesbian-gay-bisexual -transgender-queer-intersex-asexual (LGBTQIA+) population. The disempowered left less written material, because they were less likely to be literate, had less time to write, and were less likely to have their writing preserved in archival collections. Therefore, although historians still relied on the writings of the elite, they had to analyze them differently in order to glean information through them about the disempowered. For instance, nineteenth-century parliamentary hearings on factory conditions in England often involved interviews with factory workers. These workers rarely left written documents of their own, but the parliamentary record preserves their remarks. Similarly, newspaper reporting of race-related discrimination, protests, and violence in the early twentieth-century United States sometimes contained comments from working-class African-Americans, even if their own written records were not preserved.

In all these cases, historians take careful account of the bias of the person writing the record. A member of parliament might be sympathetic to the plight of factory workers and yet not understand the problems they faced simply keeping personally clean. A white reporter did not have to be a malevolent racist to fail to appreciate the everyday obstacles that official seg- regation and a hostile judicial system posed to African-Americans. Sometimes written records can reveal information about the disempowered, even though their original function had nothing to do with this goal. Casual references to servants, slaves, women, and children in correspondence about business or government tell historians much about the disempowered and the attitudes of the empowered toward them. Combined with government and business statistics, financial reports, and censuses, they piece together a picture of social relation- ships and living conditions of those unable to leave us their perspectives directly through their own writing.

Historians have also increasingly relied on sources outside the traditional government archives. For instance, cookbooks marketed to families tell us about diets, the role of women in the procurement and preparation of food, and per- meation of foreign or minority ethnic commodities into the lives of the middle and lower classes. Visual and aural artifacts provide records that often tell us as much, if not more, about the disempowered than do government reports. Advertisements, postcards, African-American spirituals, and working-class musical hall performances are all legitimate evidence for the modern historian trying to uncover the lives of ordinary people in the past.

This last point is important, because the increasing willingness of scholars to embrace media other than the written word as primary sources has also increased their willingness to consider them as legitimate secondary sources too. (A primary source is a document or artifact from the period one is investigating. A secondary source is an analysis or portrayal of that period based on primary sources.) For decades, scholarship on education has explored the use of film as a means of conveying history to students. Since the beginning of this century, it has increasingly done the same with videogames (Kee et al.). A major argument for using non-scholarly and non-written sources to convey historical knowledge is that much of the population encounters the past through it. A landmark study in 1998 demonstrated that Americans are passionately interested in history, but not as professional historians present it. Rather, they encounter history primarily through family recollections, genealogies, photographs, memorabilia, movies, documentaries, historical novels, and popular histories often written by journalists (Rosenzweig and Thelen).

Do these forms of encountering the past constitute history? Until the 1970s, most historians would have replied with a resounding "No," not so much because they believed that non-scholarly and non-written media can't convey history, but because they questioned the accuracy of popular as opposed to scholarly presentations of the past. They argued that the latter presented the actual past more accurately than former. However, starting in the 1960s, scholars began to question how well scholarship itself could uncover objective truth. French philosopher Michel Foucault argued that supposedly scientific knowledge is something that scholars "construct" in the context of their own assumptions and biases that are a product of the societies around them. For instance, early modern European concepts of what constituted insanity evolved in response to social norms more than to objective scientific inquiry. In short, the science of insanity was a social, rather than a scientific, construct. Gradually, the argument that scholarly knowledge reflects its social setting as much as the method and rigor of dispassionate inquiry spread across the humanities and social sciences. The debate soon got personal as scholars used these arguments not only to question the motives and assumptions of distant predecessors in earlier centuries, but also those of the fellow scholars with whom they interacted. Literary scholar Edward Said argued in 1978 that Western scholarship on Asia and Africa had for two centuries served the purpose of cementing Western dominance of those continents (Said). Moreover, he argued that this pattern has continued even after the collapse of formal empires.

This questioning of the integrity of scholarly methods has eroded the distinction between formal historical scholarship and popular history to the point that scholars can now argue that "Differences between popular and academic history might then be a matter of *degree* (and *purpose*), but not *kind*" (Chapman 9). Historian Robert Rosenstone argues: "history need not be done on the page. It can be a mode of thinking that utilizes elements other than the written word: sound, vision, feeling, montage" (11). He also argues that the written word has limitation just as much as other media do, and therefore benefits from history's presentation in these other formats; defined this way, videogames can easily qualify as history too, and some scholars argue that they do (Chapman; Kapell and Elliott; Kee et al.).

How historians portray the past is therefore very much a part of their present. In extreme cases, understanding this has led some scholars to argue that the past is unknowable. Yet behind the selections and interpretations are real people and events. We may never understand them fully, but that doesn't make it impossible to get closer to an appreciation of what happened in the past and understand its significance for what followed. Inasmuch as videogames help us do this, they communicate history.

Portraying historical research

Studying and writing history can be a lonely activity. In contrast to researchers in many science and some social-science disciplines, historians usually work on projects alone. However fascinating the sources historians investigate may seem to them, anyone observing the research process would probably find it dull. It hardly makes for a good screenplay, which is probably why one doesn't see many films or television series featuring historians prominently. When they do, they usually get it wrong. For instance, the *Indiana Jones* films depict archaeological research as treasure hunting, rather than the reality of painstakingly uncovering layers of debris from earlier societies. The videogame industry has produced its own versions of this genre, among them the *Tomb Raider* and *Uncharted* series. Both gaming universes are likely to spark interest among curious players regarding the historical background of the artifacts the protagonists are retrieving. Otherwise, however, their instructional value is limited, since they occur in the present and only refer to the past, and neither of them comes close to duplicating the methods of actual historians or archaeologists.

Only rarely do popular media have a historian as a protagonist. The recent American television network NBC series *Timeless* has an engineer, a soldier, and a historian returning to various times and places in the past to prevent nefarious opponents from altering the timeline. Quite apart from the fantastic premise of time travel, this series' portrayal of the historian is grossly oversimplified. The protagonist seems to know the most minute details of everything in the past, from the exact wording of a message left by ill-fated defenders of the Alamo to a particular German castle's floorplan. In reality, historians specialize according to a combination of historical period, geographic area, and theme. For instance, someone might specialize in nineteenth-century immigration into the United States and conduct research into a narrower topic within that subfield. Such a historian could teach an introductory course on US history but, given her training, she would be unlikely to know specific details of the early space program. The compartmentalization of knowledge into subfields of a discipline has occurred across all areas of knowledge, but popular media tend to distort and oversimplify this process. Inasmuch as *Timeless* actually has the protagonists experience the past through the aid of supposedly scientific machinery, the *Assassin's Creed* series perhaps comes the closest to it among videogames. However, in *Assassin's Creed*, the protagonist in the modern era is not a historian and cannot alter the past.

A much better portrayal of what historians actually do can be found in *Gone Home*, a videogame in which the player takes on the role of Kaitlin Greenbriar, a woman in her twenties who returns to her parent's home in Oregon after spending a year in Europe. She finds the house deserted. However, by exploring letters, tape recordings, cancelled ticket stubs, photographs, and other evidence she finds around the house, the protagonist (and the player) is able to get a good idea of why nobody is there to greet her. In doing so, she also uncovers some secrets going back generations earlier. Nevertheless, the context and fragmentary nature of the evidence leave some of this earlier story ambiguous and open to interpretation, just as is often the case in actual historical research. The game makes clear the main and obvious conclusion (regarding Kaitlin's sister) at the end of the basic investigation that players must complete to end it. However, it leaves much of the additional background information unexplained, except through sources that can lead to different conclusions among different players. *Gone Home*, therefore, simulates much of the process involved in historical research without openly telling the player that it's doing so (Bell). Unlike *Assassin's Creed*, it presents the past as something that one can only experience through artifacts, not through reliving it. *Gone Home* depicts a fictional story, but it reveals the difference between history, which it invites the player to construct out of the material at hand, and the past, which is forever out of reach directly.

Designer preference versus marketability

Even if we regard the historical method as providing a more accurate view of the past than do popular media, this doesn't mean that popular forms don't contribute some understanding of the past. If that understanding errs because it doesn't rely on the historical method, then we need to understand what views of history popular media instill in their audiences. This section focuses on the motives behind decisions to develop several historical videogame franchises. As we shall see, the initial pitch for a historical setting often sets up a tension between creativity and profitability.

A basic difference separating the motives of professional historians and game designers is the audiences they try to reach. Most professional historians work in universities. Although the love of history may cause them to become historians, once they have joined a faculty (or even before), the demands of their profession require them to publish in order to maintain or advance their careers. For the most part, these publications must be peer-reviewed. This process involves editors sending a scholar's manuscript to other (usually anonymous) scholars who have researched on topics similar to the one the manuscript covers. These scholars then recommend whether to publish or reject the manuscript, or recommend alterations before publication. This process distinguishes academic scholarship from unsubstantiated claims that one might find through a casual search on the Internet. Professional historians, therefore, usually write to persuade fellow scholars. To do so they must show that they have followed acceptable historical methods regarding sources, and cite them in their work. They must also persuade the reviewers and the publisher that their work makes an original contribution to their field that will interest other scholars at the very least. Historians rarely expect to make much money from their publications. The practical rewards come through recognition in their fields of study, and promotion and job security at their place of work.

The practical goals of videogame designers are very different. With some important exceptions, the goal of videogame designers is to create products that will sell and turn a profit for their company. They want their products to be well-reviewed for their entertainment value, not only for personal recognition, but also to boost sales. The financial success and popularity of videogames are the most obvious avenues to success in the careers of game designers. Some designers work for companies and nonprofit organizations that develop videogames for educational purposes. However, by far the largest market for historical videogames is as entertainment. Therefore, videogames must primarily be playable and fun. Concerns about accuracy are secondary.

The evolution of the videogame business has intensified this priority. As with many other industries in the digital age, large corporations tend to buy out small videogame startup companies, or drive them out of business. Media studies scholars Nick Dyer-Witherford and Greig de Peuter describe the videogame industry as a "hit-driven business, where 10 percent of the games make 90 percent of the money ... Little surprise, therefore, that publishers are notoriously risk averse" (43). These authors hold up California-based Electronic Arts (EA) as an example of corporate prioritization of profit over creativity. By enforcing a corporate model for game production, with top-down decision-making through a bureaucratic hierarchy, EA has churned out games the market wants, and realized high profits. Critics, however, have argued that it has done so at the expense of its employees, who must work long hours in an assembly-line atmosphere. They also claim that EA's business model stifles creativity. New ideas must be approved by senior corporate executives who often have little idea of the product they are selling, since they might have little to no experience either playing videogames or designing them. These executives might either dismiss developers' proposals as financially risky or appropriate the intellectual property that they amount to, often denying their originators the credit they deserve. EA's defenders have argued that as videogame design involves ever more expensive equipment, greater complexity, and a larger market, only large corporate structures can possibly meet these demands. As Dyer-Witherford and de Peuter explain this perspective (albeit not necessarily agreeing with it): "the 'garage invention' model at the roots of the game industry is not well fitted to meet large-scale production; the 'working anarchy' of the small studio, while perhaps favoring creativity, does not scale" (60).

Marketing concerns have been a significant obstacle to the preferences of any-body wanting to launch new videogame franchises with historical themes – even for Steven Spielberg, the world's most successful film producer. In 1997, Spielberg was passionately interested in World War II. While producing the film *Saving Private Ryan*, he proposed to his staff at DreamWorks a World War II first-person shooter (FPS) that would serve as a less graphic (i.e., bloody) introduction to the war and spark the interest of younger audiences. The game was *Medal of Honor*. Immediately, however, he met resistance from DreamWorks' corporate manage-ment. Pointing to the popularity of contemporary, fantasy, and science-fiction FPSs, they argued that gamers weren't interested in World War II. Peter Hirsch-mann, producer and writer for *Medal of Honor*, recalls: "They said, 'World War 2 is old, it's got cobwebs on it. People want ray guns, hell-spawn and laser rifles'." However, as the company's managers discovered when they saw the demo, "shooting Nazis was extremely satisfying" (quoted in "The Making Of ... Medal of Honor"). Of course, *Medal of Honor* became a best-seller and inspired other developers to focus on World War II FPSs. Developers working on *Medal of Honor: Allied Assault* (2001) formed the studio Infinity Ward, which in 2003 produced the first installment of *Call of Duty*, one of the most successful FPS franchises ("Call of Duty Q&A").

Initial corporate resistance to Spielberg hints at a tension that exists for the producers of many historical videogames. Designers may prefer historical themes because of their interest, even passion, for history, but, from a financial perspec-tive, anything straying from the most obvious preferences of the marketplace is risky. If "ray guns, hell-spawn and laser rifles" are a safer moneymaking theme than World War II, then what of Medieval assassins or ancient Romans? Sid Meier, the creator of the *Civilization* franchise, thought it was easier to follow one's passion in the early days (1980s and 1990s) of the videogame industry than it has been more recently. As one of his interviewers explains:

> During those halcyon days of the nascent PC game industry, computer game design had not yet been restrained by the single-minded adherence to narrow, hit-proven genres or skyrocketing hundred-million-dollar pro-duction budgets of today. Instead of looking at focus groups and market conditions to guide his designs, Meier says he'd simply propose potential topics for gamers, like "pirates," "trains," "civilization," or "the Civil War," and then act on them.
>
> *(Edwards)*

For the moment, the industry has arrived at a compromise of sorts, between small design studios and large corporate conglomerates. Modern videogame designers usually begin their careers with large corporations such as EA and Microsoft. Many then launch out on their own, collaborating with colleagues they meet working for their former employers. These studios then pay larger corporations, sometimes the same ones they previously worked for, to market and distribute their products. For the large corporation it becomes a way to explore innovative ideas without investing too much. Of course, if the startup design team is truly successful, it grows in size and might begin to take on the organizational features of the large corporation, thereby encouraging its most successful designers to set up on their own once again.

The brief history of the British studio Pivotal is instructive. Created in 2000 by designers who had worked for British-based Eidos Interactive, publisher of the *Tomb Raider* franchise, the studio produced the *Conflict* series of cooperative third-person action games. This series initially sold well, although its final title, in 2008, received mediocre reviews and low sales. When in 2003 Pivotal's parent company Kaboom went out of business, Sales Curve Interactive (SCi) acquired it. Five years later, SCi bought Eidos. In order to afford the acquisition, however, it shut down fourteen studios. Since Pivotal's most recent title, which was not on a historical theme, had fared poorly, it was one of them. By 2008, Pivotal's staff had grown to 100, and all but twelve were laid off (Glasser).

Pivotal was an example of an organization begun by people who loved to create games and enjoyed the themes of their creations. Media analyst Jon Dovey conducted a series of interviews with the studio's staff in 2003, who at the time had produced two games set during the two American-led wars in Iraq (1991 and 2003) and one set during World War II. The design team was working on a game set in the Vietnam War, which it published the following year. Dovey attributed the decision to focus on Vietnam, a historical theme, to its managing director, Jim Babra, "the visionary and driving force who has pushed the studio forward from its earliest days" (Dovey 69). Babra had been interested in history since childhood and had earned a degree in economics and social history. He remembered becoming interested in history through books, but also films and play.

> I always played toy soldiers, still do, and role playing games, make believe. I actually read a lot of history. I think for me it was a classic time growing up, you had Robin Hood on TV, Richard the Lion heart, Lancelot, you know. I remember them as being great but they are probably rubbish if I saw them again today.
>
> *(Quote in Dovey 69–70)*

Nevertheless, some compromises between the interests of the designer and the desire to make a profit, or at least avoid a loss, are inevitable. One of the "level designers" for Pivotal Games showed a keen awareness of the international videogame market. Although working for a British company, this designer acknowledged that the demands of American consumers guided the team's choice of historical themes for their games:

> So there are an inordinate number of wars that have happened in the
> world, but picking a war that the American market is going to be aware
> of then becomes the question. And I think really there are three wars that
> they, the majority, the industry consider they are aware of, World War II
> which is done a lot, the Vietnam event, which I think is a slightly ... trickier
> setting for a game, and then the Gulf War, the two of them, because they
> happened most recently.
>
> *(Quoted in Dovey 76–77)*

Because the United States is the world's most populous developed economy,
any game producer interested in the bottom line must consider its market.
Enrollments in undergraduate college courses in the United States hint at the
preferences of American consumers, since many college students play videogames. In most American universities, courses on American history are the most
popular, followed by those on twentieth-century Europe. Courses focusing on
other areas, such as the Middle East, tend to peak when that area is in the news.
Among major conflicts of the past, the most popular courses tend to focus on
the American Civil War and World War II.[2] As with Vietnam, Civil War
games are problematic, because of divided attitudes toward it within American
society. However, World War II has the advantage of having involved many
nations and therefore appealing to a potentially broad international market.
Moreover, because the popular American view of the war regards it as a battle
between good and evil in which the United States was on the good side, it has
turned out to be a relatively uncontroversial setting for playable American military protagonists (Adams; Bodnar). This triumphalist approach to World War II
also extends to British consumers, who tend to regard the war as "Britain's
finest hour" (Ponting). Of course, this rather self-congratulatory view of American
and British behavior during the war is problematic. In particular, the United
States' nuclear attacks on Japan and its behavior toward Japanese-Americans is a
source of controversy, as are the Anglo-American "carpet bombing" air raids on
Germany. Nevertheless, the fact that professional historians have raised these issues
doesn't appear to have significantly changed domestic popular approval of America
and Britain's roles in the war.

Choices of historical themes are trickier for producers aiming at markets
beyond the developed English-speaking countries, because other countries' consumers' narratives of the past often differ markedly from those of the United
States. French and German consumers, for instance, are less likely to regard
World War II as a heroic conflict. For French consumers the war is problematic,
not only because their country initially suffered a humiliating military defeat, but
also because historians have upended the postwar narrative that focused on the
heroic role of Free French soldiers and the French resistance to Nazi rule.
Rather, historians have revealed the great extent of French collaboration with
the Nazis, including even French President (1981–95) François Mitterand
(Rousso). Similarly, historians have shown the great extent of Hitler's popularity

among the German people of the time, which has made it difficult for Germans to separate Nazi guilt specifically from German guilt generally over the aggression and atrocities German forces committed during the war (Marcuse, *Legacies of Dachau*; Art). Not surprisingly, French and German developers of historical games have focused their attention on conflicts other than World War II, and some designers aiming at the German market believe that FPSs are less popular there. Referring to their own products, which combine strategic-level, map-focused decisions with tactical-level, battlefield simulations, developers for the British videogame studio Creative Assembly claimed that:

> Germans actually tend to like playing the strategy side of the campaign map over all the other platforms. They love all that intricate building your camp up, making sure you've got all the right buildings in every area to maximize the bonuses … and then maximizing your economy to get the most amount of money coming in.
>
> *(Grill)*

Whether this is actually the case is difficult to tell, since the development team provided no statistics to back up their claim. However, it may not matter in exploring the role of the market in game design decisions, since what the designers and the corporate sponsors believe is more important than the underlying reality.

One of the largest videogame producers in the world is Ubisoft. Based in Rennes, France, it has development teams located across Europe, Asia, Australia, and Canada. As a multi-national corporation, Ubisoft has certainly taken account of the American market. It bought and continued the *Tom Clancy* franchise of action spy-thriller games, with contemporary settings and American protagonists. It also collaborated with the US Army to produce *America's Army: Rise of a Soldier* (2005), a training simulation made user-friendly for the general market. However, Ubisoft's historical games have usually occurred in settings before the twentieth century. For instance, in 2007 Ubisoft acquired German company Sunflowers Interactive, whose major franchise was *Anno* (marketed as *A.D.* in Australia and the United States). *Anno* was the brainchild of Albert and Martin Lassing and Wilfried Reiter of the Austrian firm Max Design. Their primary focus began with historical economic simulations. The *Anno* series drew on earlier historical city-building games, which were flooding the market at the time, such as Sierra's *Caesar* series, in which the gamer played a Roman governor responsible for managing his province's economy. The Max Design team applied this concept to the age of European exploration and trade, and added cultural flavor to it by featuring different architectural styles in European, Middle Eastern, and East Asian destinations, as well as different ecological settings. However, the designers abstracted history by stripping the factions of historical names and characters ("Why Anno Is Indestructible"). This approach to the past, therefore, had the air of neutrality, designed to avoid offending any potential market.

Among Ubisoft franchises with historical settings, the most popular is the *Assassin's Creed* series. Set in a variety of locations and periods before the twentieth century, the series avoids some thorny issues of that later period. It also skirts around the central issues surrounding controversial events of the more distant past, such as the Crusades, that remain sore issues today. Patrice Désilets, who introduced the series' concept to Ubisoft's Montreal branch, received his bachelor's degree in film studies and literature. This humanities background is evident in the focus on architecture in the early games of the series. Before developing the original *Assassin's Creed* game, Désilets had worked on *Prince of Persia: Sands of Time*, whose setting evoked the *Arabian Nights*. *Prince of Persia*'s original creator was American designer Jordan Mechner, who focused in the 1980s and 1990s on producing digital games based on the swashbuckler movies that had inspired him as a boy. Désilets wanted to shift from a fantasy Middle Eastern setting to a historical one. The inspiration came from a book he read in college that mentioned the historical Assassins who flourished during the Crusades. Désilets acknowledges that his "bosses" were "concerned" about the game's marketability. However, the game's success vindicated him. As he released its sequel, he remarked that

> people are more into history than we think ... the idea of putting a game disc in your console and being in the Crusades, that is appealing ... Because it's not fantasy. It's not about defeating Orcs, but it's about being in Jerusalem and now in Florence and Venice like it was back then.
>
> *(Pham)*

Swedish-based Paradox Interactive also steered away from the twentieth century, at least initially. Its first videogame series, *Svea Rike* (Kingdom of Sweden), a strategy game set in Medieval Scandinavia, had its greatest appeal within Scandinavia – although its fourth installment was marketed to the English-speaking world as *Europa Universalis: Crown of the North*. It was, however, the original *Europa Universalis* videogame (2000) that propelled Paradox into the international gaming market. Set in the age of European expansion, this "real-time" strategy game has the player guide a sovereign state from the late fifteenth through the late eighteenth centuries. The concept for the game came from Philippe Thibaut, a French businessman who had developed the tabletop boardgame of the same title. He earned a master's degree in business administration and had "experience in international trade." However, he told an interviewer:

> History has been a passion since I was a kid and still is. Reading history has always made me dream. Similarly, confronting different books and writings told me there are so many diverse opinions and analysis of the same historical event that it could well have been the result of a game, which could have been different. So, I guess the desire to create these

games comes from the urge to explore other alternatives but within realistic patterns. Something you could call "What if … ."

("Europa Universalis")

Joining Thibaut, and eventually managing the Paradox development studio, was Swedish designer Johan Andersson. Although his background was in programming, he also was "passionate about history" (Salt). Whereas the latest setting for any game that Thibaut has designed is World War I, Andersson went on to tackle World War II – but not, as Spielberg had done, through an FPS. Rather, he designed a grand strategy game along the lines of *Europa Universalis*. Players could play any major power. The game's strategic approach to the war allowed Paradox to aim it at markets in mainland Europe as well as Anglophone countries. The game came in several language versions, including English, French, German, and Russian ("Latest Patch Is 1.06C"). Paradox has never sold games intended to bring in the revenue of *Call of Duty* or *Assassin's Creed*. Its games involve plenty of mental energy and don't emphasize impressive graphics. Nevertheless, this doesn't bother Andersson. In 2014 he praised the working environment at Paradox: "we have the luxury to be game dev[eloper]s with the creative freedom to make the type of games we ourselves love" (Salt).

One of the most daring choices for an initial game release in a predominantly Western market was *Shogun: Total War*, a 1999 game focusing on battlefield tactics in Japan's Sengoku period (1467–1603). The game's development company, Creative Assembly, established near London in 1987, focused initially on sports themes for games marketed by EA. Advances in three-dimensional (3D) graphics cards made the team want to try something new. Mike Simpson, who had previously worked with EA, drew his inspiration from Cinemaware Corporation's *Lords of the Rising Sun*, an arcade-style game published for Amiga in 1989 and set in Medieval Japan. *Shogun: Total War*'s sixteenth-century setting may have seemed remote to its Western audiences, but Creative Assembly thought it would sell (Dean). According to Simpson: "It gave us all the things we needed to make a decent game out [of] it, things like American contact, we thought Samurai against guns, so we liked that" (Grill). Here we see the importance of the American market, which has long had a fascination with Medieval and early modern Japan. The 1980 television miniseries *Shogun*, set in early seventeenth-century Japan, had earned American network NBC its highest viewing audience in its history ("Shogun"). However, Simpson goes on to admit, "but I guess if you really asked us, we just wanted to do that" (Grill) – i.e., develop *Shogun: Total War*.

These examples, by no means exhaustive, of the inspiration behind the first entries in several historical videogame series indicate the tension and complexity behind the decisions over the historical setting. For many designers, particularly in Britain and the United States, the preferences of American consumers are a significant concern, because the American market is so large. However, the market response to historical themes is also a concern for companies based on the European mainland. Perhaps more surprising than marketing is the role of personal interest among designers. The initial developers of these historical series appear to have chosen their themes, sometimes over the misgivings of their corporate offices, primarily because they found them interesting. In the industry's early days, at least, the driving force behind these historical videogame franchises appears to have been the enthusiasm of the designers. These were acts of creativity as much as business.

Designer intent and consumer reception

In the mid-twentieth century, nascent scholarship on media studies assumed that a work's consumers understood what its author intended to convey. They might appreciate it or not, they might agree with it or disagree, but both the author and the consumer understood what the work was about. Challenges to this assumption arose in the 1960s when German scholar Hans Robert Jauss argued that the meaning a reader gets from a literary work might differ significantly from the message the author intended to convey. Moreover, the meaning for the reader differs from one individual to another depending on the reader's circumstances. For instance, other literature readers have already encountered might influence their responses to a particular work, responses that the author of the work can't control. Perhaps most important, since what people read might influence their own writing, the audience's understanding of a particular work constantly evolves through the prism of subsequent literature. Jauss describes this effect as a "changing horizon of experience" (Jauss and Benzinger) that moves across time along with the audience. For Jauss this concept had historical implications, since it meant that an audience's response to a literary work could never be the same as that of the original audience who first read it, or even that of intervening generations. For instance, the modern enthusiasm for Jane Austen's novels, and the various TV miniseries and films they have spawned, can't be the same as it was for the audience first reading her publications in the early nineteenth century. Society today is markedly different from what it was then. Indeed, it is this very difference that creates the quaint appeal of Austen's turns of phrase and sense of propriety so attractive to many of her modern fans (Lynch). Obviously, these differences would not have occurred to an early nineteenth-century audience, nor to Austen herself. Yet the reception of Austen by audiences now and in Austen's lifetime are not entirely distinct. Rather they are connected by a process of reception and authorship, as well as subsequent literature, which moved the "horizon of expectation" along.

Because Jauss's "reception theory" involves change over time, it has appealed to historians interested in changes in responses to interpretations of past events. In particular, Harold Marcuse has examined the changing perceptions since World War II of the historical meaning of the Nazi concentration camp at Dachau (Marcuse, *Legacies of Dachau*). On his website at the University of California, Santa Barbara he defines "reception history" as:

the history of the meanings that have been imputed to historical events. This approach traces the different ways in which participants, observers, and historians and other retrospective interpreters have attempted to make sense of events, both as they unfolded, and over time since then, to make those events meaningful for the present in which they lived and live.

(Marcuse, Reception History*)*

"Reception history" is, therefore, an important consideration when studying any medium's presentation of the past.

This is even more the case when one considers the implications for media other than the printed page. In 1973, sociologist Stuart Hall extended Jauss's theory to broadcast and film media, but with a more political edge to his argument. He described authors of programs (television, radio, film, performance, etc.) as "encoding" meaning into their creations. The resulting program then transmits the meaning. This encoding process might be deliberate or not. Often it simply arises from the assumptions common among members of the profession of broadcast journalists. However, as viewers of the program "decode" the meaning they may interpret it in ways other than those intended by the program's author. Hall identifies three "positions" from which the receiver of the program might interpret its meaning. The first is the "dominant-hegemonic," in which the viewer takes the meaning as interpreted by the author. Hall is particularly concerned with use of the media by "political and military elites" to spread their interpretation (propaganda) to the masses. He argues this could occur even in societies with ostensibly free presses, because "broadcasting professionals" work within the same social circles as the elite and operate according to a "professional code" created in society's upper echelons. Therefore, in Western capitalist countries during the Cold War, the press could present the contrary views of major political parties while still operating within boundaries that accepted the legitimacy of capitalism and the constitutional framework within which it operated. Viewers who accept this framework also accept the "dominant-hegemonic" encoding embedded, for instance, in broadcast news reports.

The second position of decoding the message is "negotiated." This position is inherently contradictory, for while it accepts the "dominant-hegemonic" encoding at face value for general principles, it resists it in specific applications that may matter most to the receiver of the message. Hall uses the example of workers who accept that limiting the right to strike is in the "national interest," but are willing themselves to go on strike for better personal pay and working conditions. Hall's third position is "oppositional," in which the audience subverts the original intent of the author's meaning. His example here is once again political: "the case of the viewer who listens to a debate on the need to limit wages but 'reads' every mention of the 'national interest' as 'class interest'" (173).

Videogames offer even more compelling opportunities for reception analysis than literature or television, because they are inherently interactive. As historian Adam Chapman points out: "In most histories, historians are the only ones who *produce* within this story space, with audiences normally restricted to *receiving* ... The common idea of history is that it involves historians *doing* and audiences *reading*." However, "games allow *doing* as well as *reading*," and this "playful doing also produces narrative" (33). All videogames provide what people who study the psychology of human-computer interaction (HCI) call "affordances." James Gibson, the cognitive psychologist who originated this term, also refers to it as "action possibilities" (Shaw). In the context of videogames, affordances are opportunities for interaction within a game that can potentially alter, in at least some small way, what occurs in its virtual world. This might be as simple as looting a rifle off a dead soldier in an FPS. The rifle's specific strengths and weakness may then affect the player's success in the sequence. The affordance might be environmental, such as a tree that the protagonist can hide behind, or a wall that he or she must climb. It might also be a person in an action-adventure game, perhaps a guard whom the player must avoid. If the player's interaction with a feature affects play, then it's an affordance. The more open-world the videogame, the more affordances it provides players, enabling the players to shape the narrative.

All videogames allow for some variation of action within each scene, but many allow the player to shape the narrative more significantly. Although action–adventure series such as *Assassin's Creed* or *Red Dead Redemption* have basic storylines that players must follow to complete the game, they also have many side missions, some of which players must undertake, but which they can complete in a variety of sequences. Moreover, many games, whether action-oriented or strategic, allow players to apply affordances to update their capabilities. The manner and order in which they update them is, to a certain extent, up to the players. Grand strategy games such as *Civilization, Total War*, or *Europa Universalis* are even more open-ended, providing seemingly limitless opportunities for shaping the games' fictional alternate history.

Some games force players to make ethical decisions, which provide opportunities to write narratives opposing those that society approves. For instance, the game *Bioshock* gives players the option of saving victims of the game's virtual dystopia or harvesting them for one's own health and energy. To choose the former surely fits better with what society regards as ethical, but perhaps the latter is closer to society's behavior toward those not in the dominant-hegemonic group. *Total War: Rome II* gives players options of how harshly to treat the inhabitants of captured cities, and *Civilization VI* allows players to pursue nuclear disarmament or use nuclear weapons on enemy cities. Because designers build these affordances into their games, they do not strictly fit Hall's oppositional position of response to media. However, they are all ways in which players take part in constructing their own narratives.

A more significant method of responding to and even opposing the intent of videogame designers is through modifications (mods) to the original program that change the rules of play or the affordances one encounters in the game. Although modding can potentially occur for games on any theme, historical games are a particularly popular focus. Scholars have identified several reasons for this interest. First, players develop mods because they think the game is inaccurate in some way. For instance, the notes accompanying *Divide et Imperia*, a mod for *Total War: Rome II*, explain that it provides "Realistic army fixes in scale representing the army number of the period" and "[f]ormations' behavior simulating the way they worked in real life" (quoted in Chapman 38).

Second, mods address content areas within the story, adding features such units, events, technologies, or even major historical forces that the modder (person creating the mod) thinks the game is missing and should include. For instance, Gabriele Trovato (aka Rhye in the gaming community) developed the *Rhye's and Fall of Civilization* mod for *Civilization IV*, to better reflect the process of civilizations' historical patterns of rise and decline. All official versions of the *Civilization* series have the player choose a civilization at the beginning of the game and guide it through to victory or defeat. In reality, many of these civilizations were not contemporary with one another and arguably none has existed for the entire six millennia covered in the game. *Rhye's and Fall* enables players to begin with an ancient civilization (for instance, Rome) and follow it through its rise and possible decline. When a new era begins (for instance, leaving the Classical period and moving into the Medieval) the player has the option of switching to playing a different rising civilization (for instance, the Vikings). This process, which the player can repeat several times during the game, allows for a more historical feel to the successive rise and fall of civilizations.

Third, some modders simply use an existing game to generate a mod on a different theme, particularly if no existing game covers that theme. For instance, long before the publication of recent World War I-themed games, fans of *Napoleon: Total War* repurposed the game to cover the later conflict, and the *Europa Universalis* series is replete with mods adding factions and conflicts that players think it missed. The near-future action of EA's *Battlefield 2*, released in 2005, was intended as a change from earlier titles in the franchise, which had focused on World War II and Vietnam. Nevertheless, modders repurposed it for historical settings such as the Korean War and World War II (Chapman 39).

Finally, mod development can serve as a resumé builder. The developer of a mod for *Battlefield 1942* remarked: "I saw it as a great opportunity to get some real experience and something to be able to show as a reference when applying to game designer jobs" (Postigo). In 2007, media studies scholar Hector Postigo regarded videogame programming as "one of the last highly technical fields that an amateur can enter without any formal training" because it was "still in the process of formation." The proliferation of university degrees in programming and courses specifically in videogame design probably mean that formal training is more important for career entry today. Nevertheless, mods provide examples of a job applicant's talent that support professional qualifications.

Sophisticated mods require considerable programming skill and, when focusing on historical themes, reveal detailed knowledge of specific historical topics. These mods often appear on fan discussion boards hosted by game producers, or through digital rights managers (DRMs) such as *Steam*. The mods are free to download, although they require purchase of the original game to operate, so it's relatively easy for players of the original game to try them out and provide feedback on discussion boards. Although a mod's developer might be an individual or small group of enthusiasts, the more successful mods are usually the result of extensive feedback. One might argue, therefore, that similar to the experience of professional historians, modders submit their work for "peer review," albeit for a combination of playability and historical accuracy, and without formal academic oversight.

Although modding can be an act of "dissonance" – it often implies criticism of the game as originally released – much of it amounts to "negotiation," Hall's middle category of audience response. The reason is that game publishers often encourage the development of mods and host sites for their publication. Mods are advantageous to game marketers and developers for a couple of reasons. First, they amount to free labor developing and testing game concepts. The 2007 market value of modding the six most popular FPSs was anywhere between $10.1 million and $30.4 million (Postigo 303–08). Also, as software entrepreneur Scott Miller acknowledges, mods "extend the life of a game by providing free additional content for players to explore" (Au). Some mods are so successful that designers end up incorporating elements of them into later releases of a game or its series. *Rhye's and Fall* became a scenario in the *Civilization IV: Beyond the Sword* expansion (2007) and later versions and expansions of the *Europa Universalis* series have responded to many of the critiques implied by mods that aimed to expand the playability of factions outside Europe. Although videogame designers control what historical themes they present and how they present them, consumers also play a crucial role.

Most of the games mentioned above are single-player, some with options for participating in small-group multi-player scenarios. Occasionally it's the other way round. EA, for instance, marketed its *Battlefield* franchise specifically with multi-player participation in mind, and reviewers of its most recent title observed that the game is much more rewarding if the gamers play on teams with other gamers than if they play alone with artificial intelligence (AI)-supplied comrades. If single-player gameplay provides limited opportunities to shape the narrative, multi-player games, and particularly massively multi-player online (MMO) games (which involve thousands of participants) provide much greater scope. The reason for this is that once a game involves more than one human player, then the game designer and the algorithms the designer has programmed into the game are no longer the sole source of "affordances" discussed earlier. The mere existence of a character in the game is an affordance. Any character occupies virtual space and provides assistance or presents an obstacle for the player. If another player is controlling that character, then that player is effectively participating in designing the game through his or her actions. Moreover, if a player can create objects that other players interact with, then that player is designing affordances for the other players. To use Hall's terms once again, the "decoder" becomes an "encoder" within the framework that the original "encoder" intended.

However, mods and multi-player activity provide abundant opportunities not only for consumers to be creative within the designer's framework, but also to work in opposition to that framework. Skilled modders can create mayhem within communities playing games that allow consumer input. A source of several transgressive instances was *Spore* (2008), a single-player game focusing on "evolution," in which players (paradoxically) design their own species. Although the game is single-player, its designers created an online community in which one player's design could inhabit another player's game, constituting an affordance. Some subverted this provision by sharing obscene images and terms, for instance, a single creature that appeared to be two creatures copulating, and a caterpillar whose protrusions on its back spelled out an obscene word for that act. A less offensive example was a creature designed to look like Homer Simpson from the animated TV series *The Simpsons*. More harmful are programs released through multi-player game lobbies online, such as occurred in the *Call of Duty* series. Some of these mods privileged one group of players over others, for instance, giving some players unlimited ammunition, thereby disrupting game balance and angering many participants. An illicit program distributed this way in *Call of Duty: World at War* effectively served as a virus delivering unwanted invitations (a form of adware) to players' screens inviting them to visit certain lobbies (Meades 42–48, 149–52).

It's unclear to what extent these examples serve as oppositional behavior in the sense that Hall originally described, since they appear to be pranks serving no obvious political purpose. However, modern sociologists and historians define resistance very broadly, from armed rebellion and civil disobedience to "the ordinary weapons of relatively powerless groups: foot dragging, dissimulation, false compliance, pilfering, feigned ignorance, slander, sabotage, and so forth" (Scott et al. 29). It is therefore possible to consider transgressions of the game designers' rules as acts of resistance even if their target and underlying message are not apparent.

Conclusion

The production and consumption of historical videogames is a complex process. It involves a variety of motives. Entertainment corporations finance and market historical videogames primarily for profit; designers develop them often because of their love of history; and consumers buy them because they want entertainment, but also often because of their interest in history. Many consumers may buy videogames without caring about the historical setting. Particularly with FPSs and action-adventure games, the action may be all-important. However, as Chapman points out, "this doesn't really matter. Players are exposed to the offers of engagement with history and historical representations that these games entail and contain nonetheless" (14). Moreover, motives behind playing historical videogames may be more similar than are immediately apparent to motives behind reading scholarly books or taking history courses in college. After all, professional historians would not devote their lives to the subject if they didn't find it fascinating and, yes, sometimes escapist. The underlying motivations for encountering history are irrelevant. The question is what type of history does the consumer get out of it? The answer can't be limited to a simple issue of whether the representation of the past is accurate. It must also take account of the unique ability of videogames to allow players to both interact with virtual pasts and manipulate them. This is the case whether the virtual past has players guiding a character through an earlier society in an action-adventure game or developing that society from a god-like perspective in a strategy game. In either case, players aren't simply audience members. They are also narrators telling their characters' stories and writing their factions' histories in these digital worlds.

Notes

1 My thanks to Dr. Gina Martino for this analogy.
2 Based on personal observations and discussions with colleagues and administrators at Midwestern universities.

Works cited

Adams, Michael C. C., *The Best War Ever: America and World War II*. Johns Hopkins University Press, 1994.
Age of Empires, Ensemble Studios, 1997.
America's Army: Rise of a Soldier, Secret Level, US Army, Ubisoft, 2005.
Anderson, Benedict R., *Imagined Communities: Reflections on the Origin and Spread of Nationalism*. Verso, 1983.
Anno (game series), Max Design/Related Designs/Blue Byte, 1998–2018.
Art, David, *The Politics of the Nazi Past in Germany and Austria*. Cambridge University Press, 2006.
Assassin's Creed, Ubisoft Montreal, 2007.
Assassin's Creed (game series), Ubisoft, 2007–18.
Au, Wagner James, "Triumph of the Mod." *Salon.com*, 16 April 2002, www.salon.com /2002/04/16/modding/.
Battlefield 2, Digital Illusions CE, 2005.
Bell, Richard Thomas, "Family History: Source Analysis in Gone Home." *Play the Past*, www.playthepast.org/?p=4089.
Bodnar, John E., *The "Good War" in American Memory*. Johns Hopkins University Press, 2010.
Call of Duty, Infinity Ward, 2003.
Chapman, Adam, *Digital Games as History: How Videogames Represent the Past and Offer Access to Historical Practice*. Routledge, 2016.
Dean, Paul, "Creation Legend: The History of The Creative Assembly." *Eurogamer*, 27 September 2012, www.eurogamer.net/articles/2012-09-27-creation-legend-the-history-of-the-creative-assembly.

Dovey, Jon, "Why Am I in Vietnam? The History of a Videogame." *Videogame, Player, Text,* eds Barry Atkins and Tanya Krzywinska. Manchester University Press, 2007.

Dyer-Witheford, Nick and De Peuter, Greig, *Games of Empire: Global Capitalism and Video Games.* University of Minnesota Press, 2009.

Edwards, Benj, "The History of Civilization." *Gamasutra: The Art and Business of Making Games,* 18 July 2007, www.gamasutra.com/view/feature/129947/the_history_of_civili zation.php?print=1.

Europa Universalis, Paradox Development Studio, 2000.

Europa Universalis: Crown of the North, Paradox Development Studio, 2000.

"Europa Universalis: Philippe Thibaut – Interview." *Armchair General Magazine.* 13 March 2006, http://www.armchairgeneral.com/interview-philippe-thibaut.htm.

Foucault, Michel, *Madness and Civilization: A History of Insanity in the Age of Reason.* New American Library, 1965.

Gibson, James Jerome, *The Ecological Approach to Visual Perception.* Houghton Mifflin, 1979.

Glasser, A. J., "Eidos Parent SCi Axing 14 Projects- Pivotal Too?" *Gamesradar,* 1 March 2008, www.gamesradar.com/eidos-parent-sci-axing-14-projects-pivotal-too/.

Gone Home, The Fullbright Company, 2016.

Grill, Author, "Creative Assembly Interview: Huge Retrospective." *Funambulism,* 14 November 2011.

Hall, Stuart, "Encoding/Decoding." *Culture, Media, Language: Working Papers in Cultural Studies, 1972–79,* ed. Stuart Hall. Hutchinson; Centre for Contemporary Cultural Studies, University of Birmingham, 1980, pp. 163–73.

Jauss, Hans Robert and Benzinger, Elizabeth, "Literary History as a Challenge to Literary Theory." *New Literary History,* vol. 2, no. 1, 1970, pp. 7–37.

Kapell, Matthew and Elliott, Andrew B. R., eds, *Playing with the Past: Digital Games and the Simulation of History.* Bloomsbury, 2013.

Kee, Kevin et al. "Towards a Theory of Good History through Gaming." *Canadian Historical Review,* vol. 90, no. 2, June 2009, pp. 303–26.

"Latest Patch Is 1.06C." *Paradox Interactive Forums,* https://forum.paradoxplaza.com/forum/ index.php?threads/latest-patch-is-1-06c.56910.

Lords of the Rising Sun, Cinemaware, 1989.

Lukacs, John, *The Future of History.* Yale University Press, 2011.

Lynch, Diedre Shauna, "Cult of Jane Austen." *Jane Austen in Context,* ed. Janet Todd. Cambridge University Press, 2005, pp. 111–20.

"The Making of ... Medal of Honor." *Gamesradar,* 30 March 2015, www.gamesradar.com /making-medal-honor/.

Marcuse, Harold, *Legacies of Dachau: The Uses and Abuses of a Concentration Camp, 1933–2001.* Cambridge University Press, 2001.

Marcuse, Harold, *Reception History.* www.history.ucsb.edu/faculty/marcuse/receptionhist.htm.

Meades, Alan F., *Understanding Counterplay in Video Games.* Routledge, 2015.

Medal of Honor, Dreamworks Interactive, 1999.

Medal of Honor: Allied Assault, 2015, Electronic Arts, 2002.

Munslow, Alun, *Narrative and History.* Palgrave Macmillan, 2007.

Napoleon: Total War, Creative Assembly, 2010.

Pham, Alex, "Prince of Persia Creator Jordan Mechner Is Still in the Game." *Los Angeles Times,* 25 April 2011, http://articles.latimes.com/2011/apr/25/business/la-fi-himi- mechner-20110425.

Ponting, Clive, *1940: Myth and Reality.* H. Hamilton, 1990.

Postigo, Hector, "Of Mods and Modders: Chasing Down the Value of Fan-Based Digital Game Modifications." *Games and Culture*, vol. 2, no. 4, October 2007, pp. 300–13.

Prince of Persia: Sands of Time, Ubisoft Montreal, 2003.

Red Dead Redemption, Rockstar San Diego, 2010.

"Rhye's and Fall of Civilization." *Sid Meier's Civilization Mods by Rhye*, http://rhye. civfanatics.net/pages/civ4-RFC-press-coverage.php.

Rosenstone, Robert A., *Visions of the Past: The Challenge of Film to Our Idea of History*. Harvard University Press, 1995.

Rosenzweig, Roy and Thelen, David, *The Presence of the Past: Popular Uses of History in American Life*. Columbia University Press, 1998.

Rousso, Henry, *The Vichy Syndrome: History and Memory in France since 1944*. Harvard University Press, 1991.

Said, Edward, *Orientalism*. Vintage, 1978.

Salt, Chris, "The History and Future of Paradox Grand Strategy." *SpaceSector.Com*, www. spacesector.com/blog/2014/02/the-history-and-future-of-paradox-grand-strategy/.

Scott, James C. et al., *Weapons of the Weak: Everyday Forms of Peasant Resistance*. Yale University Press, 1985.

Shaw, Adrienne, "Encoding and Decoding Affordances: Stuart Hall and Interactive Media Technologies." *Media, Culture & Society*, vol. 39, no. 4, May 2017, pp. 592–602.

"'Shogun' Pushed NBC to the Top Last Week." *The Christian Science Monitor*, 24 September 1980, www.csmonitor.com/1980/0924/092429.html.

Shogun: Total War, Creative Assembly, 2000.

Sid Meier's Civilization VI, Firaxis Games, 2017.

Svea Rike, Target Games, 1997.

Timeless, created by Eric Kripke and Shawn Ryan, NBC, 2017–18.

Tom Clancy's (game series), Ubisoft, 1998–2017.

Tosh, John, ed., *Historians on History: Readings*, 2nd edn. Pearson Longman, 2009.

Total War: Rome II, Creative Assembly, 2013.

"Why Anno Is Indestructible." *Making Games*, 7 December 2015, www.makinggames.biz /feature/why-anno-is-indestructible,9615.html.

2
THEME AND MECHANICS

Introduction

Film critic Roger Ebert caused a swirl of controversy in 2005 when he declared that videogames were "inherently inferior to film and literature." Much of the debate focused on the definition of art, which Ebert believed precluded interactive media. Whatever the merits of these arguments, Ebert's opinion appears to be losing ground with major art institutions, such as the Museum of Modern Art and the Smithsonian American Art Museum, both of which have exhibited videogames as art ("The Art of Video Games"). Whether or not videogames will ever be considered high art, to be compared with that of William Shakespeare or Leonardo da Vinci, they are certainly a form of entertainment that involves artistic considerations and technological limitations, as do most movies. And just as these considerations and limitations shape the way that movies present history, so they shape the way that videogames do too, albeit somewhat differently. This chapter considers three aspects of videogame production that circumscribe their presentation of history: mechanics, compression, and hindsight bias. Each restriction has counterparts in other media forms, but the interactive nature of videogaming particularly makes the first one stand out from its predecessors.

Mechanics

In *Assassin's Creed II* protagonist Ezio Auditore must find all six assassin's seals in order to unlock his ancestor's special suit of armor. One of them is hidden in the dome of la Basilica di Santa Maria del Fiore (aka, Il Duomo), the most prominent landmark in Florence, and one of Italy's most magnificent works of architecture. In order to reach the top of the dome from inside the cathedral,

Ezio must leap among the rafters and balconies, scaling walls and stained-glass windows, working his way ever higher. Meanwhile, the game treats the player to a visual feast of architecture surrounding the effort, with pigeons providing hints regarding the way ahead (Image 2.1). Of course, the player is really navigating a digital maze. In terms of actual gameplay, the player could just as well be navigating a two-dimensional maze from one interactive field to another, stripped of all its magnificent surroundings. Even the sense of going up or down is unnecessary in terms of the game's mechanics, since the entire game occurs on a two-dimensional screen. The third dimension and the historic architectural setting are illusions, special effects designed to provide players with sufficient visual and audio cues to suspend disbelief that they are actually in the basilica.

To the extent that modern cinema relies on computer-generated images (CGIs) for special effects, the underlying structures of videogames' virtual worlds are not unique. However, unlike film, videogames rely on digital media as the means of interaction. Moreover, this interaction is central to videogames, whereas it is almost nonexistent in film. Audiences sometimes react audibly to plot developments in movies, but they usually don't have the ability to shape the outcome. Much like novels, movies present their audiences with unalterable stories. They are completed works, expressions of their authors and production teams. Although the audience can respond to a film, it can't change its outcome. (However, their audience comments through online reviews might persuade a movie's creators to alter its sequel.) Videogames, by contrast, require the player to participate in determining the outcome.

IMAGE 2.1 *Assassin's Creed II*, navigating "Il Duomo" interior. © 2009 Ubisoft Entertainment. All Rights Reserved. Assassin's Creed, Ubisoft and the Ubisoft logo are trademarks of Ubisoft Entertainment in the US and/or other countries.

Nevertheless, game designers are adept at creating the illusion of greater choice than actually exists. *Assassin's Creed II's* Duomo maze has many potential routes, but few of them avoid disaster, and only one general route reaches the goal. A much simpler maze dominates the *Sid Meier's Civilization* series' underlying technology choices. Players choose which technologies to prioritize, but they don't advance very far without first researching all the basic ones. In this case, the restrictions are intentional. By contrast, *Spore* provides more choice in reality than should be allowable given the game's theme. *Spore* purports to be a game about evolution, but as lead developer Will Wright readily admits, it more closely simulates intelligent design (Snider). The reason is a matter of gameplay and marketability, not ideology. The very nature of natural selection would leave the player with nothing to do, other than watch random effects work their way through the gene pool. In order to turn evolution into an actual interactive game, rather than a simulation, Wright had to give players the ability to manipulate the evolutionary process. Both *Assassin's Creed II* and *Spore* present illusions, concerning the levels of choice, in order to be playable and marketable. However, *Spore* is rare among recreations of the past in offering more choices than were actually available. The norm is for games to offer fewer, because it's impossible to reproduce the complexity of history in a playable way.

Perhaps more fundamental in a practical sense is the extent to which game developers determine the thematic overlay that makes the difference between whether a videogame is historical in content or not. This is the difference between mechanics and theme. The videogames industry divides games into genres according to a combination of their mechanical interfaces and thematic levels. For instance, the *Civilization* series consists of turn-based strategy games. Mechanically, they involve players making decisions and moving pieces, then allowing the artificial intelligence (AI), i.e., the computer, to do likewise. This arrangement is similar to chess. Thematically, at the most general level, the games are strategic, because they involve manipulating resources and game pieces. This is also a mechanical issue, since the games require no quick eye-hand coordination.

At the opposite end is the *Call of Duty* series. As with so many games that purport to recreate the experience of serving in combat, those in this series have the player seeing events through a soldier's eyes. They require rapid eye-hand coordination through the eyes of the protagonist and focus on shooting at enemies – thus their designation: first-person shooter (FPS). Real-time strategy (RTS) games involve continuous play with no game turns. However, the player can usually pause the game. Paradox Interactive's series of RTS games, which relate to one another but have no single name, require the player to pause frequently in order to handle the myriad decisions required in managing a faction. Gameplay takes place on a world map and through interactive charts and message screens. The *Assassin's Creed* games work much the same way as an FPS. However, players see the person they are manipulating, giving them more the feel of puppet masters. Moreover, the games focus much more on elements other than shooting at human targets. Stealth, puzzle-solving, and human interactions are major features.

There have been various attempts to bridge the gap between grand strategy, building or battlefield tactics, and action at the level of individual characters. The *Total War* series features turn-based play on the strategic map, but real-time pausable action at the battlefield level. In keeping with the scholarly concept of "total war" meaning that war permeates all aspects of society, much of the *Total War* series' strategic-level interaction involves building up a faction's economy and research abilities. Ubisoft's *Anno (A.D.)* series of settlement-building games occurs at the tactical level, in which the player builds farms and buildings and then watches simulated citizens interact without direct intervention. Longbow's *Hegemony* series, focusing on ancient warfare, allows tactical placement of units on a strategic map. City improvement also occurs on the map. The result is an apparently seamless combination of the strategic and tactical level of military operations that depends on how closely one zooms the camera.

Perhaps the most popular series attempting to combine elements of action at the individual, tactical, and strategic levels into a single interface is *Age of Empires*. These games have the player guide a major historical figure while constructing buildings and farms, and training soldiers and workers, all as part of a grand strategic story that cuts between one scene and the next. In reality, however, the *Age of Empires* series operates mainly at the tactical level, much as *Anno* or the battle interface in *Total War*. The cut scenes in between these tactical mini-games require the player to move in a linear direction at the strategic level, much as they do between missions in *Call of Duty*.

A comparison of these samples indicates at least one correlation between mechanical aspects and thematic features of videogames: those dealing with characters at the individual level are rarely turn-based. Almost all involve continuous action with the ability to pause the game. At the tactical level, some games such as *Total War* use continuous action, whereas others such as *Ultimate General: Gettysburg* and most battle-level computergames based on tabletop war games use turns. Whether building a city or fighting a battle, players perform these tasks as parts of a continuous action. (Notice I avoid using the industry term "real-time," which I consider a misnomer for reasons I'll deal with in the next section of this chapter.) The ability to play in a continuous-action environment is one of the great contributions that computer technology has brought to games with historical themes. Before the digital age, continuous action occurred in sports and in children's imaginative play, but not in games focusing on history. The latter were usually boardgames involving multiple human players. The format required turn-based play in order to calculate the effects that each player's action had on the others. Even the classic tabletop role-playing game *Dungeons and Dragons* required turns in order to enable each player to resolve combat and other activities through its complex system of dice rolls. Since computers can accomplish these calculations instantly, game turns are unnecessary for this purpose.

However, although individual-level games are rarely turn-based, the obverse is not true – plenty of strategy games use continuous-action mechanics. If anything, continuous play may be overused at the strategic level where the capacity (or lack thereof) of players to multi-task continues to limit the potential of continuous action mechanics. This limitation is obvious when comparing gameplay in *Hegemony* and *Total War*. Like *Hegemony*, *Total War* resolves battles through continuous action. (Actually, this is an option with the latter, since players can choose to resolve battles automatically on the strategic map rather than guide their armies on the battlefield.) Unlike *Hegemony*, however, *Total War* has players decide which battles they will fight in a turn-based environment on a strategic map. In *Total War*, therefore, players focus on one battle at a time. In *Hegemony*, by contrast, a player may fight battles at opposite ends of the map simultaneously in the same continuous-action environment. The result can be overwhelming for the player, and arguably unrealistic historically. Before the age of radio communications, a single commander couldn't micromanage the activities of units in two battles occurring far apart at the same time. Similar concerns arise in Paradox's games, particularly *Hearts of Iron*, which simulates the myriad decisions of each World War II belligerent in such detail that playing a major power becomes unwieldy. This contrasts with Muzzy Lane's turn-based, and less detailed, World War II simulation *Making History: The War of the World*. Paradox's solution in *Hearts of Iron III* and *IV* has been to allow players to delegate whole theaters of war to a subordinate AI, much as national leaders did to their senior generals.

Soren Johnson, one of the lead designers of both *Civilization IV* and *Spore*, argues that the most effective games have mechanics that clearly support their themes. In critiquing his own work with *Civilization IV*, Johnson argues that the game is not a good simulation of history, because "all actions in the game are conducted top-down – the player is some strange combination of king, general, tycoon, and god." The reason his team designed the game this way was to make it playable:

> The source of these conflicts with real history is the problem of player agency. In order to be fun, the player needs to be in control. Moreover, the consequence of each decision needs to be fair and clear, so that players can make informed choices, plan ahead, and understand their mistakes. Real history, of course, is much messier and difficult to understand, let alone control.
>
> (Johnson)

However, the game works because the players get what they want, which isn't history, but "the desire is to control history, which may not teach us much about it, but it is not without value." Johnson argues that a game's mechanics, more than its theme, truly engages the player.

Game designer Raph Koster agrees in part. Asserting "that game systems train us to see underlying mathematical patterns," he points to *Deathrace*, the first game ever to be withdrawn from circulation due to its violent content; the player's goal was to use a car to run over innocent pedestrians. In spite of the understandable outrage that this theme inspired, the game's underlying mechanics were almost identical to those of the far less offensive *PacMan* – i.e., "picking up objects on a two-dimensional playing field." (84) Nevertheless, Koster also argues: "the bare mechanics of a game do not determine its meaning." To make his point he provides the following "thought experiment":

> Let's picture a mass murder game wherein there is a gas chamber shaped like a well. You the player are dropping innocent victims down into the gas chamber, and they come in all shapes and sizes. There are old ones and young ones, fat ones and tall ones. As they fall to the bottom, they grab onto each other and try to form human pyramids to get to the top of the well. Should they manage to get out, the game is over and you lose. But if you pack them in tightly enough, the ones on the bottom succumb to the gas and die. I do not want to play this game. Do you? Yet it is *Tetris*. You could have a well-proven, stellar game design mechanics applied towards a quite repugnant premise. To those who say the art of the game is purely that of the mechanics, I say that film is not solely the art of cinematography or scriptwriting or directing or acting. Similarly, the art of the game is the whole.
>
> *(172)*

This example shows how important a theme can be in defining a videogame. *Tetris*, developed by a Soviet programmer in 1984, is a puzzle game in which the player attempts to stack randomly generated shapes of four connected blocks. Presumably, customers would choose to play *Tetris* or the gas chamber game described above for vastly different reasons, even if their subconscious minds responded similarly to the identical underlying problem of the two games. Series such as *Total War* or *Assassin's Creed* portray different geographic and historical settings between adjacent titles while often using only slightly altered mechanics with each new release. The differences between *Total War: Shogun 2* and *Total War: Rome II* are slight in terms of game mechanics, but significant in terms of historical and geographic setting. Yet customers continue to buy and play this series in spite of the similar mechanics across successive titles. Clearly two issues are pulling them in. They like the mechanics. Once they have become familiar with a particular game series' mechanics their learning curve for subsequent titles diminishes. Nevertheless, they need new themes to keep their interest. The combination of these two issues determines how attractive a game is to potential consumers.

Compression and focus

Although the underlying mechanics of a game are important considerations for the type of historical theme portrayed, they are not the most important way in which the videogame medium relates to the presentation of history. In order to entertain, videogames, as movies before them, must simplify the complexity of the past, compressing space, time, events, and characters to fit into a reasonable framework that consumers can manage and enjoy. They must also limit their focus to certain aspects of history in order to create meaningful interactions. This last concern is hardly unique to videogames. Even academic history books vary in focus from the very broad to the very narrow.

A photographer can't easily combine both near and distant focuses into a single shot, because one or the other is likely to be blurry. Similarly, a videogame designer can't easily attempt to recreate the experience of a World War II combat soldier and simultaneously have the player make strategic decisions that a general or national leader would. A comparison of two videogames set during World War II demonstrates this point. In *Call of Duty: World at War* the player experiences the war through the virtual eyes of two fictional protagonists, United States Marine Corps Private C. Miller and Soviet Army Private Dmitri Petrenko, the first in the Pacific Theater and second on the European Eastern Front. All decisions occur in the virtual surroundings of a given scene's battlefield. Success in one scene allows progression to the next. The program determines this progression, not the player. For instance, the player does not decide where to deploy his or her character next in the theater of a military operation. Rather, the scenes unfold much as in a novel or play, with the game establishing the setting and requiring the player to interact with AI characters and perform certain tasks to progress. The game focuses on immersion in successive battles and leaves the common-soldier protagonists with about as little choice in the game as they would have had in real life.

By contrast, *Hearts of Iron IV* has the player in charge of a nation's entire war effort, deciding what to research and produce, where to deploy forces, and when and where to attack. Since the game spans the entire globe, there is no decision-making imposed from above, nor are there any scenes. The entire world is the single scene of all play. Even so, *Hearts of Iron IV* excludes many aspects of history. Nowhere does a player experience the war as an individual soldier or civilian. Nowhere does the game simulate an actual battlefield. The *Total War* and *Hegemony* series appear to bridge the gap between the grand strategy and tactical battle level. However, to do so, both make compromises. The *Total War* series combines the two levels by enacting individual battles as separate mini RTS games within the grand strategy turn-based game. Decisions made at the strategic level determine the composition of the player's army and the terrain on which it fights. The *Hegemony* series provides apparent seamless integration between both levels. In reality, however, the game designers achieve this effect by choosing small theaters for their wars. Greece, the scene of the series' first game, does not cover a very large area, thus making it easier to conduct tactical-level activities on a strategic map. Moreover, *Hegemony*'s armies are disproportionately large for the scale of their virtual surroundings in order to avoid the necessity of zooming in at too detailed a level of terrain. Microsoft's *Age of Empires* series attempts to combine all three levels in an RTS format, in which players can actually control a military leader, and individual soldiers, while mustering armies and navies to fight at the tactical level and conquer territory at the strategic level. In order to do so, however, it drastically compresses time and space. The gap between the individual and strategic level is so great that attempts to bridge it in a single simulation are awkward at best.

If the choice of game level is one area in which physical limitations force designers to exclude many aspects of history, in this case the player's attention, another is time. This restriction is not so much a function of game mechanics as of human endurance. Paradox developers could allow the *Hearts of Iron* games to progress in true real time, virtual second for actual second. Assuming World War II lasted the same amount of time in the game that it did in reality, a single game would require six years of constant attention to complete. Obviously, few people would be interested in playing such a game. The developers, therefore, allow players to accelerate the clock, watching days fly by until some meaningful action or event occurs. This tendency to compress time is typical of all sorts of entertainment, from novels to movies. It even occurs in historical scholarship, which focuses on the moments when events meaningful to the book or article's topic occurred. Significantly, however, while first- and third-person character games skip time as they skip scenes, they are less prone to compress time. That occurs more in strategy games covering large swaths of history. The *Assassin's Creed* series saves the player time by allowing "fast travel," effectively skipping areas between cities or locations in a city. It also frequently compresses geographic space to a small fraction of its true extent. The Paradox series simply lets the player speed time up rather than skip it.

Another aspect of time compression occurs in the *Civilization* series. *Civilization VI* begins in 4000 BCE and ends in 2050 CE. It lasts 500 turns, unless the player achieves one of the four specific victories or loses to a rival before reaching the end date. However, these numbers do not mean that each turn is equal to 12.1 years. On the contrary, every installment of the *Civilization* series decreases the number of years that each turn covers as the game progresses (Table 2.1). This distribution allows most of the gameplay to occur after 1500, when the pace of technological development was more rapid. Nevertheless, this arrangement treats the recent past as more important than the distant past. Given life expectancy in the ancient past, the forty-year turns at the beginning of *Civilization VI* are each about the equivalent of a contemporary lifetime, or at least two-thirds of a lifetime for those fortunate enough to survive disease and war. By contrast, in the rich economies of the twenty-first century, the six months that each turn stands for at the end of the game is the equivalent of about 1/160th of a lifetime. There can be little doubt that most people treat the recent past as more important than the distant past. Popular interest, however, does not equate to balanced history. By privileging the recent past the *Civilization* series is no doubt more marketable – but perhaps less historical.

Time compression can create apparent distortions of logic and scale in games focusing on history. Historian Jeremiah McCall estimates that the Macedonian

TABLE 2.1 *Sid Meier's Civilization VI*, Turn Length in Years

Time period	Years per turn	Number of turns
4000–1000 BCE	40	75
1000 BCE–500 CE	25	60
500–1000	20	25
1000–1500	10	50
1500–1800	5	60
1800–1900	2	50
1900–2020	1	120
2020–2050	0.5	60

Adapted from the "GAMESPEED_STANDARD" subroutine in "Data/Civ6/Base/GameSpeed Values," *Civilization Wiki*, http://civiliza tion.wikia.com/wiki/Module:Data/Civ6/Base/GameSpeed_Values.

cavalry in *Hegemony: Philip of Macedon* travels a mere ten miles per day, less than half, or possibly only a quarter, of its true historical speed. On the other hand, the games' sieges are too short. As McCall points out: "Without siege engines, however, and often even with them, besieging armies would have to wait for starvation in the city or, more commonly, someone in the city to betray it. Sieges generally took on the order of months." However, one of McCall's unassisted sieges took the equivalent of eighteen virtual days. What the designers considered good for game balance in fact distorts historical reality.

Similarly, time compression is apparent in the *Total War* series. Table 2.2 shows ship speeds in four *Total War* games, based on the distance covered in a single turn and the time the game assigns to a turn. Although the historical speeds have wide margins of error depending on contemporary accounts and variable winds in the age of sail, it is clear that the *Total War* series slows down

TABLE 2.2 *Total War*, Ship Speeds and Turn Lengths

Game	Game speed*	Historical speed*	Turn length†	Number of turns
Rome	1.0	55	0.5	568
Medieval II	0.3	75	2.0	225
Empire	20.0	110	0.5	200
Rome II	0.5	55	1	300
*miles per day	†in years			

In-game ship speeds are based on personal observation and online discussions. See "Speed of Ships in Total War – Medieval II: Total War Message Board for PC," *GameFAQs – Medieval II: Total War*, 17 April 2012, www.gamefaqs.com/boards/931592-medieval-ii-total-war/62566744; historical speeds depended on the winds. Estimates are based on Lionel Casson, "Speed Under Sail of Ancient Ships," *Transactions of the American Philological Association* 82 (1951): 136–48; and Klas Rönnbäck, "The Speed of Ships and Shipping Productivity in the Age of Sail," *European Review of Economic History* 16, no. 4 (November 2012): 469–89.

ship speeds by orders of magnitude and does so inconsistently between titles. The reason is not designer ignorance, but playability. In order to simulate the historical ability of fleets to intercept enemies at sea, players mustn't complete long-distance voyages in a single turn. However, *Total War* games cover such long time periods that to have turns representing the equivalent of a few weeks would create games totaling thousands of turns. *Rome: Total War*'s 586 turns was an outlier for the turn-based genre. Creative Assembly limited later titles to roughly half as many turns, thus requiring the distortion in ship speeds. Note that *Empire: Total War*, the game in Table 2.2 that covers the shortest historical period also has the least distortion in ship speeds.

Creative Assembly's decision resulted in yet another distortion in *Total War: Rome II*. The design team wanted to cover a 300-year period in the same number of turns, thus requiring that each turn represent one year. However, they also wanted to simulate the different combat and travel conditions between the four seasons. In *Rome: Total War* this was no problem because the design team simply allotted the necessary large number of turns. *Empire: Total War* limited the number of turns while preserving seasonal variation because it covered only 100 years. The solution in *Total War: Rome II* was initially not to have seasons. When developers introduced them in a later patch, they maintained the game's one-year turns, but had each turn successively represent one of the four seasons ("How Many Turns per Year"). Each turn, therefore, may last anywhere from three to fifteen months depending on where it lies in the four-year cycle among the seasons. None of the game's accompanying dynamics, in terms of transit or production time, takes account of this variable turn length. To observe these temporal distortions is not to condemn the game. As a work of entertainment, it requires distortions in order to make it playable. The developers considered this issue and made necessary compromises with historical accuracy. Nevertheless, it's important when analyzing any game's presentation of history to take such compromises into account, no matter how necessary they may be.

An interesting distortion in the opposite direction occurs in *Assassin's Creed IV: Black Flag*, because it attempts to play out the individual level of interaction on a strategic scale without obviously transporting the main character from one scripted scene to another. The mapping system in the *Assassin's Creed* series allows players to know how far their protagonists are from their targets. In the narrow city streets of Florence or Havana, the series measures these distances in meters. However, *Assassin's Creed IV: Black Flag* takes place on the Caribbean Sea, which serves as an open world in which the player can have the protagonist, Edward Kenway, roam at will. To cross the Caribbean in a schooner such as Kenway's ship would have taken several days. Clearly, gamers would not put up with long, boring voyages over open water, so the designers conflated distance between their map of the Caribbean and the actual gameplay on its surface. To illustrate the point, Image 2.2 shows Kenway at his ship's helm heading toward a target on the coast of Cuba near Cardenas. The skull just above the ship's starboard is accompanied by the distance: 7700 meters. Switching to map mode (Image 2.3) at this point in the game shows Kenway's position, the hooded

IMAGE 2.2 *Assassin's Creed IV: Black Flag*, distance measured shipboard. © 2013 Ubisoft Entertainment. All Rights Reserved. Assassin's Creed, Black Flag, Ubisoft, and the Ubisoft logo are registered or unregistered trademarks of Ubisoft Entertainment in the US and/or other countries.

IMAGE 2.3 Positions of ship and destination from Image 2.2 on map of Caribbean. © 2013 Ubisoft Entertainment. All Rights Reserved. Assassin's Creed, Black Flag, Ubisoft, and the Ubisoft logo are registered or unregistered trademarks of Ubisoft Entertainment in the US and/or other countries.

assassin's head, relative to the target, once again a skull. However, Kenway is just north of the Turks and Caicos Islands. The actual distance between the two points is about 750 kilometers. Therefore, the game is compressing the time it takes to reach the destination by a ratio of about 100:1, a stark contrast to the

Total War series, which *lengthens* sea voyages in order to allow for the possibility of interception. These two very different responses to the problems of distance demonstrate how the interaction of game mechanics and playability trump historical accuracy. Yet it's difficult to criticize such compromises. Without them, the games would be unplayable.

If at the strategic level games often conflate and distort time, at the individual level they do the same with characters. Indeed, a notable feature of popular character-focused games is that their playable characters are rarely historical figures. These games are, therefore, more analogous to historical novels than biographies, whereas many strategy games at least purport to recreate historical forces that professional historians might examine in their scholarship. Indeed, many character-focused titles are quite openly fantastic in their plots. The *Assassin's Creed* series incorporates an intricate backstory dealing with an advanced prehistoric civilization. *Bioshock: Infinite* falls into the creative category of steampunk, set in an alternate universe in which nineteenth- and early twentieth-century technologies developed capabilities with steam age technology that are commensurate with the oil- and electronic-based technology of actual twentieth-century society.

Yet amid their fantastic frameworks, both series introduce players to many aspects of the periods in which they are set. For instance, the virtual settings of the *Assassin's Creed* series involve carefully reconstructed street maps of cities ranging from ancient Alexandria to Victorian London. Moreover, many of the characters that the fictional protagonists encounter are historical. If Ezio Auditore is the James Bond of Renaissance Italy, then Leonardo da Vinci, a truly historical figure, is his Q, supplying him with the latest technology for his exploits. In reality, while da Vinci did conceive of much of this technology, such as tanks and flying machines, he never produced workable prototypes. Furthermore, some of the events in Ezio's fictional life actually occurred, such as the 1476 assassination attempt on Lorenzo di Medici, which the player guides Ezio to foil. Similarly, Haytham Kenway, the fictional protagonist of the early scenes of *Assassin's Creed III*, is credited with assassinating General Edward Braddock, the commander-in-chief of British forces in North America during the Seven Years' (French and Indian) War. Braddock in fact died in combat in 1755. Not only do these protagonists affect historical characters (in the previous instance, by killing one) in ways that are unhistorical; they also, implausibly, encounter a large number of them. During his fictional career, Ezio befriends da Vinci, Lorenzo di Medici, Niccolo Machiavelli, Piri Reis, and Suleiman the Magnificent. He has an affair with Caterina Sforza. He confronts as enemies Rodrigo (aka Pope Alexander VI), Cesare and Lucrezia Borgia, and Girolamo Savanarola. In featuring this plethora of notable cameo appearances in a single person's life *Assassin's Creed* follows the practice of many historical films and television dramas.

Much further removed from historical events than *Assassin's Creed* is the *Bioshock* series, which occurs in fantastic settings, albeit during historical periods imbued with their societal contexts. However, the series emphasizes the dark side of these contexts to explore racism, eugenics, and American exceptionalism.

In a post-apocalyptic submarine art-deco dystopia, *Bioshock* presents the player, through the protagonist, with the moral dilemma of killing children in order to survive, or saving them, thus jeopardizing personal survival. In the early twenti-eth-century airborne city of Columbia, *Bioshock Infinite*'s dystopia reflects con-temporary America's below. The only way to fit in is to accept the racism and hyper-nationalism of the period. Neither the *Assassin's Creed* nor the *Bioshock* series claim to enable players to recreate history. Rather, they use fictional char-acters to play out fictional stories in the context of historical places and events in the former and social norms in the latter.

Why do developers of character-focused videogames prefer their characters to be fictional? Why not choose a real character, for instance da Vinci himself, to have as the protagonist of *Assassin's Creed II*? The advantages of using fictitious characters are readily apparent. They allow designers to develop their own story lines unencumbered by the tedious details of a real person's life. No historical characters fit the profile of the protagonists in the *Assassin's Creed* series. None provides the balance of life experiences and personal characteristics that the designers needed to drive their stories forward and capture the interest of play-ers. As with other entertainment media, therefore, the compression of characters, events, and time itself is intrinsic to videogames' portrayal of history.

The problem of hindsight bias

So far we have seen that the underlying design of videogames, whether they focus on action or strategy; and the demands of consumers, their levels of inter-est, and attention spans; restrict the ability of game designers to reconstruct the past. Perhaps an even more fundamental problem is our knowledge of the past. We already know how things turned out, but people at the time did not. How, then, can game designers simulate the lack of knowledge inherent in the people living in past times? This problem is called "hindsight bias," a concept observed by psychologists and historians for over forty years (Fischer 209–13; Fischhoff). Games exhibit many forms of hindsight bias. Much of this is error for which careful historical perspective can adjust. One form of hindsight bias, however, is a logical problem that no designer can overcome when developing a game aimed at players with even a basic knowledge of history.

This problem is evident when comparing exploration in *Europa Universalis* to that in *Civilization*. *Europa Universalis* covers the period from the fifteenth through the eighteenth centuries, when Europeans connected lands hitherto unknown to them into a unified world system of ecological, economic, popula-tion, and cultural interaction. Because *Civilization* covers the entirety of human history over the last 6000 years, much of the early game involves exploration as players send out scouts to discover resources and encounter other factions. A crucial difference, however, is that in *Europa Universalis* the player is discover-ing continents, resources, and other civilizations on a map of the real world in the locations in which they appeared in reality. In *Civilization*, by contrast, the player explores a randomly generated world in which the program distributes resources and civilizations unpredictably. (There is an option to play on a map depicting the real world, but it is not the standard for the game. Similarly, *Europa Universalis IV* offers an expansion pack, *Conquest of Paradise*, with a randomized New World.) *Europa Universalis'* design team boasts its game's "unparalleled ... historical accuracy," ("About") but the dramatically different approaches between it and *Civilization* to discovering the world raise fundamental questions about the meaning of "accuracy" and the limitations inherent in developing any game attempting to simulate the past. For instance, Images 2.4 and 2.5 show turn 67 (1320 BCE) from *Civilization V* playing the Aztecs, but from different playthroughs. It's immediately apparent that the surrounding environment is unpredictable from game to game.

Which is a more accurate presentation of history: to explore a map of the real world whose outlines and resources one already knows through reading history; or to uncover a map of a computer-generated world of whose outlines and resources one is as ignorant as the historical explorers really were? To focus on the first is to stress the historical accuracy of the game's world and environment. To focus on the second is to emphasize the historical accuracy of the player's perspective in relationship to that world. To focus on both simultaneously is a logical impossibility. One might argue, therefore, that in its portrayal of humanity's lack of geographical knowledge, *Civilization* is the more accurate game, even though the world it portrays varies drastically in its geography from the real world.

Even more pronounced problems of hindsight bias involve technological advances. The blogosphere is replete with advice on how best to manipulate the technology trees of games such as *Civilization* and *Total War* in order to gain an

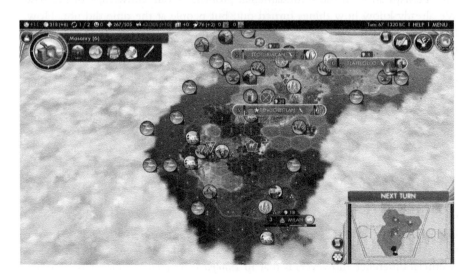

IMAGE 2.4 *Sid Meier's Civilization V: Brave New World*, first playthrough, turn 67. Licensed Asset Courtesy of Firaxis Games, Inc. and 2K Games, Inc.

IMAGE 2.5 *Sid Meier's Civilization V: Brave New World*, second playthrough, turn 67.
Licensed Asset Courtesy of Firaxis Games, Inc. and 2K Games, Inc.

advantage over one's rivals. The problem, of course, is that people living in the
past didn't know what technologies would arise. For instance, the benefits of
agriculture never occurred to hunter-gatherer communities until environmental
issues forced them to adopt this revolutionary new method of sustenance. Nor
could they have known that technological advances such as pottery-making and
bronze-working, which in some cases accompanied the development of agriculture, would lay the groundwork for later ancient innovations such as wheels and
iron tools and weapons, much less that these technologies would in turn support
the development of advanced sailing ships and steam engines.

Players, however, do know this history, and game designers have done little to
avoid the obvious, resulting hindsight bias. Indeed, players often need only call up
a game's technology tree to view exactly which technology they need to acquire
immediately in order to qualify them to acquire a later technology. For instance,
Empire: Total War attempts to simulate the global commercial rivalries of the great
powers of the eighteenth century and the wars these rivalries spawned. This period,
the "Age of Reason," was one of immense and rapid technological innovation, cul-
minating in the Industrial Revolution. Players may know that Thomas Newcomen's atmospheric steam engine in 1711 led to James Watt's considerable
improvement in 1763, which ultimately powered factories, ships, and locomotives.
Empire's technology tree charts this sequence, along which players must proceed in
order to unlock later technologies. (Image 2.6.) The players know that in order to
gain access to steam-powered factories, they must first research the Newcomen
engine. (If they are unfamiliar with the history, the chart explains the sequence for
them.) However, Newcomen knew nothing of the sort. He was trying to pump
water out of mines and, although he did envisage steam-powered boats, he did not

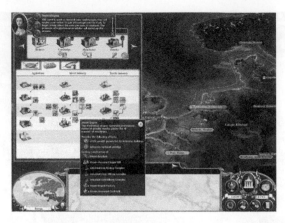

IMAGE 2.6 *Empire: Total War* technology tree, steam engine. Images from *Total War* videogames developed by Creative Games and published by SEGA; published with kind permission of SEGA.

foresee the role that refinements of his invention would play in bringing about an industrial revolution. The long-term goal-driven nature of *Empire: Total War* therefore distorts players' experiences of the eighteenth century by removing the veil of ignorance regarding the future that surrounded inventors of the age.

While the *Total War* series encourages counterfactual developments, these are within the limitations of the world as it actually existed. All its games play out on maps of the actual regions in which the historical content occurred. It should not come as a surprise, therefore, that the series attempts to recreate the actual sequence of technological innovation as faithfully as it does the map of the world in which these innovations arose. Yet even *Civilization*, which artificially generates alternate world maps for gameplay, does not attempt to generate a random technology tree. A couple of reasons may account for this restriction. First, generating alternate technology trees may make for implausible histories in which more advanced technologies precede earlier ones. More likely, however, is the difficulty that game designers, or anyone else, have conceiving of an alternate technology tree. Perhaps there was only one possible sequence to acquire many of our modern technologies. If so, however, it does not alter the fact that we know what this sequence was, and inventors of earlier ages did not. Whatever the limitations that the actual history of technology presents for game designers, it also limits the ability of players to truly appreciate the world as it appeared to its contemporaries in the past. Attempts to simulate history may inevitably present inherent obstacles of hindsight bias that no game designer can overcome.

Game designers can correct some forms of hindsight bias. When they don't, it often results from an overly deterministic view of history. These forms of bias are a major focus of the next chapter. However, the forms of hindsight bias covered above may be logically inherent in any simulation of the past. Gamers can't play in a simulation of the real past and simultaneously possess the ignorance of the future or the world around them that the people of that past had. It's simply a logical impossibility, which forever restricts our ability to truly simulate the past through gameplay.

Conclusion

Like any other medium portraying history, videogames depict their subjects under the physical constraints of the medium and the demands of the marketplace. "Playability" takes into account both these concerns. Time compression and space distortion are often necessary because players tire of games that have too little action or player participation over too long a time. Character compression and the use of fictitious characters respond to the same concerns, plus the need to reduce complexity in order to make interaction manageable. Underlying these thematic considerations are the mechanics of the game, which whether based on turns or continuous play ultimately amount to how the designer presents a complex series of decisions to the gamer. Just as music can be understood simply as a series of tones, and life itself as a complex set of chemical interactions, so can virtual reality ultimately be seen as bits and bytes – a seemingly endless series of decisions. Whether one views games (or reality) this way largely depends on how reductionist an approach one chooses to take. Analyzed at the most reductionist level, the historical content of videogames is mere window dressing. However, if one applies the same reasoning to reality, so is history itself. The rest of this book will focus on the extent to which game designers' presentations of history fit with the way historians and experts in related fields view the past. However, the mechanics of videogames will continue to be an issue, since the limitations of the medium often present designers with difficult choices. Nevertheless, mechanics and players' preferences are not the only issues influencing designers. So are their own and their audiences' assumptions about the past. Exploring these assumptions is a major task of the ensuing chapters.

Works cited

"About." *Europa Universalis IV*, www.europauniversalis4.com/about.

Age of Empires (game series), Ensemble Studios, 1997–2005.

Anno (game series), Max Design/Related Designs/Blue Byte, 1998–2018.

"The Art of Video Games." *Smithsonian American Art Museum*, http://americanart.si.edu// exhibitions/archive/2012/games/index.cfm.

Assassin's Creed II, Ubisoft Montreal, 2009.

Assassin's Creed III, Ubisoft Montreal, 2012.

Assassin's Creed IV: Black Flag, Ubisoft Montreal, 2013.

Bioshock, 2K Boston/Australia, 2007.

Bioshock Infinite, Irrational Games, 2013.

Call of Duty (game series), Infinity Ward, 2003–18.

Call of Duty: World at War, Infinity Ward, 2008.

Ebert, Roger, "Why Did the Chicken Cross the Genders?" *Movie Answer Man | Roger Ebert*, 27 November 2005, www.rogerebert.com/answer-man/why-did-the-chicken-cross-the-genders.

Empire: Total War, Creative Assembly, 2009.

Europa Universalis (game series), Paradox Development Studio, 2000–18.

Europa Universalis IV, Paradox Development Studio, 2013.

Fischer, David Hackett, *Historians' Fallacies: Toward a Logic of Historical Thought*. Routledge and K. Paul, 1971.

Fischhoff, Baruch, "An Early History of Hindsight Research." *Social Cognition*, vol. 25, no. 1, February 2007, pp. 10–13.

Gygax, Gary and Ameson, Dave, *Dungeons and Dragons*. TSR, 1974.

Hearts of Iron III, Paradox Development Studio, 2009.

Hearts of Iron IV, Paradox Development Studio, 2016.

Hegemony: Philip of Macedon, Longbow Games, 2010.

"How Many Turns per Year Is Vanilla Rome 2?" *Reddit*, www.reddit.com/r/totalwar/comments/36n4av/how_many_turns_per_year_is_vanilla_rome_2/.

Johnson, Soren, "Theme Is Not Meaning." *GCD Vault*, www.gdcvault.com/play/1012750/Theme-is-Not.

Koster, Raph, *Theory of Fun for Game Design*. Second edition, O'Reilly Media, 2013.

Making History II: The War of the World, Muzzy Lane, 2010.

McCall, Jeremiah B., "*Hegemony: Philip of Macedon* and the Inspiration of Simulation Games." *Play The Past*, www.playthepast.org/?p=2785.

Rome: Total War, Creative Assembly, 2004.

Sid Meier's Civilization (game series), Microprose/Firaxis Games, 1991–2018.

Sid Meier's Civilization IV, Firaxis Games, 2005.

Sid Meier's Civilization V, Firaxis Games, 2010.

Sid Meier's Civilization VI, Firaxis Games, 2017.

Snider, Mike, "'Spore' Creator Inspired by Intelligent Design, Social Networks." *USATO DAY.Com*, 8 September 2008, http://usatoday30.usatoday.com/tech/gaming/2008-09-08-spore_qa_N.htm.

Spore, Maxis, 2008.

Tetris, created by Alexei Pajitnov, 1984.

Total War (game series), Creative Assembly, 2000–18.

Total War: Rome II, Creative Assembly, 2013.

Total War: Shogun 2, Creative Assembly, 2011.

Ultimate General: Gettysburg, Game-Labs, 2014.

3

CONTINGENCY AND DETERMINISM

Introduction

The year is 1777 and Indians are besieging the Spanish fort of St. Augustine in Florida. However, these Indians don't come from the Americas. Rather, they are Sikh and Maratha, line infantry and camel cavalry from Punjab and Deccan expanding the thirty-year-old Republic of India's empire from its New World base in the Caribbean. The closest Native American power, the Cherokee Nation, is allied with Spain. India's ally, Great Britain, controls the North American seaboard from Virginia to Newfoundland. Over the previous ten years, India has taken advantage of the collapse of Spain's ally France in the face of the expanding empire of Poland-Lithuania, which now dominates the European mainland north of the Alps and the Pyrenees, and threatens the Spanish homeland.

India's remarkable strength so far from home arises from the development of a vibrant capitalist class. Responding to the growing presence of Europeans on its shores, this class started in the early eighteenth century to trade aggressively along the entire Indian Ocean shoreline and the coast of southwestern Africa. Complementing and supporting their bold ventures was the rise of the Maratha state, which supplanted the collapsing Mughal Empire (hastening its demise) and built up a powerful, modern navy to escort Indian dhows as they exported spices, cotton, tea, and sugar to their newly developed, far-flung markets. In order to serve the trading houses of Kerala and Karnataka, stock exchanges arose in Puna and Surat, and Indian entrepreneurs developed mills to produce cotton from their plantations into the world's finest, and least expensive, cotton cloth. In 1747, however, tensions between the Maratha Peshwa, who ruled on behalf of the Bhonsle dynasty, and the merchant class erupted into a revolution, in which the latter overthrew the former, establishing a republic. Freed from the fetters of traditional land usage and aristocratic impediments to market forces, the commercial class applied new technology to production, sparking an industrial revolution. Meanwhile, India expanded its war against Spain, ousting it from its Caribbean possessions in an effort to eliminate its main commercial rival. Firmly in control of the New World's most lucrative territory, India sent Brahmin priests to enlighten the indigenous and creole population and thoroughly Indianize its new possessions. The rest is history.

Or not. The above scenario is based on my experience playing the strategy game *Empire: Total War*. (Images 3.1 and 3.2.) That almost all the details described

IMAGE 3.1   *Empire: Total War*, industrialization in India. Images from *Total War* videogames developed by Creative Games and published by SEGA; published with kind permission of SEGA.

IMAGE 3.2   *Empire: Total War*, India's Caribbean empire. Images from *Total War* videogames developed by Creative Games and published by SEGA; published with kind permission of SEGA.

in this account occurred in the scenario I played is evidence of the depth, complexity, and sophistication of many historical videogames. The issues that this game covers also raise a unique aspect of many videogames that makes them powerful tools for studying history – their capacity to enable the exploration of alternative developments to those that actually occurred historically. This chapter explores the scholarly debate surrounding speculation about what might have been, and the extent to which videogames facilitate this type of thinking. It also examines deterministic traps that game designers sometimes fall into when constructing the parameters within which players can choose to alter historical outcomes in their virtual worlds. As is the case with all other aspects of videogames, their inherent limitations as a medium, the demands of the marketplace, and even the difficulties that game designers have conceiving possible counterfactual worlds set the boundaries within which players explore alternative historical outcomes.

The scholarship of counterfactual history

The value of exploring counterfactual scenarios in history is still a contentious issue among historians. Until recently, most scholars dismissed the exercise as futile fantasy, more appropriate for science-fiction authors than professional historians. To these scholars, history is the preserve of what happened rather than what did not. Nevertheless, proponents of counterfactual speculation argue that all historians who discuss causal relationships in the past – and that is all historians – are in fact indulging in counterfactual speculation. For any given proposition, if one argues that x caused y, then one is implicitly arguing that if x had not occurred, then neither would y. For instance, scholars who argue that the atomic bombings on Japan in August 1945 ultimately saved more lives than they cost are in fact engaging in an argument regarding a counterfactual scenario in which the bombs were not dropped. If these scholars argue that more American, and possibly Japanese, lives would have been lost in an American invasion of Japan's main islands through conventional military means, then they are speculating on what might have been rather than what actually was. The same, of course, applies to the other side of the argument. Scholars arguing that the bombs were unnecessary are also speculating on what might have occurred in the absence of their use.

Historians apply such thinking routinely in their publications, whether assessing the importance of a very specific event, such as Pickett's Charge in the Battle of Gettysburg, or the effects of a condition with global implications, such as the relative absence of domesticable animals in pre-Columbian America. To even contemplate such causal relationships implies speculation on alternate scenarios, in the former case Confederate forces not frontally assaulting Union positions, and in the latter, the presence of large domesticable animals in the New World.

Even if all historians engage in some level of counterfactual speculation, however, these two examples demonstrate that not all counterfactual scenarios are on a par with one another. In advocating for the use of counterfactual scenarios in the classroom, Richard Ned Lebow divides them into "plausible" and "miracle"

(160–61). Pickett's Charge clearly falls into the former category because, within the framework of actual history up to that point, it is quite plausible that this event need not have occurred. The same is true of other "near-misses" of the past. Lebow provides, as a famous example, the assassination of Archduke Franz Ferdinand of Austria, which triggered World War I. This event was truly a "near-miss," or more accurately a "near-hit," because the initial attempt to kill the archduke during his visit to Sarajevo had failed. Only when his cavalcade halted, because it had taken a wrong turn, was the assassin able to shoot the archduke and his wife. Any number of slight changes in the minor events of that day could have resulted in the archduke's survival – better security for the visit, a decision to abort the festivities after the initial assassination attempt, or the leaders of the cavalcade simply not taking the wrong turn. The consequences of not going to war might have profoundly affected the subsequent unfolding of history, for World War I created the context for the rise of fascism. Without World War I it is reasonable to assume there would not have been the vicious race war that we know as World War II. The number of lives spared would have been immense. Millions of Jews, non-Jewish Poles, and Russians would have survived to have their own children; the United States would not have been forced into immediate mobilization; and a beleaguered Britain would not have had to go into *de facto* receivership to its American ally. The consequences of such a scenario are incalculable.

The apparent role of chance makes such narrow, clearly defined, plausible events popular topics of counterfactual speculation. Such events also spark debate between those who view history as deterministic and those who view it as contingent. Perhaps the most famous deterministic view of history is Karl Marx's. Declaring that the "history of all hitherto existing societies is the history of class struggle" (Marx and Engels 8), Marx mapped the past in terms of successive economic systems in which the laboring class overthrew the dominant one, only to replace it as the exploiter in the new social order that arose in the process. For Marx the outcome of this process was inevitable. While detailed events, such as the assassination of Archduke Franz Ferdinand, might be contingent on specific chance events, whether or not these events occurred would not affect the general course of history. Contemporary Marxists tended to regard World War I as nothing more than a conflict among the bourgeoisie (business class); although to their disappointment, most socialist parties supported their respective nations' war efforts. Marxists could dismiss the war in these terms, because Marx had predicted that ultimately the proletariat (industrial working class) would overthrow the bourgeoisie. Of course, things didn't turn out that way, but this only proved Marx's powers of prediction faulty, not his analysis of the past. Many historians still regard conflict between economic haves and have-nots as the major force driving political change.

When determining the historical significance of Franz Ferdinand's assassination, one does not need to be a Marxist to argue it made little difference in the long run. Historians have identified a host of trends and events during the late nineteenth and early twentieth centuries, all pushing Europe's major powers toward war, and it's just as easy to envisage some other combination of events triggering the conflict. Historian Paul Schroeder observes: "The fact that so many plausible explanations for the outbreak of war have been advanced over the years indicates ... that it was massively overdetermined" (320). For him a major war was inevitable. Although the details of its beginning might have differed, the general trend of historical events would have remained similar.

By contrast, the presence of several species of domesticable livestock in pre-Columbian America is an implausible circumstance that would very likely have profoundly affected the entire course of history over the last 500 years. Geographer and biologist Jared Diamond argues that the presence of varied species of domesticable animals in the Old World and their almost complete absence in the New gave the former a massive technological boost by greatly augmenting human labor. He also argues that the presence of livestock in the Old World exposed the population of Africa, Asia, and Europe gradually to crowd diseases building its immunities. More fundamentally, he claims that the North-South orientation of the Americas discouraged trade across its diverse climate zones, while the East-West orientation of Eurasia presented far fewer obstacles. The result was greater transmission of technology among Eurasian societies than among pre-Columbian American ones. When Europeans began to settle in the Americas, the combination of superior technology and the diseases they brought killed off over 90 percent of the indigenous population (Jones 703). Given these circumstances, the extinction or subordination of indigenous New World societies seems inevitable.

Some scholars recoil at the apparent determinism of Diamond's environmental emphasis. Nevertheless, the determinism of this argument does not alter the fact that it implies a counterfactual – because in order to appreciate the impact of livestock and diseases, we must imagine how things might have turned out if these contrasting circumstances between the Old and New Worlds had not existed. Even Diamond posits a counterfactual. What makes his argument appear so deterministic is the impossibility of the counterfactual existing unless not only prehistory but the physical evolution of the Earth had occurred differently. This clearly, then, is one of Lebow's "miracle" scenarios. Yet, as Lebow points out, such implausible counterfactuals still have analytical value, because they "help us work through moral and scholarly problems" (Lebow 161). For Diamond the disparity of technological development among human societies is a moral problem, because it has so often served as a reason to argue that technologically more advanced ethnic groups are somehow more intelligent, hardworking, or innovative than their less advanced counterparts. Diamond uses theories about the impact of livestock, disease, and continental orientation to debunk such racial or ethnocentric thinking. The counterfactual, however implausible in the world as we know it, therefore serves an explanatory end for understanding actual history and the real world around us today.

Understanding the different levels of plausibility that counterfactuals present is important for appreciating the different scenarios possible in historical video-games. *Ultimate General: Gettysburg* presents players with quite plausible alternate outcomes on the simulated battlefield. *Empire: Total War*, by contrast, occurs on a map of the real world, but allows dramatic departures from the historical record that can propel regions on economic, political, and military trajectories quite opposite to those they actually experienced during the eighteenth century. At the far end of "miracle" counterfactual reconstructions of the past is the *Sid Meier's Civilization* series, in which the program randomly generates continents that bear little relationship to their actual terrestrial counterparts, and in which the distribution of resources only rarely occurs the way it did on Earth. In *Civilization* the Aztecs and Incas often have access to horses and iron, with predictably different outcomes in their competition against Old World civilizations. The next section explores these issues in greater depth.

Contingency and technology in *Sid Meier's Civilization*

Ever since the release of its first edition in 1991, *Sid Meier's Civilization* has dominated historical strategy games, often in market share, and always in name recognition. It has received plenty of praise from professional game reviewers. Although some historians have advocated its use as a teaching tool in the classroom, it has also been the object of withering criticism from others (Kapell). The game covers the entire period in which civilizations have flourished, from 4000 BCE to the twenty-first century CE. Players begin the game by choosing what type of environment they want their virtual planet Earth to have, and which civilization they want to play. The environmental options can differ significantly from Earth as we know it. The planet can be more or less arid, hotter or colder, and more or less mountainous. Among other options the player can also choose whether to have an earthlike distribution of large continental land masses with occasional islands, a single continental landmass ("Pangaea"), a world filled with islands, or a landlocked world with a large inland sea in the middle. There is also the option to play on a physical map of the Earth as we know it. A wide variety of civilizations is available from many regions of the world and periods of history. The choices are not limited to the cradles of civilization that would be historically appropriate to the fourth millennium BCE. For instance, one can choose to play the United States, even though in historical terms this civilization only existed during the last twentieth of the period the game covers. Each civilization has unique attributes. Each civilization also has a leader, a great person from that culture's history, who serves as the player's default avatar to guide that faction through the ages.

Unless one chooses to play on a map of the actual Earth, the game then generates a random map with randomly distributed resources and civilizations, including the player's own civilization, which may appear almost anywhere on the planet. The player begins with a settler (representing the civilians of the band or tribe) and a warrior (representing all the warriors of that tribe) surrounded by a single circle of squares or hexes (depending on the edition of the game). The rest of the map is blank, waiting for agents of the player's civilization to explore it. The first turn usually involves two commands to units. The first is to the settler, to build a city, thereby eliminating the settler and having it become the city's first population increment. The second is to the warrior, to explore the surrounding territory. As the warrior unit explores, it uncovers varied topography, such as ice, jungles, forests, hills, mountains, deserts, plains, rivers, flood plains, and coastline. It also uncovers different livestock, crops, minerals, and marine resources, all of which exist permanently in the square or hex in which they are discovered. Particularly important early in the game are the strategic resources of iron and horses, which enable the player to build swordsmen and cavalry – far more powerful than warriors. Exploration also uncovers ruins or villages, which provide various small bonuses to the player's civilization; barbarians, which threaten civilizations but also provide opportunities for military units to gain experience; and other civilizations, which provide trading opportunities but also the potential for war. All these features are affordances, as explained in Chapter 2. They provide players with features and objects that they can manipulate or respond to in ways that alter subsequent gameplay.

Meanwhile, the first city is producing. Initial choices are usually (depending on the faction) a worker, a monument, another warrior, or another settler. In *Civilization V* and *VI* the monument is valuable because it increases culture and the boundaries of the civilization. The worker unit is necessary for developing any of the resources that the warrior uncovers, and for connecting cities with one another. Another settler is necessary for creating further cities, which should be located near to major resources. Only resources in a civilization's zone of control, or acquired from other civilizations (or in *Civilization V* and *VI*, city-states) can be used to develop military units, feed the population, increase happiness, or enhance scientific knowledge. As scientific research uncovers new technologies, new buildings and units become available, thereby increasing the power and prosperity of the civilization.

This brings us to *Civilization*'s technology tree. In order to advance to later technologies, one must first research earlier prerequisite technologies. Each technology adds to the capabilities of a player's civilization (see Images 3.3 and 3.4). For instance, in order to enable workers to build roads in *Civilization V*, a player must research "The Wheel," and in order to research this technology the player must first have researched "Animal Husbandry." That animal husbandry should be a precondition for acquiring the wheel is not surprising, since cultures that did not domesticate any large mammals could not harness vehicles to them and did not therefore see much point in wheel technology. Significantly, Mesoamerican culture used the wheel on what were probably toys, but not on practical large vehicles. However, the assumption that one must have the wheel in order to build roads is in fact ahistorical. Most famously, the Inca

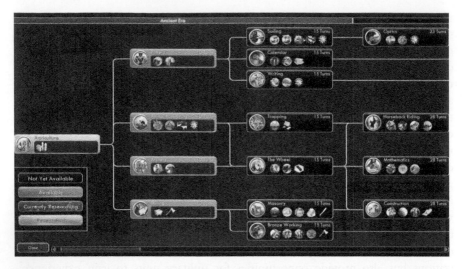

IMAGE 3.3 *Sid Meier's Civilization V: Brave New World*, Ancient Era technology tree. Licensed Asset Courtesy of Firaxis Games, Inc. and 2K Games, Inc.

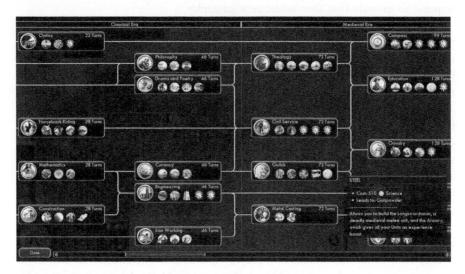

IMAGE 3.4 *Sid Meier's Civilization V: Brave New World*, Classical Era technology tree. Licensed Asset Courtesy of Firaxis Games, Inc. and 2K Games, Inc.

Empire had an extensive network of roads without developing wheel technology. These roads facilitated the movements of armies and couriers. Certainly, the absence of wheels affected their construction, since Inca roads, unlike those of the Old World civilizations, scaled mountains with staircases. However, they were roads nonetheless. The logic of *Civilization V*'s tech tree becomes even more problematic by making the wheel a necessary precondition for mathematics. Perhaps the thinking is that wheels encouraged geometry. However, some of the ancient world's most adept mathematicians were the Mayans, who developed a sophisticated calendar and the concept of zero. Yet they didn't use the wheel. This departure from historical possibilities may reflect a cultural bias among the games' designers, based on the development of technology in the Middle East and Europe. Whatever the reason, it introduces a level of determinism not supported in the historical and archaeological record.

The problems surrounding the position of the wheel in *Civilization V*'s technology raise broader problems with technology trees in general. As all civilizations have encountered one another, particularly over the last 500 years, the resulting exchanges of technology have created a situation in which there is usually only one historical instance of the initial development of a new idea from inception to fruition. This is most apparent with some of the major technological advances of the twentieth century, which required teams of scientists and engineers working under government sponsorship. With the space race and atom bomb, even highly secretive national rivalries arose initially in the context of widespread international exchange of scholarly information. Rocketry was born from the ideas of Konstantin Tsiolkovsky, Robert Goddard, and Hermann Oberth (Russian, American, and Austro-Hungarian-turned-German, respectively), who concluded that multi-staged rockets using liquid propellants were the only feasible way of breaking the Earth's gravitational pull. (While Goddard and Oberth were aware of each other's work, it is not clear that either knew of Tsiolkovsky's.) All these interchanges occurred before these scientists' respective governments enveloped transnational discussion in shrouds of secrecy (Burrows 36–73).

Similarly, the concept of atomic power and weaponry arose in the 1930s amid widespread scholarly exchange among physicists including Werner Heisenberg and Neils Bohr, pioneers of quantum physics, and Albert Einstein, the father of relativity. As late as Spring 1940, when France and Britain were already fighting Germany, Leo Szilard had difficulty persuading Enrico Fermi, a fellow immigrant to the United States, not to publish the results of his nuclear experiments at the University of Chicago (Baggott 46–47). After the United States dropped atomic bombs on Japan, Soviet scientists used reverse engineering, and important information passed to them by communist sympathizers working in the American and British programs, to design their own bomb. The examples of rocket science and nuclear physics therefore demonstrate that, as far as we know, there is only one basic way to escape Earth's gravity and only one basic way to design a fission bomb, each of course displaying minor variants reflecting the priorities of the design teams involved. Most notably, Heisenberg's team, working for the Nazis, failed to produce an atom bomb, in part because its members had not realized the compression technique necessary to create a chain reaction using relatively small amounts of uranium.

Nevertheless, in other areas of technology, alternative solutions to solving the same problem have developed, and it's unclear whether the reasons for the adoption of different methods are the result of the superiority of the technology in a given situation or the influence of culture and politics. For instance, in most of North America train travel is associated with the period from the mid-nineteenth to the mid-twentieth centuries, having subsequently yielded to the airplane and automobile. Yet in Europe and many parts of Asia diesel rail technology has moved on to high-speed electric versions and continues to compete with the automobile. The reluctance of the United States, Canada, and Australia to follow this developmental path may be a result of their dispersed populations, which may not benefit so obviously from high-speed rail. However, it may also result from the influence of oil companies and car manufacturers over these countries' political systems. This influence is particularly evident in the United States, whose government consciously chose in 1954 to invest in highways rather than railroads, even in California, the Great Lakes region, and the Eastern Seaboard, where the population is relatively dense (McShane).

Similarly, the demise of the dirigible airship (aka Zeppelin) on the eve of World War II may owe as much to a few spectacular disasters, predating the era in which fixed-wing aircraft could carry many passengers and have disasters of their own, as it does to the superior speed of the airplane. World War II highlighted the superiority of the airplane, whose faster speed and smaller size made it less vulnerable to attack than dirigibles. Vulnerability to attack would have been less a concern in peacetime. Moreover, the United States stockpiled most of the helium required to keep airships aloft, and denied Germany, which had invested the most in dirigible technology, access to it during the war. Although dirigibles probably could not have competed with airplanes for transatlantic travel after commercial jet carriers became relatively safe and viable in the late 1950s, the age of the airship ended twenty years before this point. Furthermore, it is conceivable that dirigibles might have continued to fill a niche between the automobile and the airplane many years after. The demise of the dirigible in the late 1930s may therefore owe as much to the political circumstances surrounding its heyday as it does to its suitability as a transport technology at that time (Robinson).

Such examples underscore the contingent nature of the adoption of technology. The question is to what extent videogames acknowledge such contingencies. The answer is complicated. *Civilization IV* allows the construction of airships, but the technology trees of *Civilization V* and *VI* do not. However, *Civilization V: Brave New World* includes a scenario, "Empires of the Smoky Skies," based on the premise that steam continued to power technological development in the twentieth century. A comparison of Images 3.5 and 3.6 shows the differences between what *Civilization V*'s designers considered to be their simulation of reality and the counterfactual technological development. Note the absence of electricity in the alternative technology tree and the dependence of all subsequent technologies on steam power, rather than on biology, and dynamite. This technological bottleneck sets the stage for the absence of machinery dependent on oil and electricity. Thus, we see the development of analog, rather than digital, computers and tanks and airships powered by steam rather than gasoline.

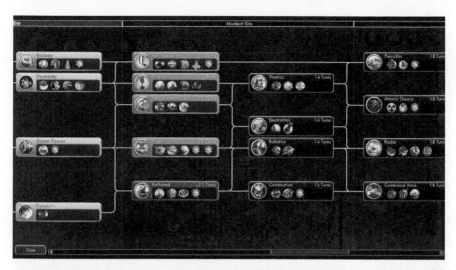

IMAGE 3.5 *Sid Meier's Civilization V: Brave New World,* Modern Era technology tree. Licensed Asset Courtesy of Firaxis Games, Inc. and 2K Games, Inc.

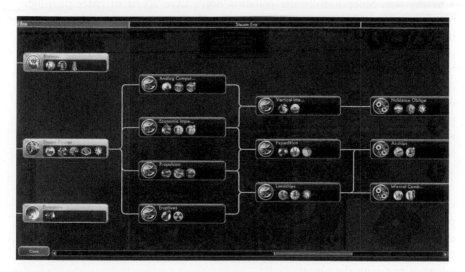

IMAGE 3.6 Equivalent of Image 3.5 technology tree in *Sid Meier's Civilization V: Brave New World* "Empires of the Smoky Skies" scenario. Licensed Asset Courtesy of Firaxis Games, Inc. and 2K Games, Inc.

A whole genre of literature and the arts, called "steampunk," has arisen around such counterfactual scenarios (Brummett), and some videogames occur in this type of setting. Most acclaimed by critics is *Bioshock Infinite,* set in 1912 and taking place in the fictional aerial city of Columbia. It is a dystopic alternative past in which a fundamentalist-Christian, American nationalist, and racist government has broken away from the United States. Massive balloons keep the city aloft, lending an air of technological plausibility to the virtual world. Nevertheless, neither *Bioshock Infinite* nor *Civilization V*'s "Empire of the Smoky Skies" scenario addresses the issue of more recent choices in alternative technological solutions to the environmental challenges of fossil fuels. Indeed, an exclusively steam-powered world would be at least as dependent on fossil fuels as the world we live in now. In fact, the main technology tree of *Civilization V* does a better job of addressing such issues in its nod to alternative forms of production, with hydro-electric, solar, and nuclear power becoming available alternatives or supplements to coal-burning factories. It does not, however, address the use of modern rail technology, treating the railroad instead solely as a product of the age of steam. This may result from both games being products of American design teams and therefore drawing on the United States' technological trajectory. French developers might have included high-speed rail, and Danish ones, wind farms.

Perhaps *Civilization*'s most comprehensive effort to envisage alternative paths of technological developments is set not in the past, but in the future. *Civilization: Beyond Earth* has gamers play a faction from Earth that has survived an unspecified catastrophe and set out to colonize an earthlike planet circling a nearby star. Since initially the colonists don't have access to faster-than-light travel, they must forge new societies in a hostile alien environment in competition with the colonists of rival civilizations from Earth, all in the absence of any support or communication with the home planet. *Beyond Earth* envisages three "affinities" that a player might follow: one is "purity," which involves terra-forming the new planet and destroying its native species to make the new environment as much like Earth as possible. This philosophy toward colonization is perhaps most reminiscent of the way British settlers approached their occupation of North America and Australia. Another "affinity" is "supremacy," in which humans embrace technology to transform their environment, and even themselves, into cybernetic organisms. Since victory in this case involves ultimately returning to Earth and "liberating" humans there from their organic existence, the player's goals take on a nightmarish quality. Finally, in "harmony" the player coexists so thoroughly with the alien environment that his or her civilization begins to merge with it, and humans themselves become hybrid alien beings. Victory for this affinity is "transcendence," in which the player's faction becomes one with the planet.

Each "affinity" requires a different emphasis in technological development. Although all players begin with "Habitation," and the early game almost requires them to develop the subsidiary "leaf" technologies of "Pioneering" and "Planetary Survey," incentives to research particular technologies increasingly diverge as players move further away from the center of the technology web. Image 3.7 shows the bottom-right quadrant of this web from the perspective of a player (late in the game) pursuing the "harmony" affinity. The technologies with light circles to the left are those that the player has already researched; the technologies in darker tone are those that can be researched immediately; and

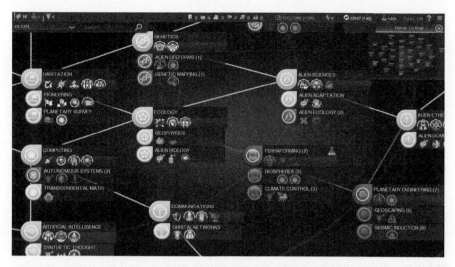

IMAGE 3.7 *Sid Meier's Civilization: Beyond Earth* technology tree, bottom-right quadrant. Licensed Asset Courtesy of Firaxis Games, Inc. and 2K Games, Inc.

the technologies with dimmed circles require intermediate technologies to be researched before the player can begin working on them. Technologies with upright arrows provide a "purity" affinity; those with inverted arrows, a "supremacy" affinity; and those with spirals, a "harmony" affinity. The game totals eighteen of each type of affinity, and the player becomes more powerful by amassing all eighteen of a single type of affinity. (Although an update made it possible to win through a combination of affinities, the initial release discouraged this approach.) There is insufficient time in the game to research the technologies necessary to acquire more than one complete set of any type of affinity. (Even in the update there isn't time to research all the technologies in the web.) Image 3.7, therefore, shows a policy of scientific research that has bypassed the more mechanistic technologies, favoring the "purity" and "supremacy" affinities, in favor of the holistic biological technologies, favoring the "harmony" affinity. It's neither necessary nor desirable to research those other technologies if a player is following the path of "harmony."

Western scholarship has a tendency to assume that the basic outline of technological development followed by the Western world was, with minor variations, the only path possible to modernization. Other routes of technological development are difficult to imagine, and may in fact require utterly implausible counterfactual scenarios. It perhaps takes a version of *Civilization* occurring 500 to 1000 years in the future to indulge in such speculation. Almost all of the technologies in *Civilization: Beyond Earth* are speculative, many of them based on existing works of science-fiction. Even in this futuristic game, freed from our knowledge of what actually will occur, the "purity" episode seems most likely, since it best approximates the behavior of humans in the past.

Perhaps invented alternative technology trees for historical videogames would appear even less plausible when set alongside the technologies that actually developed. Significantly, so far it appears that no game developer has tried.

Great individuals and events

So far, we have dealt with counterfactual alternatives to actual history in terms of major impersonal historical forces, whether environmental, technological, social, or economic. Perhaps the most popular speculations in counterfactual history, however, revolve around great people and dramatic events, particularly battles. This should not be surprising, since high-profile individuals and events appear to have effects well beyond the daily events of millions of people's lives. Moreover, they also tend to interest the average reader or game player more than the larger forces that have been the focus of most historians for many decades. The "great man theory" is one of oldest ideas debated among professional historians, dating well back into the nineteenth century, and it's worth examining its validity and seeing how videogame designers have incorporated it.

The most famous proponent of the "great man" theory of history was Thomas Carlyle, who in 1841 argued that:

> Universal History, the history of what man has accomplished in this world, is at bottom the History of the Great Men ... They were the leaders of men, these great ones; the modellers, patterns, and in a wide sense creators, of whatsoever the general mass of men contrived to do or to attain; all things that we see standing accomplished in the world are properly the outer material result, the practical realisation of embodiment, of Thoughts that dwelt in the Great Men into the world: the soul of the whole world's history ... were the history of these.
>
> *(Carlyle 1–2)*

Although Carlyle's approach to history was popular among historians in the nineteenth century, it raised considerable opposition even during his lifetime. Marx objected to Carlyle's view because it contradicted his own that the masses, or even completely impersonal forces, shaped history. Carlyle's most ardent opponent, however, was Herbert Spencer. As a founding father of Social Darwinism, Spencer regarded history as the result of purely impersonal evolutionary forces and argued that great individuals are more products than creators of the cultures in which they arise:

> If it be a fact that the great man may modify his nation in its structure and actions, it is also a fact that there must have been those antecedent modifications constituting national progress before he could be evolved. Before he can re-make his society, his society must make him. So that all those changes of which he is the proximate initiator have their chief causes in

the generations he descended from. If there is to be anything like a real explanation of these changes, it must be sought in that aggregate of conditions out of which both he and they have arisen.

(35)

Both Carlyle and Spencer's arguments were racial in their underlying assumptions. Long after his death, Carlyle's great-man theory supported the fascist "cult of the personality," which extolled the leader as the driving force behind a nation's destiny. Similarly, in framing his opposing argument, Spencer claimed:

> by no possibility will an Aristotle come from a father and mother with facial angles of fifty degrees, and ... out of a tribe of cannibals ... there is not the remotest chance of a Beethoven arising.

(34)

Nevertheless, the Social Darwinist nature of Spencer's arguments doesn't undermine the general assertion that the significance of any individual's contribution to society depends partly on the accumulation of experience on which that individual builds and the set of circumstances constraining or propelling that person's actions. However racist the basis of Spencer's assertion, his argument in favor of impersonal forces set the tone for professional historians ever since. For most of the nearly 150 years since, they have increasingly turned their attention to studying larger social, economic, and environmental forces, focusing on individual people and events more for their illustrative value than to argue that these anecdotes themselves made enormous differences in the outcome.

This tendency among historians, to regard great people and events as reflecting, more than shaping, historical processes, does not however mean that all of them entirely dismiss the ability of major events to influence the world around them. As historians have increasingly focused on the extent to which developments in their fields were contingent on combinations of circumstances and occasionally random events, they have implicitly raised the possibility of such events at least altering history in the short term. Since individuals are more likely to have a measurable influence over single, important events, these events provide the opportunity to speculate on counterfactual scenarios had these individuals acted differently. Nevertheless, most professional historians focus on trends rather than events, and processes rather than individuals. When they do focus on specific events or individuals, it is usually to illustrate the greater trends and aspects of the surrounding society. Questions of group agency and the contingent nature of events may challenge the economic or evolutionary determinism of Marxism and Darwinism respectively, but they have not restored great individuals to the center of historical analysis.

The general public, however, has largely ignored the last century or more of historical scholarship in this regard. Battles, revolutions, heroes, and villains all provide much more compelling reading than grand processes, and the academic micro-studies that illustrate them. Not surprisingly, the most popular historical games, such as *Call of Duty* and *Assassin's Creed*, follow individuals through historical events and sometimes include great individuals in the story lines. For instance, *Call of Duty: Black Ops* introduces Cuban leader Fidel Castro into the game as the focus of the protagonist's assassination plot. The *Assassin's Creed* series introduces its fictional main characters to a long list of famous individuals, including Richard the Lionheart, Leonardo da Vinci, Benjamin Franklin, Edward Teach (aka Blackbeard), and Cleopatra. In *Assassin's Creed* the protagonists often influence history by performing tasks accomplished by lesser-known or nameless figures in the past. Yet, curiously, such first- and third-person action games are less likely to pursue major counterfactual scenarios than are the less personal strategy game series, such as *Civilization* and *Total War*.

When action games present counterfactual scenarios, they may be completely discrete from their main narratives. This is the case with *The Tyranny of King Washington*, an add-on set of scenarios to *Assassin's Creed III*, which is set during the American War of Independence. In reality the United States' first president chose to step down after two terms, setting an example that only Franklin Delano Roosevelt did not follow. Washington's gesture set an important precedent for the rule of law and due process at the beginning of the republic. In *The Tyranny of King Washington*, however, the victorious general falls under the influence of an orb left over by a long-lost technologically advanced civilization that preceded all historical civilizations. This orb makes Washington lust for power, forcing *Assassin's Creed III* protagonist Connor Kenway to oppose him. If one ignores the science-fiction premise behind Washington's turn toward megalomania, the scenario posits an issue that other historians have noted: the importance of Washington's willingness to yield power. This discussion not only implies the counterfactual of him not willingly yielding power, it also implies that the actions of a great individual affected the development of the early American republic. The game scenario clearly applies the "great man" theory to Washington.

Grand strategy games deal much more with major historical processes. This too can be a problem in terms of historical scholarship, which is often suspicious of sweeping generalizations. Nevertheless, the approach of most of these games to great individuals adheres more closely to most historians' views on the matter. In *Civilization* and *Total War* important individuals arise fairly often during gameplay. Moreover, they bear the names and rough areas of expertise of historical figures. However, they appear as part of a process resulting from the general level of research and development in the civilization. In *Civilization VI* the player can actually see a chart estimating how many turns remain before the next "great person" appears. In *Empire: Total War*, the player assigns "gentlemen" to work in colleges and universities advancing knowledge in their areas of expertise. In *Europa Universalis* advisors work for the government, adding their special attributes to the progress of the state. Paradox's *Crusader Kings II* (preceding *Europa Universalis* chronologically) makes the connection between individuals and the faction even more obvious, since the player's faction is a dynasty rather than a state. The aim is to maintain and expand the dynasty. In this context the state merely expresses the dynasty's power. As a result, players must pay particular care in *Crusader Kings II* to ensure that their lineage is secure through marriages and offspring. In all these games military leaders enhance armies or navies' abilities to win battles. However, no single great individual is likely to transform the destiny of a civilization radically unless other contributing factors are at a tipping point. All these three game series provide abundant opportunities to alter history and pursue counterfactual scenarios, but with the possible exception of *Crusader Kings II* the way to achieve this goal is much more through processes over time than through the actions of any individual. In this sense, these games place great individuals in much the same position they occupy among professional historians.

Wars and battles: Hastings and Gettysburg

Perhaps the greatest potential for individuals to shape the course of history is through war, particularly through battles that determine the outcome of war. As an area of research, military history has fallen out of favor among most professional historians. This is particularly the case for the traditional form, focusing on decisions and circumstances that led to victory or defeat. Modern historians of war and the military often examine their social aspects, such as camaraderie among soldiers, or the use of gender in propaganda. No matter how much historians emphasize social and cultural history in their research, however, few of them would deny the importance of decisions on the battlefield for what they study. For instance, historians focusing on British society in the second half of the twentieth century would surely be studying a very different place if it had been under Nazi occupation. To take a fairly mundane example, how would such an occupation have affected the development of youth culture in the thirty years following the war? Given Nazi objections to any music that drew on non-"Aryan" influences, and given the oppressive nature of Nazi governance, it's hard to imagine that the Beatles and the Rolling Stones would have ever found an outlet for their adaptations of rhythm and blues. A far grimmer outcome of Germany's conquest of Eastern Europe is that the social history of the large Yiddish-speaking communities of that region effectively ended with the Holocaust. Without those German victories, these communities may well still be in existence today. If few historians focus on the course of crucial wars and battles, it's because earlier historians already did so, and because there are so many other aspects of the past deserving analysis. The fact that historians' attention has turned in other directions does not mean that they think the outcomes of these events were unimportant.

As with counterfactual scenarios in general, the further back a military event, the more profound its effect on the twenty-first century is likely to have been if its outcome were different. An example of how profoundly such events might influence subsequent developments is the Battle of Hastings, fought on 14 October 1066 between the armies of Harold Godwinson, the recently elected Anglo-Saxon king of England, and William, the Norman duke claiming his throne. Had William failed to conquer England, our world would surely be significantly different. Most obviously, the very sentences you are reading now would for the most part be unrecognizable. Norman dominance of England accounts for the enormous infusion of French words, which set English apart from other Germanic languages and provided it with such a varied vocabulary. Politically, England would have continued to share more ties with Scandinavia than France. Since it was the Norman connection that served as the basis for the late Medieval English claims to much of France, there would presumably have been no Hundred Years' War had Harold prevailed at Hastings. In the second volume of *What If?*, a collection of essays speculating on counterfactual outcomes, contributor Cecelia Holland muses on possible far-reaching effects of an English victory. Pointing to the recent Norse colonization of Greenland and attempted colonization of Newfoundland, she argues that English attention would have turned to the west rather than the south, leading to a much earlier establishment of English settlements in North America. Such a development would have been less disastrous for Native Americans, since the gap in military technology between the Old World and the New was not so great at this point (79–80). Holland does not mention the impact of disease, but this too might have been more gradual, and therefore less devastating to Native American cultures than what actually occurred centuries later. Holland's speculation may border on fantasy, so difficult is it to demonstrate the economic and political effects she claims would have occurred, but few scholars would dispute that Hastings was one of history's most consequential battles.

The contingent nature of history is particularly evident in the Battle of Hastings, because its outcome was far from a foregone conclusion. The composition of the two armies favored the Normans. Harold's forces, made up solely of infantry, and lacking even archers, suffered a serious disadvantage compared to the mix of infantry, cavalry, and archers that comprised the Norman expedition. Balancing this benefit to the Norman side, however, was the home-field advantage that Harold enjoyed. Surrounded by a hostile population and separated by open water from his home base, William knew that he would soon run out of supplies. Rather than placate the locals, as many would-be rulers might do when planning on annexing a kingdom, William raided nearby estates, foraging for food. Not only did this increase his army's supplies, it also encouraged Harold (whose own estates William raided) to engage in battle almost immediately. The Norman duke needed a quick decision before his army of 5000–10000 (fairly large by Medieval European standards) went hungry, and before Harold could raise a much larger force from the surrounding population (Bradbury 162–68).

William got his wish, but even so, the circumstances of the two armies' encounter allowed the English to fight from an advantageous position. Whether Harold had a chance to pick the location of the battle is uncertain, but William clearly did not. Some of the Norman forces were absent, because they were foraging. Standing in close formation, English forces formed a "shield wall" at the top of a hill. Harold intended to exhaust and erode William's forces by letting them charge uphill against this shield wall. It would certainly have helped the English side if it had included a larger number of archers, who could fire over their comrades onto the assaulting Norman forces. Against the English were Norman cavalry on the wings, who in more open terrain might outflank the English. In this case, however, the presence of woods on either side of the English shield wall made such a maneuver more difficult (Bradbury 184–85).

Adding to the uncertainty of the outcome was the presence of both claimants on the battlefield. Both leaders served as their army's commanders, and neither commanded from afar. Rather, they too engaged in battle to inspire their men. If either fell in battle, not only would their forces be demoralized, but much as in a game of chess, the war would be over – because the whole point of the conflict was to determine which individual contender gained the throne. This personal stake in combat added a feature of uncertainty to many ancient and Medieval battles that was largely missing in later times, when monarchs, presidents, and even generals directed their forces from a greater distance.

The personal vulnerability of the leaders presented the first great counterfactual possibility of the battle. For after an initial assault against the English shield wall failed, and the Norman army retreated in apparent disarray, the rumor spread that William had fallen and was dead. Indeed, he may have fallen from his horse, but he soon appeared before his men pulling off his helmet to reassure them that he was alive and well. In doing so he halted the Norman retreat and rallied his forces to turn on the English, some of whom had now broken from the shield wall in pursuit of William's fleeing men. These English soldiers fell to the Normans, who spent the rest of the day assaulting the shield wall and feigning retreat, all the while tempting Harold's forces to break from their secure position atop the hill so that William's cavalry could pick them off. At some point during the battle not only did Harold die, but both of his brothers as well. With all the obvious Anglo-Saxon heirs to the throne dead, the shield line broke and fled, and William marched on to London and the throne (Bradbury 185–208).

Players can appreciate the tactical and personal issues at stake in *Medieval II: Total War*'s recreation of the Battle of Hastings, available in the game as a historical battle scenario distinct from the main campaign. Image 3.8 shows the arrangement of Norman forces at the bottom of the hill and English forces at the top. Knowing in hindsight what actually occurred, it is relatively easy for the player, as William, to run a series of attacks against the English shield wall followed by retreats that tempt Harold's forces down the hill where one can overrun them. However, alternative tactics, such as a full-frontal assault without retreats, can lead to disaster, as Image 3.9 shows. *Medieval II: Total War* only gives gamers the option of playing the Normans in this

IMAGE 3.8 *Medieval II: Total War*, "Hastings," order of battle. Images from *Total War* videogames developed by Creative Games and published by SEGA; published with kind permission of SEGA.

IMAGE 3.9 *Medieval II: Total War*, "Hastings," William's death. Images from *Total War* videogames developed by Creative Games and published by SEGA; published with kind permission of SEGA.

scenario. It is, therefore, impossible to change English behavior directly by, for instance, having Harold adamantly refuse to let his troops be drawn down the hill. This restriction makes the battle entirely William's to lose. By contrast, the BBC's history website features an untitled game about Hastings in which a player can choose either side. Rather than depicting "real-time" continuous action, however, it presents players with a series of decisions, each dependent on the previous one, followed by graphics depicting the outcome. Significantly, however, there appears to be no way to win if one chooses the English faction, while it is possible to lose as the Normans if one chooses any other course of action than those that William pursued. In other words, only William's alternate decisions can change the outcome, not Harold's, and the only way for William to win is if he follows exactly what occurred.

Historical treatments of the battle do not take such a deterministic approach. Historian Jim Bradbury observes: "Part of the fascination of the battle of Hastings is that it was such a close-fought thing" (201). Although his analysis in no way purports to entertain counterfactual scenarios, he leans in this direction in describing the immediate aftermath of the Norman's first assault, when the rumor spread of William's death:

> This was the crisis point for William. His troops were in disarray. The
> beginnings of a flight can very easily turn into broader panic. The rumour
> of his death could have been cause enough for a general flight.
>
> *(192)*

Holland clearly considers Hastings to have hung in the balance, as do the editors of the volume containing her essay. The Battle of Hastings presents an interesting example of contingency in history, the counterfactual possibilities of which players could explore in videogames. Curiously, so far commercial videogame designers have not seized this opportunity.

More options to play counterfactual history are available for players exploring the Battle of Gettysburg, the largest battle of the American Civil War. Sid Meier published a "real-time" title (*Sid Meier's Gettysburg*) in 1997 and Matrix Games currently sells a 2012 Gettysburg title as part of its *Scourge of War* series on the Civil War. The 2014 independent release *Ultimate General: Gettysburg* uses a terrain map based on satellite imagery to provide a unit-level continuous-action (albeit sped-up) version of the battle, with breaks at the end of each day. During these breaks the game assesses a player's progress and provides opportunities for planning tactics for the following day. Players can choose either side, and it's quite possible, counter to history, for the Confederacy to win the battle.

The object of the Confederacy was to secede from the United States, in order to safeguard the institution of slavery, which was under pressure from Northern states that had abolished it. The military goals of the Southern states were, therefore, defensive. They had to prevent Union armies from occupying their territory and imposing US law. In order to accomplish this goal, however, the Confederate States needed to attract support from other powers, particularly because the states remaining in the Union were more industrialized and better able to equip its army. Confederate leaders also hoped to persuade Northern voters in the upcoming 1864 election to replace Abraham Lincoln with a president willing to make peace on Southern terms, or at least to sway members of the United States Congress to withdraw their support from the war effort. To achieve these goals the Confederate States required a victory that would embarrass the anti-secessionist politicians of the North. Such a victory would ideally demonstrate that the Union could not even defend its member states, let alone impose its will on the South. A symbolic area of vulnerability lay in the location of the United States' capital, Washington, DC, on the border of Maryland and Virginia. Virginia's secession left the Union capital just across the Potomac River from one of the Confederacy's most powerful states. If a Confederate army could penetrate deep into Union territory and cut off communications between most of the Union and its capital, it would provide a symbolic victory that, the reasoning went, might bring enough external and internal pressure on the US government to force it to let the Southern states secede.

Leading this effort in the field was General Robert E. Lee. In June 1863, he led a force of 72,000 men through western Maryland into southern Pennsylvania. Tracking his forces further east (but unsure of Lee's location) was a Union army, 94,000 strong, under the command of Major-General George Meade (Busey and Martin 125, 260). Besides the political goals listed above, a more immediate one for Lee was to forage for supplies lacking in Virginia. In spite of Lee's directive to avoid engaging the enemy, a Confederate commander ordered a reconnaissance in force, against Union forces stationed on three hills west of the town. Thus began, almost by accident, the first day of the battle.

The chance nature of the battle's beginning explains some of its central features and outcomes. Since neither side anticipated a major confrontation near Gettysburg, both sides were slow to deploy their forces to the engagement. As a result, the battle lasted three days, with combat abating during the nighttime as both sides rested and replenished supplies. Each day further reinforcements arrived after their commanders learned of the clash of arms nearby. Crucially, because Lee had dispatched his cavalry division (under Major-General J. E. B. Stuart) in an effort to outflank the Union army, it was unavailable until the third day of combat. If these forces had been present on the first day of the battle, the Confederate forces might have won in a single day.

As the battle turned out, however, Confederate forces were unable to turn early success into outright victory the following day. Meade arranged his forces in the shape a fishhook, holding the high ground formed by Cemetery Ridge and Cemetery Hill. In the midst of enemy territory, Confederate forces needed to gain the high ground, break the stalemate, and establish dominance over the surrounding countryside, or they would lose the campaign. This situation led to Lee's loss of the battle. Because the Union army's artillery commander decided to conserve ammunition by halting a two-hour long volley on the afternoon of the third day, Southern commanders assumed that the Northern side had exhausted its supply. They were wrong. When Confederate Major-General George Pickett led an infantry charge up Cemetery Hill to dislodge Union forces from the high ground, he encountered an artillery barrage (and stiff resistance from the Northern infantry) that halted the Confederate advance. By the end of the day, Lee decided to withdraw his forces to Virginia. Meade, controversially, chose not to pursue the Confederate general, thus possibly allowing the war to drag on until 1865. However, the South never tried such an audacious invasion of Northern territory again.

Ultimate General covers this complex engagement in considerable detail. It allows players to direct their forces by clicking and dragging them to the positions they are to hold. At the end of each day, it provides the player with options for the next day's strategy and, according to the player's decisions, deploys forces for that day's battle. Since the player is in the position of either Lee or Meade, commanding their entire army depending on which side the player chooses, individual units may become demoralized and withdraw. Other than this challenge, common in videogame portrayals of battlefield tactics, players are in complete control of their forces within the context of what was already occurring at the beginning of the battle. For instance, Lee can deploy the forces that were available to him on Day 1, and whatever forces are left on the following two days based on what survived the first day. However, he can't get Stuart to appear with his cavalry until the third day. This circumstance is determined by the actual past at the game's beginning.

Ironically, *Ultimate General: Gettysburg* provides for better possibilities of alternative outcomes than do the digital portrayals of Hastings discussed above – this in spite of the general agreement among historians that both battles could have gone either way, and that Hastings was more clearly a turning point in history. Although Gettysburg was the largest battle of the American Civil War, a Southern victory would probably have achieved no more for the Confederacy than delaying its defeat at the hands of a numerically and industrially superior North. As military historian Thomas Goss notes, "Even if Lee had succeeded in smashing the Army of the Potomac at Gettysburg, victory would not have been a fatal blow to the Union. Vicksburg would still have fallen, and the Confederacy would still have been split in half" (14). Hastings, on the other hand, was the only major battle in Harold's struggle against William. It changed the history of England, and arguably much of the rest of the world. The difference between the two battles lies in their technological and political contexts. Like most wars of the nineteenth and twentieth century, the American Civil War required the full deployment of a country's resources to support large armies and the equipment attending them. Political leaders stayed far from the battlefield and were often representing governing structures that could survive their personal demise. Hastings, on the other hand, involved comparatively small retinues led into battle by hereditary leaders, whose personal demise would undermine the rationale for the conflict.

Significantly, none of the historians contributing pieces on the Civil War to the *What If* volumes chose Gettysburg as potentially changing the conflict's outcome. However, perhaps the most influential writer of history in the twentieth century (although not a professional historian) did believe Gettysburg determined the outcome of the war. This was Winston Churchill, who contributed an essay to *If: Or, History Rewritten*, in 1931. Not only did Churchill have Lee prevail on the battlefield, but in a wholesale acceptance of the states' rights argument for the cause of the war, the British statesman then has the Southern general proclaim emancipation after capturing Washington, DC. This implausible maneuver allows Churchill to get around the problem of British opposition to siding with a country that was seceding in order to preserve slavery. It thus allows Churchill to have Britain help secure the Confederacy's independence. Such counterfactual thinking may have encouraged subsequent generations to exaggerate the importance of Gettysburg. Unaffected by historians' more recent statements to the contrary, Matrix's description of *Scourge of War: Gettysburg* declares that the engagement "became well-known as the turning point in the American Civil War." In this case, the large American market, with its fascination with the epic conflict that nearly tore its country apart, guarantees that the largest engagement of that war will receive greater coverage whether or not it was truly decisive.

Conclusion

The ability to participate in or create virtual alternate versions of history sets videogames apart from other media focusing on historical themes. As with film, strong marketing pressures on this new medium cause it to exaggerate the influence of great individuals in history, because the stories of great individuals often make more compelling drama than larger, seemingly impersonal behaviors of masses of people over long stretches of time. Unlike film, however, one genre of videogames, strategy games, allows for and even encourages viewing history through this wide lens. These games, along with many battle games, most easily allow for, and even encourage, players to alter history and support possible alternative scenarios to those that actually occurred. The ability to do so is one of the most powerful and beneficial aspects of videogames, one that other media have difficulty permitting. One of the quickest ways to gain knowledge on any subject is to practice it. Unfortunately, it is impossible for anyone to "practice" or "do" the past, since historical events occur only once. Similarly, it is impossible to analyze history experimentally as one might chemistry or physics, because the almost infinitely complex set of conditions that set the context for any historical event are not going to be repeated in the same combination. Historical simulations are as close as we can come, and, for the average consumer, the closest to a simulation one can use is a historical videogame.

This is the power of videogames, but it is also a danger – because no videogame can possibly simulate the complexity of past contexts in which events unfolded. Game designers must, therefore, choose what to include and what to leave out. In doing so, they are influenced by their own worldviews and assumptions about history. They are also influenced by market forces and playability, both of which constrain what they can and cannot include in order to make the game successful financially. The result is arguably much more a work of art than historical analysis. There is nothing wrong with this, and few game designers would claim otherwise. Game players, however, should not assume that every alternative outcome they achieve in a game could actually have occurred. Exploring counterfactual scenarios is a great way to understand why things turned out the way they did, and what might have occurred if they hadn't. However, players should realize that the context they are playing in is a creation of the game designer, whose biases it reflects.

Works cited

Assassin's Creed (game series), Ubisoft, 2007–18.

Assassin's Creed III, Ubisoft Montreal, 2012.

Assassin's Creed III: The Tyranny of King Washington (DLC), Ubisoft Montreal, 2013.

Baggott, Jim, *The First War of Physics: The Secret History of the Atom Bomb, 1939–1949*. Pegasus Books: Distributed by W.W. Norton & Co., 2010.

BBC History – British History in Depth: The Battle of Hastings Game., www.bbc.co.uk/history/ interactive/games/hastings/index_embed.shtml.

Bioshock Infinite, Irrational Games, 2013.

Bradbury, Jim, *The Battle of Hastings*. Npi Media Ltd, 2002.

Brummett, Barry, ed., *Clockwork Rhetoric: The Language and Style of Steampunk*. University Press of Mississippi, 2014.

Burrows, William E., *This New Ocean: The Story of the First Space Age*. Random House, 1998.

Busey, John W. and David G. Martin, *Regimental Strengths and Losses at Gettysburg* 4th edn, Longstreet House, 2005.

Call of Duty (game series), Infinity Ward, 2003–18.

Call of Duty: World at War, Infinity Ward, 2008.

Carlyle, Thomas, *On Heroes, Hero-Worship, & the Heroic in History: Six Lectures; Reported, with Emendations and Additions*. James Fraser, 1841.

Churchill, Winston S., "If Lee Had Not Won the Battle of Gettysburg." *If: Or, History Rewritten*, ed. Philip Guedalla, Viking, 1931, 257–84.

Cowley, Robert, ed., *What If? 2: Eminent Historians Imagine What Might Have Been*. Putnam Adult, 2001.

Cowley, Robert and Stephen E. Ambrose, *What If?: The World's Foremost Military Historians Imagine What Might Have Been: Essays*. Berkley Books, 2000.

Crusader Kings II, Paradox Development Studio, 2012.

Diamond, Jared M., *Guns, Germs, and Steel: The Fates of Human Societies*. W. W. Norton & Company, 1999.

Empire: Total War, Creative Assembly, 2009.

Europa Universalis (game series), Paradox Development Studio, 2000–18.

Goss, Thomas, "Gettysburg's 'Decisive Battle'." *Military Review*, vol. 84, no. 4 (August 2004), 11–16.

Holland, Cecelia, "Repulse at Hastings, October 14, 1066." *What If? 2: Eminent Historians Imagine What Might Have Been*, ed. Robert Cowley, Putnam Adult, 2001, 68–86.

Jones, David S., "Virgin Soils Revisited." *The William and Mary Quarterly*, vol. 60, no. 4 (October 2003), 703–42.

Kapell, Matthew, "Civilization and Its Discontents: American Monomythic Structure as Historical Simulcrum." *Popular Culture Review*, vol. 13, no. 2 (Summer 2002), 129–36.

Lebow, Richard Ned, "Counterfactual Thought Experiments: A Necessary Teaching Tool." *History Teacher*, vol. 40, no. 2 (February 2007), 153–76.

Marx, Karl and Engels Friedrich, "Communist Manifesto." Transcribed from the 1888 English translation by Samuel Moore. www.gutenberg.org/cache/epub/61/pg61.html.

Matrix Games – Scourge of War: Gettysburg., http://matrixgames.com/products/441/details/Scourge.of.War:Gettysburg.

McShane, Clay, *Down the Asphalt Path: The Automobile and the American City*. Columbia University Press, 1994.

Medieval II: Total War, Creative Assembly, 2006.

Robinson, Douglas Hill, *Giants in the Sky: A History of the Rigid Airship*. University of Washington Press, 1973.

Schroeder, Paul W., "World War I as Galloping Gertie: A Reply to Joachim Remak." *Journal of Modern History*, vol. 44, no. 3 (September 1972), 319–45.

Scourge of War: Gettysburg, Matrix Games, 2012.

Sid Meier's Civilization (game series), Microprose/Firaxis Games, 1991–2018.

Sid Meier's Civilization IV, Firaxis Games, 2005.

Sid Meier's Civilization V, Firaxis Games, 2010.

Sid Meier's Civilization VI, Firaxis Games, 2017.

Sid Meier's Civilization: Beyond Earth, Firaxis Games, 2014.

Sid Meier's Gettysburg!, Firaxis Games, 1997.

Spencer, Herbert, *The Study of Sociology*. Henry S. King, 1873.

Total War (game series), Creative Assembly, 2000–18.

Ultimate General: Gettysburg, Game-Labs, 2014.

4

ECONOMICS AND RESOURCE MANAGEMENT

Introduction

The Depression-era economist Lionel Robbins described economics as "the science which studies human behaviour as a relationship between ends and scarce means which have alternative uses" (Robbins). For this reason, the art of controlling any economy is a matter of time and resource management, often in the context of rivals seeking to use the same resources. If this were not the case, then money would presumably be unnecessary and nobody would have to make difficult decisions about how to spend it. Since computers began as number-crunching devices, it is hardly surprising that some of the earliest digital games focused on resource management and the impact of external forces on this process. One of these was *The Sumer Game*, which Doug Dyment developed in 1968 to demonstrate FOCAL programming on a Digital Equipment Corporation PDP-8, the first mini-computer. The BASIC version was released in 1975 under the title *Hamurabi*, misspelled perhaps in order to adhere to the eight-character naming convention required by early computer files. The game presented the player with a series of text-based dialogs, in which the player is the autocrat Hammurabi, receiving information from an obsequious minister of state, requiring a decision expressed in a typed response. Below is an example of the way the game worked taken from the online Atari Archives. The information questions and format are all standard, but the outcome numbers (in bold) vary based on Hammurabi's (the player's) previous responses.

> Hamurabi: I beg to report to you
> In the Year 1, 0 people starved, 5 came to the city,
> Population is now 100
> The city now owns 1000 acres.
> You harvested 3 bushels per acre.
> Rats ate 200 bushels.

You now have 2800 bushels in store.
Land is now trading at 24 bushels per acre.
How many acres do you wish to buy? **10**
How many bushels do you wish to feed your people? **2000**
How many acres do you wish to plant with seed? **990**

Each year the game resets with numbers based on the previous year's production. Eventually, the people oust the player who ruins the economy, declaring him or her a "national fink." Note the role of random events, whether rats or plague. All these factors appear as quantifiable events that impact the city's population. The rest is simple calculation.

Along with *The Oregon Trail, The Sumer Game/Hamurabi* served as an inspiration for many of the city- and empire-building titles of later years, whether or not they occurred in historical settings. Their core concepts are present in Maxis's *SimCity*, Sierra's *Pharoah* and *Caesar*, Ubisoft's *Anno*, and Firaxis' *Sid Meier's Civilization*. It's also the ancestor of the plethora of tycoon games, most notably *Sid Meier's Railroad Tycoon*. All these games involve some simulation of production and trade. In doing so, they deal with a very old field of historical scholarship, economic history. In order to understand how well videogames portray economic aspects of history, it's necessary to see what scholars have to say about the impact of these issues on past societies. The story is long, complex, and full of controversy.

Economic history

If the oldest focus of historical scholarship is the affairs of great men (such as war, diplomacy, religion, and high politics), the second-oldest is surely economics. The development of early modern financial institutions, such as stock exchanges and insurance companies, and the profound social changes accompanying the movement of people into large towns surrounding factories, gave rise to economics as a discipline of study. Anyone remotely aware of the economic theories underlying the last two centuries of political debate is probably familiar with at least the names of Adam Smith and Karl Marx. The former, who published *An Inquiry into the Nature and Causes of the Wealth of Nations* in 1776, has long served as an inspiration to supporters of the free market. His arguments against government regulation, embodied in his day in the mercantile system, continue to resonate with parties on the right in the politics of the developed world. By contrast, Marx's ideas, most systematically set forth in *The Communist Manifesto* and *Capital: Critique of Political Economy*, have long inspired politicians and scholars on the left, whether or not they subscribed to most of Marx's prescriptions for curing society's ills. The first of these treatises, co-written with Friedrich Engels, was a response to the Revolutions of 1848, which Marx regarded as the triumph of capitalism over the earlier "feudal" order. It served as a call to arms for the working class. The second work (published in three volumes from 1867 to 1894) is a scholarly critique of the late nineteenth-century capitalist economy.

Since Marx, far more than Smith, regards economic relationships as the driving forces in history, it is fair to consider him an economic historian.

Of course, Smith and Marx are only the two most famous, and among the oldest, in a vast discipline of economists. Perhaps more influential than Marx in Western democracies since World War II was John Maynard Keynes (1883–1946), whose *General Theory of Employment, Interest and Money* (first published in 1936) advocated that governments should respond to the Great Depression by increasing spending, even if this led to short-term deficits. In particular, he supported the idea of increasing the supply of money in ways that would increase demand, and therefore presumably create conditions favorable for hiring more workers. These newly employed workers would in turn use their money to create further demand, thus creating a cyclical effect that would generate ongoing economic expansion. His championing of government intervention within a capitalist framework was popular throughout the Western democracies from the 1940s (when government had to invest in production to fight World War II) through the 1970s, after which it receded in the face of "monetarist" and "supply-side" economic theories. Both these theories gained popularity among conservatives during the late 1970s as the Western economies suffered from "stagflation," a combination of high unemployment and high inflation. Monetarists argued that the production of currency should increase at a constant modest rate rather than as a government response to financial crises. Most famous among these economists was Milton Friedman, whose ideas arose in part from his analysis of central banks' responses to the onset of the Great Depression. He argued that government interference with the money supply had transformed a mere recession into one of the world's worst economic crises (Friedman and Schwartz). This assertion was the opposite of Keynes's, that the government should go into debt in the short term in order to create more jobs. Supply-side economists advocated cutting taxes for the wealthy and allowing free trade so that entrepreneurs would in turn create or expand businesses and hire more workers. The result, these economists claimed, would be higher employment and greater economic growth. The debate between monetarists and supply-siders on the one hand, and Keynesians on the other, continues today.

From a historian's perspective, however, all these theories share two important features. First, they all rely on data from the past. Of the theories mentioned above, only Marx's focuses on arguments about history. The others use examples from the past to justify their assertions regarding the proper way to manage the economy in the future. Second, inasmuch as these theories rely on history, they adopt a material approach to it. They regard humans as rational actors, pursuing what is in their material interest. Granted, the authors of these theories may acknowledge the role of irrational behavior, but they tend to see it as incidental to material motivation. Indeed, Marx saw one of most powerful "irrational" forces in history, religion, as little more than a tool in the hands of wealthy elites who cynically deployed and manipulated it in order to distract the working class from pursuing their rational material interests (Introduction to *Critique of Hegel's Philosophy of Right*). In this sense, therefore, Marx described even religion as having an underlying material purpose.

For many historians in the twentieth century, Marx provided the framework for demonstrating how ideas that the establishment of the day often portrayed as just or benign were actually used by that establishment to oppress the lower orders of society and prevent them from organizing and resisting the status quo. In particular, British and American historians tended to focus on the struggle for liberties already attained and congratulate their societies for these achievements. By contrast, Marx decried this perspective for ignoring the economic oppression of the masses. What use was political liberty if only the wealthy elite could enjoy it? For Marx, this freedom merely signified another stage in the dialectic of the class struggle. The English, American, and French Revolutions, and the Revolutions of 1848, were simply the triumph of the bourgeoisie (business-owning class) over the "feudal" aristocracy (land-owning class) that had dominated Europe's economy since Medieval times. Any freedoms the bourgeoisie had achieved no more affected the average inhabitants of these societies than did the privileges of the nobility before them. Marx inspired many twentieth-century historians to highlight ways in which prevailing economic and social systems had exploited the lower classes for the benefit of the elite (*Communist Manifesto*, Part I).

Because of the political implications of Marxism, it's important to note that just because some historians accept Marx's basic belief in the centrality of economic classes in politics and ideology does not necessarily mean that they support communism. While many self-proclaimed Marxist historians have actively supported left-of-center parties in democracies, most of them distanced themselves from communism during the Cold War era, regarding its attempt to impose a top-down revolution on agrarian masses as un-Marxist. Moreover, the materialist basis of Marxist analysis has even influenced many conservatives focusing on economic history. Many scholars have borrowed some ideas from Marx even if they do not consider themselves Marxist, profoundly disagree with many aspects of Marx's analysis, and actively oppose parties that claim to be Marxist.

A group that was influenced by Marx but went well beyond his analysis in its own influence on history was the *Annales* school of historians. Starting between the two world wars, and growing in prominence after World War II, this school arose around the French academic journal *Annales*,[1] which emphasized history from the "bottom up." Starting with Marx's argument that developments of historical importance arose from class conflict over the means of production, the editors of and contributors to *Annales* focused on evidence that challenged the earlier narrative of great men advancing civilization through revolutions empowering elected legislatures. Much of *Annales*'s emphasis was on social history. However, since its authors considered social and economic history to be closely connected, they made important contributions to the field of economic history as well. In particular, Fernand Braudel (editor 1956–68) developed a new approach to history in his study of the Mediterranean economy during the reign (1556–98) of Spanish King Philip II. Rather than focus on great people and events, he emphasized the impact of long-term social and economic forces, which he demonstrated were closely intertwined. Indeed, he portrayed the entire Mediterranean basin as an avenue for the transmission of goods, armies, and ideas, mainly based on economic motives. His work inspired American historian Immanuel Wallerstein to write *The Modern-World System*, in which he argues that a worldwide system of economic and cultural interaction first emerged in the fifteenth-century Mediterranean and spread, through European exploration and colonization, to include the rest of the globe. The sinews of trade that European companies of this period established served as the conduits for armies, commodities, and ideas. Therefore, aspects of civilization, such as religion, that are seemingly unconnected with economics nevertheless rest on its scaffolding. Inasmuch as Wallerstein sees economics as the root cause of many other historical developments, and inasmuch as he sees the differences between the haves and have-nots as fundamentally a relationship based on the exercise of power, he shows the influence of Marx.

Fellow scholars focusing on the world system may agree with Wallerstein regarding the economic basis and power relationships of the system, while disagreeing with him on some central features of his approach to history. In particular, Wallerstein's original argument has come under criticism for its apparent Eurocentrism. For instance, Andre Gunder Frank and other historians have argued that the world system did not begin in Europe and the Mediterranean in the fifteenth century CE, but rather in the Middle East and southern Asia in the third millennium BCE. From the trade network between the first three cradles of civilization, in what today are Iraq, Egypt, and Pakistan, it had spread by 1 CE to include the Mediterranean, eastern Africa, China, and Southeast Asia. The European inclusion of the Americas and Oceania was merely the latest phase in this expansion. Since China and India were the agricultural powerhouses of the pre-industrial world system, and since they had the largest populations, they came to account for most of this system's production of wealth at the time of the Roman Empire (Frank and Gills). Recent research into the economies of India and China indicates that these areas continued to account for nearly half of the world's productivity into the late eighteenth and early nineteenth centuries (Pomeranz), long after Western European maritime powers had conquered most of the Americas. Only the industrialization of Western Europe and the United States propelled the West into the position of economic dominance that it held during the nineteenth and twentieth centuries. Frank, therefore, argues that Western dominance of the world system is an anomaly that will yield in the twenty-first century to something approaching its previous balance, in which India and China resume their natural place as economic superpowers.

Although economics plays a major role in many strategy games, and a significant one in some action games, the extent to which they incorporate the issues mentioned above is less obvious. The rest of this chapter examines how well videogames deal with economics in their historical settings, and how obvious they make economic processes to players.

Resource management

One of the first best-selling strategy games for computers in the early 1990s was *Sid Meier's Railroad Tycoon*. Although later versions branch out across the globe and into the twentieth century, the core of the game focuses on building a railroad company and defeating artificial intelligence (AI) rivals in nineteenth-century North America, particularly building a transcontinental railroad from the Mississippi to the West Coast. In order to make your company prosper, you must identify resources and markets *en route*, and build stations to harness these resources and serve these markets. The challenge is to expand rapidly enough to beat your rivals, but not so rapidly that you go into bankruptcy. Build too small a station, buy too little rolling stock, or stick with obsolete locomotives and you won't be able to take advantage of all the resources and markets available. Build too large a station, buy too much rolling stock, and upgrade your locomotives too quickly and you will run into so much debt that won't be able to turn a profit. You can invest in the stock market and borrow money, but the former is risky and the latter often incurs high interest penalties. *Railroad Tycoon* is, therefore, essentially a resource management game. In order to win you must plan carefully and constantly monitor the ebb and flow of supply and demand, expanding and reducing the number of locomotives on a route and their rolling stock's capacity to transport particular goods accordingly.

Railroad Tycoon (and its later versions) works so well because its scope is limited to purely economic aspects of history over a narrow period. The computer you play on serves as a complex calculator, tabulating your investments and profits. Sid Meier's next historical game, *Civilization*, applied many of the same principles to a vastly more complex subject, the entirety of human history. Unlike *Railroad Tycoon*, the goal of *Civilization* is not simply to make your company more profitable than your AI rivals', it is to exceed them in one of four possible paths to victory, in the most recent version: domination, science, culture, and religion. Wealth isn't one of these goals, but it is an essential component of achieving each one. The *Civilization* series encourages players to take care how they place their cities' inhabitants in a city's environs in order to maximize resources.

Image 4.1 demonstrates how this feature works in *Civilization VI*. Kyoto has ten population units. One is working in the city center (surrounded by walls). The remainder are working in the hexes surrounding the city with the highlighted heads. Kyoto controls five other hexes (with darkened heads) that its citizens could work, but it doesn't have enough population units to do so. The AI assigns population units to work in the hexes that it considers optimal. However, the player can override the AI's preference in two ways. One is by choosing a particular emphasis on the line of options immediately above the city name in the bottom-right-hand corner. The following symbols represent these emphases from left to right: culture – treble clef, food – ear of maize, production – copper gear, science – test beaker, faith – wings, and wealth – coin.

IMAGE 4.1 *Sid Meier's Civilization VI*, Kyoto city screen.
Licensed Asset Courtesy of **Firaxis Games, Inc.** and 2K Games, Inc.

However, another way of overriding the AI's preference is to assign population units to work in specific hexes. Each hex that can generate one of the above items indicates the amount by the number of that symbol visible in the hex. For instance, the population unit, highlighted in the hex immediately northwest of the two-hex mountain range to the west of Kyoto, is generating two food points and one production point. Immediately to Kyoto's east, another population unit is working in a hex containing an iron mine. The anvil indicates the presence of iron. The player has already built a mine on the location using a "builder" unit. The hex generates one food, four production, and one science point. It also provides iron to support military units that specifically require it, such as swordsmen in the early game and frigates mid-game.

Civilization VI also has a feature, new to the series, in which the player chooses to devote certain hexes to certain types of productivity. Faith and science both benefit from locations next to mountains, presumably because holy sites and observatories are often built in high places. In this playthrough, I built science and religion districts on the hexes between Kyoto's city center and the mountain range to the west. The game treats population units assigned to these hexes as "specialists." The science district to the southwest of Kyoto has one specialist generating two science points. However, it also has a library and a university, each of which generates another science point, totaling four science points from the hex. The holy site to the northwest of the science site has two "specialists," plus three religious buildings, a shrine, a temple, and a meeting house. That hex generates eight faith points.

All of this fits with historians' understanding of the basic elements of civilization. Specialization of labor, with some workers tending farms and others mines, provided the food and raw materials that allowed other segments of society to concentrate on activities, such as religion and science, that required greater education and a more sedentary lifestyle. This specialization enabled civilizations to acquire new knowledge exponentially in a way that had not occurred through the previous 200,000 years of modern humans' existence. The *Civilization* series demonstrates this historical process well through the multiplying effects of buildings and specialists in city screens such as the one in Image 4.1. Moreover, social and political support for institutions, such as libraries, temples, and barracks, undoubtedly encouraged greater productivity and innovation in the areas of science, culture, and military preparedness respectively – although it remains impossible in reality to measure the benefits of knowledge and expertise as precisely as videogames do in their virtual worlds.

Nevertheless, the need of games and computers to quantify everything leads to rather simplistic calculations for the effects of buildings and resources. Obviously not every market actually increased a city's generation of wealth by the same amount, as it does in *Civilization VI*, but the tendency to provide specific equivalents permeates almost every videogame for a number of reasons. First, because videogames are software programs running on computers, they all rely on calculations. Even if they weren't digital, however, these games would require calculations. Most strategy boardgames require the role of dice or the drawing of cards to emulate the element of chance that enters into most experiences in real life. The extent to which acquisitions of features in a boardgame augment a player's position usually works through percentages or specific numbers as well. The only difference is that the players have to make the calculations according to the game's rules rather than the computer doing it for them. As things stand, various other augmenting features, such as religion, terrain, trade, and characteristics of individual civilizations, interact with the market to determine precisely how much extra income it generates.

Trade

If productivity is one aspect of many videogames, particularly the strategic ones, so is trade. *Civilization V: Brave New World* has a robust trading system that clearly shows players how their trade routes are affecting their faction. More than many other games, it reveals the role of trade in spreading knowledge and ideology. Image 4.2 shows the "Establish Trade Route" drop menu for Heliopolis, an Egyptian city. Carthage controls those shown in the image. Each of the three visible cities (the remainder are accessed through scrolling the menu) lists the effects that trade will have on both Heliopolis and the city it trades with. For instance, trading with Hippo Regius will earn six units of wealth (coins) for Heliopolis and two for the target city. Such an arrangement obviously favors the human player (Egypt). However, the other effects are more ambiguous or even negative to Egypt. On the plus side, Hippo Regius will experience +6 pressure points to convert to Zoroastrianism, Heliopolis's dominant religion. Conversely, Heliopolis will

IMAGE 4.2 *Sid Meier's Civilization V: Brave New World*, "Establish Trade Route" drop menu.

Licensed Asset Courtesy of **Firaxis Games, Inc.** and 2K Games, Inc.

receive +6 pressure to convert to Protestantism, Hippo Regius's dominant religion. This is not necessarily detrimental to Egypt, since under special circumstances cities can gain some of the positive traits of religious minorities. However, if Zoroastrianism arises in Egypt, and is that country's dominant religion, the Egyptian player will not welcome the wholesale conversion of any Egyptian city away from it. More disturbing still are the +2 science points that Egypt will export to Carthage via this trade route. This icon indicates that Egypt has two technologies that Carthage lacks, and that this trade route will speed Carthage's acquisition of them. The absence of any number and science icon going in the opposite direction shows that Carthage has no technology that Egypt lacks. This trade route will therefore narrow the technology gap between Egypt and Carthage, a development that the Egyptian player would rather not occur. The Egyptian player therefore must balance these choices when deciding with whom to trade.

Did these considerations actually occur historically? In modern times, governments often have considerable control over whom their businesses trade with. Even a pro-business government like that of the United States maintains strict laws prohibiting its private corporations from trading with hostile states, such as North Korea and Iran. Further back in time, however, governments were less capable of regulating trade to other countries. China presents an excellent example of the problems and benefits for both merchants and rulers of regulating trade. The Han Dynasty of China was perhaps the most organized and technologically advanced government of the ancient world. The Han emperors recognized the value of the Silk Road crossing west from the Yellow River Valley across Central Asia to the eastern shore of the Mediterranean Sea. The money and goods that Middle

Eastern and Central Asian merchants traded for Chinese silk stimulated the Chinese economy, and the taxes on these transactions enriched the Han treasury. However, the Silk Road was hazardous for merchants, not only due to the formidable terrain it crossed, but also because powerful nomadic cavalry controlled much of the Central Asian Steppe and raided the caravans crossing it. Han armies helped to reduce this threat through a series of military victories over these nomads during the second century BCE. Nevertheless, they went further, by extending the Great Wall westward and encouraging military families to settle the western frontier. At the western end of Han possessions a customs house, the Jade Gate, issued visas to foreign merchants legitimizing their business within the realm, but also tracking it for taxation purposes. By providing security for merchants, control for rulers, and wealth for both, this system was mutually beneficial.

However, a later example, also from China, reveals the opposite. In order to deal with the Japanese piracy along the Chinese coast, the Ming Dynasty imposed a ban on private overseas trade. The result was simply an increase in smuggling and piracy, as the trade continued in spite of the ban. In 1685, the Qing Dynasty lifted the ban, recognizing the damage it was doing to the Chinese economy. Meanwhile, scientific and religious influences continued to enter China along these trade routes, particularly from Europe.

Much knowledge passed along the Silk Road, mainly from East to West, as China unintentionally provided Europeans with the knowledge of gunpowder, paper, and the compass, and India provided the West with the all-important concept of zero. Even early rocketry came to the West from China through India, where British East India Company forces experienced the receiving end of it in the late eighteenth century. They then refined military rocketry using metal rather than cloth or paper casing and used it against the United States during the War of 1812, inspiring Francis Scott Key's reference to "the rocket's red glare" in the American national anthem. Of course, the transmission of technology through trade and warfare operated in reverse, as Indian and Chinese forces adopted the parade ground drill that was so important to warfare in the age of muskets.

Governments therefore had only limited control over what ideas their merchants transmitted, and even the most strenuous attempts to regulate this process did not succeed for long. To the extent that *Civilization V* shows the risks of transmitting technology through trade, it reflects this fact. However, in providing players with the ability to decide which cities caravans and cargo ships visit, the game overstates the usual level of government involvement.

Mercantilism in games portraying the early modern era

Another series of games simulating trade is *Europa Universalis*. Like *Civilization V* and *VI*, this complex reconstruction of the early modern world quantifies the effects of a player's trading decisions. Moreover, as with *Civilization V* and *VI*, the *Europa Universalis* games overemphasize government involvement in determining where merchants traded. Today, fans of Adam Smith tend to cite him in

order to criticize socialism or even simply Keynesian economics. Smith, however, preceded socialist economists. Rather, he criticized mercantilism, the dominant overseas trading system of his day. In a mercantile system, a European
monarch or legislature issued a charter to a company to trade with a region or
establish a settlement. In the case of trade, the European government would
usually grant that company the sole right to sell goods in the home country
from the region in which it was trading. These companies frequently raised
shares from multiple investors who knew that the company's products faced no
competition at home, although, like other companies, they had to pay taxes to
the government.

Such monopolies may seem like they were a sweet deal for investors until
one takes into account the hazards of trading overseas in the seventeenth and
eighteenth centuries. Storms are far less likely to sink modern cargo ships than
they were the wooden merchant vessels of centuries past. Today a multi-national
company's office in a distant country can call its headquarters in an instant to
discuss any difficult financial transaction its agents are considering. If a revolution
occurs and their office is attacked, these agents know that their headquarters and
home government will learn of it almost immediately. Moreover, when shipping
products to their markets, modern corporations can count on major powers to
protect their cargoes from pirates. While well-publicized hijackings, such as
that of the *Maersk Alabama* in 2009, highlight the continuing threat of piracy
in the early twenty-first century, they have also drawn a response from major
powers that has diminished their incidence. By contrast, in the seventeenth and
eighteenth centuries, company ships required constant escorts or had to arm themselves to ward of equally well-armed pirates. Of equal concern were the companies
of rival European countries competing in the same region. Before the age of even
the telegraph, merchant ships often discovered they were at war only when a rival
country's merchant ship or naval vessel opened fire on them. None of these ships
could contact their home country for immediate assistance, since the fastest that
news could travel was the speed of the ships themselves. These companies, therefore, armed themselves both at sea and on land. If their ships doubled as military
vessels, so did their regional offices, or trading posts, often amount to fortified city-
states defended by regiments of soldiers recruited both in the home country and
locally near the fort. The quasi-military nature of these companies explains why the
British East India Company was ultimately able to conquer the entire Indian subcontinent during the late eighteenth and early nineteenth centuries. Certainly, this
was an example of monopoly corporate power run amok, but it arose out of the
insecurities brought about by the technological limitations of the age. Shielding
investors from competition in their home market was necessary to convince them
to risk their money on such dangerous ventures.

Monopoly companies also established settlements. Many of these, such as the
Virginia Company and the Massachusetts Bay Company, are famous in American
history. France, the Netherlands, and Sweden made similar arrangements with
companies to exploit the resources of the New World. The protections that the

European governments offered these ventures were essential in order to help them succeed initially. As late as the 1760s, residents of the British colonies on North America's eastern coast welcomed the presence of British forces during their war against French and Native American forces on their borders. Unfortunately for these colonists, however, British protection came with British control. American schoolchildren usually learn about the burden of British taxation as the major cause behind the American Revolution, but many other issues contributed as well. Among them was American merchants' resentment over the mercantile system, under which British law forbade them to trade directly with the colonies of competing European powers. Merchants in British colonies in North America could not, for instance, sell cotton in Quebec before Britain's conquest of it. Nor could they buy sugar from Cuba. Each European power tried to maintain a closed self-sufficient economic system – what in the twentieth century became known as autarky – rather than take the risk of trading with their rivals. Worse still, many commodities exported from other parts of these empires had to go through the home country before going to another colony in the same empire. The addition of the middle men in the home country raised the price of commodities for colonial consumers.

Perhaps the most famous example of this practice was British East India Company shipments of tea from southern China (before the East India Company developed tea plantations in India) to Britain's North American colonies. The East India Company would ship the tea to London, where it was stored in large warehouses. Then it sold the tea to other British merchants to ship to the American colonies. This system enriched the British merchants responsible for the Atlantic leg of the shipment, but it raised the cost of the tea for American consumers. In response to American protests against the British government's tax on tea, Prime Minister Lord North persuaded Parliament in 1773 to allow the East India Company to sell its tea directly to America without involving other British companies. The aim was to lower the cost of the tea and thereby placate colonial protesters. Lord North's plan amounted to too little, too late. By the time he allowed this circumvention of the mercantile system, the protesters were more concerned about the principle of "no taxation without representation" than the actual price of tea. As a result, one of the East India Company's tea shipments ended up at the bottom of Boston Harbor anyway.

The portrayal of the mercantile system in commercial videogames is mixed. Although *Civilization IV: Colonization* notoriously omits the Golden Triangle and slavery from its portrayal of the Atlantic economy, it does capture some of the flavor of the colonies' dependence on trade with their respective mother countries. They can't trade with the colonies of rival European powers. However, companies and investors are not present in the game, nor is dependence on trade originating from other parts of European empires that passed through their capitals. Similarly, Nitro Games's *East India Company* models trading between Europe and the Indian Ocean with players buying commodities in Eastern ports and filling cargo holds for return to the home country. As with

Colonization, unfortunately, the game fails to show the Indian Ocean trade's relationship to the rest of the imperial economy. The player therefore gets little sense of how the mercantile system actually worked. In order to do so a game would have to include the European, North American, and Indian Ocean theaters during the early modern period. Two games, *Empire: Total War* and *Europa Universalis IV*, do this. In focusing on these three theaters specifically, *Empire* emphasizes their connection in the eighteenth century. Moreover, since the game requires the development of a faction's economy in order to support its military, and since the conquest of certain regions is the sole objective for victory, *Empire* highlights the importance of economic development in ways that mercantilist theorists would have agreed with. However, by omitting the Golden Triangle and the operation of trading companies, *Empire* fails to demonstrate the operations of mercantilism. Rather, the economic model it portrays is more akin to the planned economies of twentieth-century Communist countries than the more complex and nuanced interactions between governments and corporations, and mother countries with colonies, that characterized early modern mercantile systems.

Game developers have not addressed the reasons for these omissions in *Colonization, East India Company*, and *Empire*, but the most obvious is playability. Mercantilism was a complex system. While modeling it in a game is mechanically possible, it would add a layer of complexity that players might find daunting. One game series that attempts to tackle early modern trade more deeply is *Europa Universalis*, now in its fourth release with accompanying expansions. Since this game covers the entire globe it's structurally at least as well positioned to address the mercantile system as is *Empire*. It does so by having players assign merchants to zones and by clearly excluding rival factions from these zones in a faction's colonies (Image 4.3). With the game's *Dharma* expansion, European powers can even create charter companies in a mercantile system. The level of complexity involved in simulating this system, however, makes the *Europa Universalis* appeal to a narrow niche market of hardcore strategy gamers.

Like their strategy counterparts, the few action games portraying early modern economics only deal with mercantilism tangentially and inadequately. *Assassin's Creed III* shows trade between the rebellious British colonies of the 1770s and Cuba. *Assassin's Creed: Liberation* has the main character directing trade with various Spanish-speaking destinations in the Caribbean at a time when her native city of New Orleans was controlled by Spain. Both cases are plausible scenarios. The first would have violated British mercantile laws, but since the colonies were at war with Britain anyway, there is no contradiction in this activity. Moreover, even before the American Revolution, smuggling was rife in the British colonies. Indeed, smugglers no more welcomed the prospect of an end to mercantile restrictions than modern drug cartels welcome the legalization of their products. Both cases promised to reduce smugglers' profits. In the case of *Assassin's Creed: Liberation*, the trade would have been legal since it occurred between Spanish colonies. However, as Image 4.4 shows, *Liberation* allows trade with any colony and even three European ports of

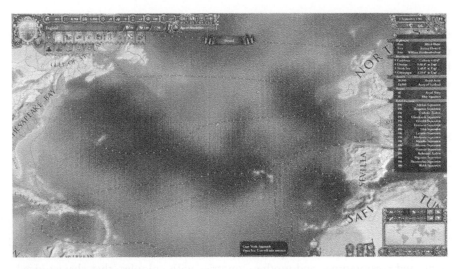

IMAGE 4.3 *Europa Universalis IV*, trade route. Copyright © 2019 Paradox Interactive AB. www.paradoxplaza.com

IMAGE 4.4 *Assassin's Creed: Liberation*, trade routes. © 2012 Ubisoft Entertainment. All Rights Reserved. Assassin's Creed, Ubisoft and the Ubisoft logo are trademarks of Ubisoft Entertainment in the US and/or other countries.

Seville, Bordeaux, and Liverpool, no matter which power controls New Orleans. In neither case do these games deal with the implications of mercantilism. While neither game is historically inaccurate in this regard, neither pays attention to the system and its effects on eighteenth-century colonial economies.

Mercantilism is a complex aspect of economic history, and it may be too much to expect any game to delve into it adequately. Since commercial games exist primarily to be fun, it's understandable that designers may be wary that the subject will spark a collective yawn among potential customers. This would be a pity, since some of the issues most central to the formation of the modern world, such as American independence, the abolition of slavery, and the development of modern capitalism, occurred in the context of mercantilism. Failure to take account of it by pretending that trade occurred freely between colonies of rival European powers, or by ignoring the infamous middle passage of the Golden Triangle, does not merely simplify history, it distorts it. However, as the next section shows, these distortions are no greater than those of many video-games portraying the economies of the last two centuries.

Laissez-faire and planned economies

Commenting on whether the evolution-themed game *Spore* is really about intelligent design, the game's senior producer, Will Wright, explains:

> We put the player in the role of an intelligent designer. When we first started the prototypes (of *Spore*) that wasn't the case. We had the game carefully mutating things and it just was not emotionally engaging. When we put the players in the role of intelligent designer then people were much more emotionally attached to what they made.
>
> *(Snider)*

The problem with evolution is that it makes for boring gameplay, or even no gameplay at all. In a true simulation of evolution, the player would simply watch events unfold without interfering. In attempting to make a game about evolution fun, therefore, *Spore*'s designers made it about creation rather than evolution. The result drew criticism from a team of scientists assessing the game for the journal *Science*. As one of the team's members put it: "*Spore*'s biology grades rolled in like a slow-motion train wreck" (Bohannon).

Economic history suffers similar problems when translated into gameplay. At the micro-level of running one's own business, as in *Railroad Tycoon*, it works reasonably well, since the player assumes the role of the tycoon deciding where to invest. At the macro-level, however, problems develop. In modern capitalist economies, most economic decisions occur at the micro-level. Companies build buildings and make investments while cities provide much of the infrastructure. For games set at the strategic level, however, this reality leaves players with little to do. For instance, players develop plantations in *Empire: Total War*. Yet who are the players supposed to be? Most of the game operates at the level of the national or imperial government. Yet even under the mercantile system, governments rarely made decisions about setting up individual plantations or buildings. Even most military decisions had to occur locally, because the technology of the time made communications so slow. The sources of such decisions are even more nebulous in the *Civilization* series. In this series players guide their civilizations from 4000 BCE to the present, about eighty lifetimes. Yet the same players also decide whether to build a granary in a particular city and determine whether that city focuses on culture, science, or manufacture. These decisions do not resemble the functioning of real economies in ancient times or the present.

One game in particular, Paradox's *Victoria II*, attempts to model free-market capitalism. Countries can follow one of four economic policies: *laissez-faire*, interventionism, state capitalism, and planned economy. Image 4.5 shows Britain's factory production screen in 1836. Note the plus buttons on the right-hand side are faded. These buttons allow players to add factories if their country has an economic policy of either state capitalism or planned economy, but not if it has a policy of *laissez-faire* or interventionism. Since Britain starts the game with *laissez-faire*, players cannot build factories directly, as the tool tip next to the button for the Midlands "state" indicates. Rather, they must encourage capitalism so that the entrepreneurial class will build industries to meet market demands. What players give up in control by adopting *laissez-faire*, they gain in economic growth, because the production cost of factories for the capitalists is so low (*Beginner's Guide*). To the extent that this system works in the game, it fits supply-side economic theories that have been popular with the governments of developed economies since the 1980s.

Free-market capitalism is difficult to model in a grand-strategy game, because the decisions do not occur in the real world at a grand-strategy level. No such

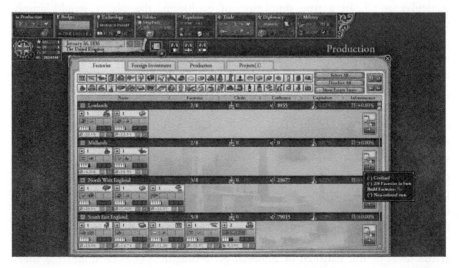

IMAGE 4.5 *Victoria II*, factory production screen. Copyright © 2019 Paradox Interactive AB. www.paradoxplaza.com

problem exists with centralized state planning. We have already seen how central planning tends to be the default model in strategy games, because it involves the player. Since central planning was, in fact, a feature of many twentieth-century economies, it can actually enhance gameplay while staying true to the past, depending on the theme of the game. The era of twentieth-century total war is particularly amenable to these mechanics. Strategy games dealing with World War II usually highlight the importance of state-sponsored research and production to the war effort. In other words, these games are not just about fighting; they are also about the mobilization of society to support the fighting. Probably the most in-depth attempt to reproduce this period is Paradox's *Hearts of Iron* series.

In particular, *Hearts of Iron II*'s technology system does a good job of capturing the flavor of relations between governments and autonomous actors during the war. Depending on which power they play, players can assign up to five technologies to research at a time. In each case, the player must assign a team to work on the technology. Image 4.6 shows the United States's aircraft technology tree. Clicking on a project, such as the development of advanced tactical bombers, reveals icons under the tree. These icons represent technology points in specific areas required to complete the project; in this case 16 aeronautic (propeller), 8 chemistry (test tube), 8 electronic (light bulb), and 8 machine tool (gear). To the left of the tree are research teams available to work on this project, with the icons representing their areas of expertise. Some of these are individual scientists, such as mathematician and physicist John van Neumann, who actually worked on the Manhattan Project during World War II. In this case, he

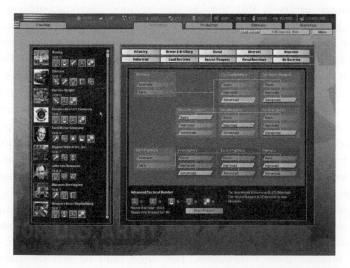

IMAGE 4.6 *Hearts of Iron II*, research project assignment screen. Copyright © 2019 Paradox Interactive AB. www.paradoxplaza.com

would bring expertise in chemistry to the project, but nothing else relevant. Note that the light bulb next to him is highlighted, but the atom (nuclear physics) and the square-root sign (mathematics) are not, because they are not needed for this particular project. (One might dispute whether a knowledge of mathematics would have been irrelevant in aeronautics, but this is the way the Paradox developers decided to portray this technology.) By contrast, two companies, Boeing and Douglas Aircraft, have all the requisite technical expertise. The only difference is that the Boeing team has a skill level of 8 whereas Douglas has one of only 7. Douglas's descendant firm, McDonnell-Douglas, may disagree with this assessment, but the important issue here is that this system of research shows the relationship between government and corporations in an era of total war. The Soviet Union's technology screens, by contrast, have design teams that are clearly divisions of the government, as would have been the case in its centrally planned economy. Missing in the United States's screen is the government entertaining bids from different companies for contracts to develop these technologies. Nevertheless, *Hearts of Iron II* comes closer than any other World War II strategy game to acknowledging the roles of business and scientists by name.

Conclusion

Economics is at the heart of most strategy games, and is an important feature in some action-adventure games. However, its appearance in videogames is often problematic. Much of the failure to simulate economics accurately arises from the need to make the games playable. In particular, two features exert limits. One is the need for simplicity. If commerce is shown in all its complexity, it becomes too difficult and tedious to play. In fact, a frequent complaint regarding many strategy games is that they require tedious micromanagement. While enhanced graphics may be the most obvious aspect of these games' improvement over their earlier versions, streamlining of decisions, including economic ones, has been no less important in making them attractive to consumers. The other problem is player agency. A game is not really a game if a player can't play it, and watching Adam Smith's "invisible hand" of the marketplace develop an economy can be boring, particularly if economic development is a central feature of a game. Paradox took considerable risks in taking the development of free-market economies out of the players' hands in *Victoria II*. While the game received generally excellent reviews from critics in the industry, it has hardly been a best-seller commercially. Players may not want to micromanage their economies, but they do want to manage them.

Still, given the nature of computers as calculating machines, economics may be the least controversial subject that videogames portray. While productivity and transactions may not be as easily measurable as games make them, economists do measure them nonetheless. The same can't be said for many other activities that historical videogames attempt to measure, such as political unrest, religious fervor, or culture. Their portrayals of these aspects of history are the subjects of later chapters. In the meantime, however, there is a less easily predictable aspect of the material world to turn our attention to: the environment.

Note

1 This journal has appeared under several different full titles since its first publication in 1929: *Annales d'histoire économique et sociale* (1929–39); *Annales d'histoire sociale* (1939–42, 1944); *Mélanges d'histoire sociale* (1942–44); *Annales. Economies, sociétés, civilisations* (1946–94); and *Annales. Histoire, Sciences Sociales* (since 1994). n.d.

Works cited

Ahl, David, *Hammurabi*. BASIC Computer Games, 1978. http://atariarchives.org/basic games/showpage.php?page=78.

Anno (game series), Max Design/Related Designs/Blue Byte, 1998–2018.

Assassin's Creed: Liberation, Ubisoft Sofia, 2012.

Beginner's Guide - Victoria 2 Wiki. www.victoria2wiki.com/New_player_guide.

Bohannon, John, "Flunking Spore." *Science*, vol. 322, no. 5901 (October 2008), 531. www.sciencemag.org, doi:10.1126/science.322.5901.531b.

Caesar (game series), Impressions Games, 1992–2006.

East India Company, Nitro Games, 2009.

Empire: Total War, Creative Assembly, 2009.

Frank, Andre Gunder, *ReOrient: Global Economy in the Asian Age*. University of California Press, 1998.

Frank, Andre Gunder and Barry K. Gills, eds, *The World System: Five Hundred Years or Five Thousand?* Routledge, 1993.

Friedman, Milton and Anna Jacobson Schwartz, *The Great Contraction, 1929–1933*, 1st edn. Princeton University Press, 1965.

Keynes, John Maynard, *General Theory of Employment, Interest and Money*. Palgrave Macmillan, 1936.

Marx, Karl, *Capital: A Critique of Political Economy*. Modern Library, 1906.

Marx, Karl, *Critique of Hegel's Philosophy of Right*, translated by Joseph O'Malley. Oxford University Press, 1970. www.marxists.org/archive/marx/works/download/Marx_ Critique_of_Hegels_Philosophy_of_Right.pdf.

Marx, Karl and Friedrich Engels, "Communist Manifesto." Transcribed from the 1888 English translation by Samuel Moore. www.gutenberg.org/cache/epub/61/pg61.html.

Minneapolis Oregon Trail: How Three Minnesotans Forged Its Path - City Pages. www.citypages. com/content/printVersion/1740595/.

Naoroji, Dadabhai, *Poverty and Un-British Rule in India*, 1st Indian edn. Publications Division, Ministry of Information and Broadcasting, Government of India, 1969.

Pharoah, Impressions Games, 1999.

Pomeranz, Kenneth, *The Great Divergence: China, Europe, and the Making of the Modern World Economy*. Princeton University Press, 2000.

Railroad Tycoon, MicroProse, 1990.

Railroad Tycoon (game series), MicroProse, 1990–2006.

Robbins, Lionel, *An Essay on the Nature and Significance of Economic Science*. Ludwig von Mises Institute, 2007.

Sid Meier's Civilization, MicroProse, 1990.

Sid Meier's Civilization (game series), Microprose/Firaxis Games, 1991–2018.

Sid Meier's Civilization IV: Colonization, Firaxis Games, 2008.

Sid Meier's Civilization V: Brave New World, Firaxis Games, 2013.

Sid Meier's Civilization VI, Firaxis Games, 2017.

SimCity (game series), Maxis et al., 1989–2014.

Smith, Adam, *An Inquiry into the Nature and Causes of the Wealth of Nations*. London: W. Straham and T. Cadell, 1776.

Snider, Mike, "'Spore' Creator Inspired by Intelligent Design, Social Networks." *USATODAY.Com*, 8 September 2008, http://usatoday30.usatoday.com/tech/gaming/2008-09-08-spore_qa_N.htm.

Spore, Maxis, 2008.

5

ECOLOGY AND ENVIRONMENT

Introduction

The development team at Paradox Interactive in Stockholm prides itself on its "unparalleled freedom, depth and historical accuracy" (*Europa Universalis IV*). Its "real-time" historical strategy games include a wealth of details, events, and decisions based on the real past. In perhaps its most famous historical game series, *Europa Universalis*, players guide a political power from the period of the Renaissance to the early Industrial Revolution. In *Europa Universalis IV* players can choose to play any sovereign political power from 1444 to 1821. Since the game attempts to recreate the actual historical abilities of the different societies of the time, one is unlikely to get very far starting with a pre-Columbian civilization at the beginning of the game. The Europeans, and possibly Asians, will eventually show up with technologies far in advance of these societies. Nevertheless, some skilled players have taken on the challenge and fared well. An important part of some factions' strategies involves establishing colonies. Originally, the game series, as its title suggests, focused on playing a European power expanding across the globe. When explorers "discovered" other lands, the game revealed the primary resources of those "provinces" for development and trade. When playing as Spain, for instance, as one discovers the provinces of Central America, they might turn out to be sources of coffee or sugar. Indeed, a pop-up screen tells the player what the chances are of the province yielding a particular resource. At first glance, there may appear to be no problem historically in revealing the primary resource of a territory in this manner. After all, Spanish settlers grew these cash crops in Central America under colonial rule, and these products continue to be major products of the region today.

The historical problem becomes apparent only if one chooses to play as the Aztecs or Mayans at the start of the game, before European contact. Under these conditions the world beyond Central America and Mexico is *terra incognita* (Latin for "unknown land") and only the local resources are revealed. As the Aztecs or Mayans expand into the area, they too encounter pop-up screens indicating that their potential resources include coffee and sugar (see Image 5.1). However, coffee beans and sugar cane were originally Old World crops, from Ethiopia, and India or New Guinea, respectively. They didn't exist in the New World until the Spanish and Portuguese set up plantations there to grow them (Pomeranz 88–92).

The reason for pointing out this error is not to fault Paradox for getting some facts wrong. *Europa Universalis IV* incorporates massive historical detail, and this was likely a conscious decision in order to avoid the complex solution suggested later in this chapter. However, whether by mistake or intentionally, the Paradox team treats the production of commodities in a given territory as a timeless feature of that territory, rather than a temporary phenomenon contingent upon historical events and developments. The presence of coffee and sugar in Central America today tells an important story. It's the story of the "Columbian Exchange," the transfer of people, commodities, and diseases between the Old and New Worlds, and among regions of both groupings of continents, in the centuries following Columbus's opening of regular contact between the Americas and Afro-Eurasia. This story is a central focus of modern historical analyses pertaining to European expansion, and European expansion is one of the major themes of *Europa Universalis*, as well as other grand strategy games that cover the period, including *Sid Meier's Civilization*. In fairness to Paradox, the development team includes the Columbian Exchange as an "institution" that modifies productivity in Europe. This institution is supposed to emulate the effect of certain commodities, such as potatoes, in the European diet. However, this level is much more abstract than, for instance, having Europeans find a Central American territory producing chocolate (a New World crop) and turning it over to

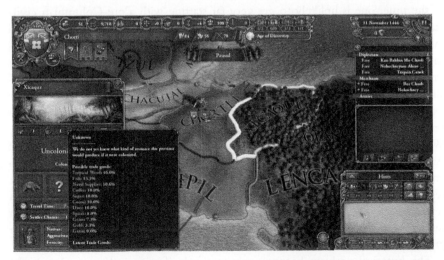

IMAGE 5.1 *Europa Universalis IV*, pop-up list of potential resources in pre-Columbian Central America. Copyright © 2019 Paradox Interactive AB. www.paradoxplaza.com

coffee cultivation. That neither the *Europa Universalis* nor *Civilization* series highlight the Columbian Exchange is evidence of at least two potential challenges to portraying the impact of humans on the environment and vice versa. One is the limitations inherent in making commercial videogames simple enough to attract a large market. The other is the extent to which game designers consider environmental aspects of history to be a priority. These challenges are important because human interaction with the physical environment has played an increasingly important role in the work of historians and other scholars dealing with the past. This chapter examines how well videogames deal with environmental issues while explaining how scholars have argued that the environment and human history are interconnected. As with all other areas of historical inquiry, disagreements abound.

Environmental history and the Columbian Exchange

Human concerns about their relationship to the environment go back a long way. The 4000-year-old *Epic of Gilgamesh* serves in part as an allegory of the relationship between settled agrarian civilizations and the wild hunter-gathering predecessors. It also contains a flood story, underscoring the impact that climate had on ancient societies. However, it was not until the twentieth century that scholars focused on the impact of the environment on historical developments. It's hardly surprising that environmental history came into existence after economic and social history, since it needed the other two to build on. In particular, the *Annales* School, discussed in previous chapters, encouraged historians to analyze large-scale developments unfolding over long periods. The first volume of Braudel's *The Mediterranean and the Mediterranean World in the Age of Philip II* (published in 1949) focused on the Mediterranean's environmental and geographical setting and observed the impact of environmental changes, such as the role of deforestation in the rise of construction costs in shipping. One of Braudel's students, Emmanuel Le Roy Ladurie, went on to bring the concept of the "Little Ice Age," a period of global cooling from roughly 1300 to 1850, into mainstream scholarship. Meanwhile, in the United States, the concept of the "frontier," as an environment that shaped the cultures on it, had been around since Frederick Jackson Turner published on it in 1893. These two strands, French and American, came together in the 1960s and 1970s to create what we know as environmental history, a topic that generates greater interest as increasing scientific evidence points to the enormous changes that humans have had on the environment and vice versa. Environmental history encourages a long view of the past, since its effects unfold over centuries and even millennia. For instance, John L. Brooke's *Climate Change and the Course of Global History* begins with the formation of the Earth and only reaches the dawn of civilization a third of the way through the book. The term "environmental history," however, only came into existence around 1970, and it was at this point that Alfred Crosby's *The Columbian Exchange* (Hughes 31–29, 84–100) gave its name to the process discussed above.

Crosby highlighted the environmental impact of European exploration and conquest from the late fifteenth through the nineteenth centuries. In doing so, he set the European encounter with the Americas in a class apart from the type of contacts Braudel had written about. In contrast to the fifteenth-century Mediterranean exchange of goods, ideas, and people, Columbus began an encounter between two ecosystems that had been separate since the end of the last ice age. There is evidence of some pre-Columbian contact, for instance, Polynesians reaching South America and Vikings briefly settling Newfoundland. Nevertheless, from a historian's perspective, such contacts made little to no mark on the development of societies in the Americas or Afro-Eurasia. By contrast, Columbus's voyages began regular communication between the Old and New Worlds. A wide range of crops went in both directions, with Europeans and Asians consuming and planting maize, tomatoes, potatoes, chocolate, and tobacco in the Old World while European planters and African slaves grew sugar, coffee, and wheat in the New.

Other exchanges tended to occur in one direction, from Afro-Eurasia to the Americas. In part, this was a reflection of the greater diversity of Old World plants and animals. The variety of livestock in the Old World meant there was no demand for the llama and alpaca from the New. Disease also traveled from East to West, with Europeans and Africans unleashing "virgin soil" epidemics of smallpox, typhoid, influenza, cholera, and gonorrhea on Native American populations that had not built up immunities to these pathogens. These epidemics, combined with European aggression and settlement, reduced the indigenous population of the Americas by over 90 percent. Finally, the people of the Old World settled the New, not vice versa, because the Europeans wielded power to expropriate indigenous people from their lands, set up plantations, and force Africans to labor on them.

The Columbian Exchange, however, was not limited to the interaction of Europe and Africa with the Americas. It also affected Asia and Australia. As the Spanish sailed west, the Portuguese sailed south and east, reaching India in 1498. Over the following three centuries the Dutch, French, and British followed them, spreading New World crops throughout the Old World and Oceania. Europeans also sped up the dissemination of Old World commodities within Africa and Eurasia. The result can be seen today in the variety of dishes, some of them closely identified with national or regional cultural heritage, that are in fact combinations of Old and New World crops (sometimes incorporating Old World animals). For instance, much of Mexican cuisine relies on beef and chicken, Eurasian animals, which it combines with corn tortillas and tomato-based salsa, both home-grown for millennia. Cheese was unknown in pre-Columbian Mexico, since Mexicans had no livestock producing milk for human consumption. The northern Asian-Indian dish aloo ghobi (potato and cauliflower in a curry) is another example of transcontinental combination, since potato originated in the Andes and cauliflower in the Middle East. The turmeric, which forms the distinctive feature of the curry in which aloo ghobi is cooked, comes from Southeast Asia.

By highlighting the importance of the Columbian Exchange, Crosby helped to displace European technological superiority from the center of the historical narrative of Europe's conquest of the Americas. In order to answer why so much of the traffic was one-way, geographer Jared Diamond looked back 13,000 years before Columbus's voyage. We discussed Diamond's thesis in Chapter 3 as it applied to Lebow's "miracle" scenario of contingency and counterfactuality. In this chapter we need to consider the importance of Diamond's explanation for environmental history and videogames' portrayal of the issues it emphasizes.

To recap Diamond's central argument in *Guns, Germs, and Steel*: the Western Europeans who arrived in the Americas (and Australia) were inheritors of millennia of influence from a band of societies stretching from the Mediterranean to East Asia. These societies had been connected through trade since prehistoric times, and as civilizations arose in the regions they occupied, the trade among them became ever more frequent and intense. By contrast, there was far less trade among the societies of the Americas, and barely any at all between Australia and the regions surrounding it. Diamond attributes the relative lack of contact in the latter cases to the difficulties of temperate-zone crops traversing tropical zones before the introduction of long-range seafaring technology. For instance, for the potato to get from Peru to Mexico, it had to cross the jungles of Columbia and Central America, which are inhospitable to raising that crop. Similarly, for any crop or domesticated animal to get from China to Australia, it had to be able to flourish in the rainforests of Indonesia. By contrast, trade, migration, and conquest had brought to Europe the suite of livestock and crops mentioned above that was unavailable in the Americas and Australia. The presence of livestock (often in the same rooms as people slept) led in turn to the spread of diseases that flourished in the crowded cities of Europe, Asia, and North Africa. Science and technology also spread to Western Europe from elsewhere: the concept of zero from India; writing, algebra, and the lateen sail from the Middle East; and printing, paper, gunpowder, and the compass from China. This combination of disease, livestock, and technology enabled the Europeans to settle the Americas and Australia, pushing aside or dominating the indigenous populations.

Although *Guns, Germs and Steel* became a best-seller it drew plenty of criticism from other scholars. The most prevalent was that Diamond's explanation pays insufficient attention to contingent events in the meeting of Old and New World populations. For instance, political divisions in both Mexico and Peru enabled conquistadors to recruit native factions to fight with them against their rivals. Others argue that modern scholarship's characterization of the impact of disease relies too much on the assumption that these differences were genetic. Disease often spreads in the wake of war, and for Native American adults to be hit by a series pathogens, which none of them had encountered as children, could account for the high mortality rates accompanying the arrival of Europeans (Tomlinson; Blaut; Jones).

However, none of these objections undermines the basic point that European expansion in the sixteenth and seventeenth centuries unleashed an unprecedented exchange of crops, livestock, and people that forever changed the ecologies of large parts of the world. Nor do these criticisms seriously undermine the evidence that the indigenous population of the Americas suffered catastrophic decline during this same period. It's true that Diamond's argument, like most assertions regarding the effects of the environment on history, works best on a grand scale. If the circumstances of initial human settlement of the world made it more likely that an Afro-Eurasian civilization would bring the various parts to together for the first time under its dominance, it wasn't inevitable precisely how this would happen, or even which Afro-Eurasian civilization it would be. Just as games can approach history at a grand strategic level, a more tactical short-term view, or in terms of single-character interactions, so can scholars. Each view has its limitations, but these limitations do not necessarily delegitimize its entire framework of understanding history.

Applying the Columbian Exchange in the virtual world

Any game covering themes of early modern European exploration and colonization should deal somehow with the Columbian Exchange. Unfortunately, none so far has done so particularly well. The problem is not with geographically variable access to resources. In both *Civilization* and *Europa Universalis* players often have to conquer or trade with other regions in order to gain access to resources they need. The problem is that these resources are fixed at the beginning of the game, waiting for players to "discover" them. In order to duplicate what really occurred historically, these games would have to assign certain territories, squares, or hexes (depending on the game's smallest unit of area) as suitable for the growing of certain types of crops (dependent on the topography and climate). Players would have access to certain crops at the beginning of the game, but not other crops, to which they would only acquire access through conquest or trade. As they acquired territory, they would be able to use farmland and plantations to grow crops to which they already had access, as well as anything originally grown on that land. The same would apply to pasture land. Horses might be available on one continent and not another. This already occurs sometimes in *Civilization*. However, there is no sense that a civilization might export the ability to raise horses elsewhere, through colonization or trade. One can argue that inasmuch as trade in *Civilization* speeds research, it indirectly speeds up acquisition of the "Horse Riding" technology. But "Horse Riding" is separate from access to horses. Players can have one without the other. Also players can trade products they produce for horses from another faction. In doing so, however, they don't gain the ability to raise horses themselves. Similarly, as playing the Mayans in *Europa Universalis IV* demonstrates, resources in that game series are fixed at the beginning of the game in the territories in which they were grown *after* European expansion, not before.

The history of sugar provides an excellent illustration of how the transfer of crops worked historically, and doesn't work in these games. Sugar cane was cultivated in India around 300 BCE (and possibly earlier in New Guinea) and reached Europe through Arab and Italian merchants during the Middle Ages.

Earlier people in the Mediterranean relied on sugar from honey to sweeten their food, or they simply ate sweet fruits. The Turkish conquest of the Middle East and the northern coast of Africa closed off European access to Egypt, the main source of sugar, opening opportunities for European landowners to raise it on their own plantations in the late Middle Ages (roughly 1300–1500). The only problem with this new commodity was that there were so few areas in Europe suitable to grow it. Sugar is a tropical crop and most of Europe lies far north of the tropics. In the late Middle Ages, the only areas under European control that were also suitable for growing sugar were in the southern reaches of Italy and the Mediterranean islands. This territory expanded slightly as the Christian kingdoms of the Iberian Peninsula (Portugal, Castile, and Aragon) conquered the Muslim sultanate of Granada, established footholds in the northwest corner of Africa, and colonized the Cape Verde and Canary Islands off the West African coast (Pomeranz 94–96). The breakthrough came with the European colonization of the Americas. Brazil and the Caribbean were ideal environments for the cultivation of sugar, and became the prized jewels in the colonial crowns of several European powers. Significantly, during the negotiations concluding the Seven Years' (French and Indian) War, Louis XV of France considered a handful of islands in the Caribbean to be more valuable than the vast majority of his possessions on the North American mainland east of the Mississippi River. Sugar, therefore, became most closely identified with regions in which it was unknown before European colonization.

Perhaps the series that focuses the most on early modern trade is Ubisoft's *Anno* (*A.D.*), whose origins we discussed in Chapter 1. The first three titles in the series, *1602, 1503,* and *1701,* focus on European expansion across the world, emphasizing overseas trade and colonization. Unfortunately, they also suffer from some of the problems described above regarding *Civilization* and *Europa Universalis.* In the early installments, players simply find resources in place and raise them, rather than importing crops or seed. Ironically, the installment of this series that comes the closest to simulating the Columbian Exchange, at least for crop diffusion, is the one set before Europeans crossed the oceans. This is the series' most recent historical title, *Anno 1404* (marketed as *Dawn of Discovery* in North America).

Anno 1404 occurs on a map that combines the strategic (exploring and trading between continents) with the tactical (developing colonies at the city-building level). It does so in a number of ways. First, the game's setting clearly mimics the conditions of fifteenth-century trade among European societies, and between them and the Islamic societies of North Africa and the Middle East. Yet it's abstract. No historical names, either for countries and empires or for prominent individuals, occur in the game. The landmasses are computer-generated, as in *Civilization.* Omitting specific names allows the developers to compress space and time without appearing to do violence to the historical record. Rather than a world with large continents (accompanied by nearby islands) with vast oceans separating them, *Anno 1404*'s map is dotted with what, if scaled to reality, would be small islands, equivalent in size to those of the Lesser Antilles in the Caribbean. The waters separating them are more the size of channels or small seas than oceans or even the Mediterranean Sea.

Just as the game compresses and simplifies space, so it also simplifies ecology. Islands in the northern half of the map have temperate climates, and those in the southern half, tropical. There are two classes of crops: northern, which includes cider, hemp, wheat, herbs, grapes, and beeswax; and southern, which include dates, spices, indigo, silk, coffee, and almonds. However, at this point *Anno 1404* shows greater ecological nuance than do *Civilization* or *Europa Universalis*. Just as coffee was not indigenous to China, nor silk to Ethiopia, these two items do not necessarily occur together on any single tropical island in the game. Rather, each island has land with a particular "fertility" to one or more of these crops. The player (as merchant) has to purchase the requisite "seeds" to plant the crop. For instance, if players want to plant dates, they have to find an island with land that has the correct "fertility" for growing dates. They must then buy date seeds from "Oriental" supplier Grand Vizier Al Zahir to start developing their plantation. (Images 5.2 and 5.3 show this transaction and the corresponding creation of a date plantation.) If players want to develop wheat or barley (identified generically as crops), they must find an island with land that has the correct fertility for growing them. They must then buy seed from "Occidental" supplier Lord Northborough to start developing a crop farm. Some of these goods

IMAGE 5.2 *Anno 1404*, buying date seeds. © 2009 Ubisoft Entertainment. All Rights Reserved. Ubisoft and the Ubisoft logo are trademarks of Ubisoft Entertainment in the US and/or other countries. Anno, Anno 1404, Sunflowers and Sunflowers logo are trademarks of Ubisoft GmbH in the US and/or other countries. Ubisoft GmbH is a Ubisoft Entertainment company. Produced by Blue Byte. Blue Byte and the Blue Byte logo are trademarks of Red Storm Entertainment in the US and/or other countries. Red Storm Entertainment Inc is a Ubisoft Entertainment company.

IMAGE 5.3 *Anno 1404*, planting dates. © 2009 Ubisoft Entertainment. All Rights Reserved. Ubisoft and the Ubisoft logo are trademarks of Ubisoft Entertainment in the US and/or other countries. Anno, Anno 1404, Sunflowers and Sunflowers logo are trademarks of Ubisoft GmbH in the US and/or other countries. Ubisoft GmbH is a Ubisoft Entertainment company. Produced by Blue Byte. Blue Byte and the Blue Byte logo are trademarks of Red Storm Entertainment in the US and/or other countries. Red Storm Entertainment Inc is a Ubisoft Entertainment company.

support an industry. For instance, "crops" support the production of both bread and beer. The *Anno* series is about the process of early modern trade, not the specifics of early modern history. In providing a representative set of crops, it partially models some elements of early modern trade, and the Columbian Exchange.

Nevertheless, because *Anno 1404* is set before regular European contact with the Americas, it does not simulate other key elements of the ecological revolution that early modern European expansion unleashed. Take, for instance, live-stock. The game has three species of livestock: goats, pigs, and cattle, which players can raise wherever the land is fertile. There is no equivalent of the seeds for crops required for them. In other words, the game assumes that these live-stock already exist throughout its virtual world. This is in keeping with the situ-ation that existed in the fifteenth century between Europe and North Africa. If the game were to extend the principle of seeding to a model of the Columbian Exchange a century later, it would have to require Europeans to bring livestock in the holds of their ships in order to breed them in the New World. Moreover, the game lacks horses, which may not be as important as cattle, goats, and pigs for purposes of developing an economy, but were some of the most prized pos-sessions of the early modern world and served as a major asset for armies.

There is, therefore, considerable scope for strategy videogames to do a better job of simulating the exchange of crops and livestock that accompanied

European expansion across the oceans. Moreover, it's not difficult to see how designers might achieve this goal. However, the Columbian Exchange involved much more than the transfer of flora and fauna. As we have already seen, it also included the transfer of people and pestilence. We will discuss how videogames deal with encounters between people from different cultures in the next chapter. For the moment, let's turn our attention to the aspect of the environment that devastated societies more than any other before the twentieth century: disease.

Disease

With life expectancies in the developed world ranging from around 73 to 83 years at birth, it's easy for us to forget how tenuous health was before the introduction of modern sanitation, antibiotics, and the ability to conduct invasive surgeries without torturing patients. Epidemics regularly killed off thousands, young and old. People died in the prime of their lives from illnesses that are easily treatable today. Families could expect to lose at least one offspring to disease in childhood. In assessing how well historical videogames model disease we need to take into account how well they model both the causes of their diseases and their effects.

There is no better illustration of how important these issues are than that most notorious of epidemics, the Black Death, which ravaged Old World civilizations, the ones privileged with Diamond's "guns, germs, and steel," during the late Middle Ages. In the movie *Monty Python and the Holy Grail*, the Python comedians depict a "dark ages" in which plague flourished – presumably due to ignorance and unsanitary conditions. However, this popular impression of the relationship between the Middle Ages and disease is inaccurate. First, the Middle Ages, conventionally dated from around 500 to 1500, were not entirely dark. To the extent that there was a decline in commerce, overall production, and scientific advancement, it occurred mainly in Western Europe during the period 450–800 CE. Elsewhere, civilization flourished, most notably in the rising Islamic caliphate, which by the latter date stretched from western India and Central Asia to Morocco and Spain, and also in Hindu India, which was experiencing what is commonly referred to as a "golden age." Second, although the Justinian Plague occurred during this period, it was in the Byzantine Empire, arguably the most "civilized" corner of Europe.

A lack of civilization didn't create the conditions for the Black Death in the mid-fourteenth century. Rather, the late Medieval flourishing of commerce and urban populations made the transmission of disease so easy. The plague spread from the borders of China westward along the trade routes of the time – whether the Silk Road across the Central Asian deserts and Eurasian steppe, or the shipping routes of the Indian Ocean and Mediterranean Sea. In the crowded trading centers dotting these routes, the disease easily hopped from person to person before the carriers succumbed to it and ceased to be contagious. The disease required bustling populous cities connected by active trade, not our picture of the "Dark Ages" (Kelly). If the transformation of Europe's Medieval economy encouraged the spread of plague, so the same plague sped the transformation of European society. The Black Death contributed to the end of serfdom across much of Western Europe, because it so depopulated the land that aristocrats could no longer afford to return runaway serfs to their masters. In any case, the elite families who controlled the serfs were often in disarray due to their own high mortality.

As discussed above, this picture of interregional interaction as prerequisite for catastrophic epidemics extends to the Columbian Exchange. As long as the Americas and Afro-Eurasia remained separated by impassable oceans, disease did not spread. As soon as these oceans became highways of commerce, however, devastating epidemics visited the indigenous populations of the Americas, which lacked the immunities to Afro-Eurasian diseases that the Europeans had built up through either genetic inheritance or exposure earlier in life. The result was per-haps the world's second-largest mortality from disease in recorded history – after the Black Death, which spread across a zone of much greater population. In terms of the percentage of the population they killed, the epidemics following in the wake of the Columbian Exchange (over 90-percent mortality) were much worse than the Black Death (between 33-percent and 50-percent mortality).

If trade and exploration spread disease, so did war. In fact, until the turn of the twentieth century the disease that accompanied war killed more soldiers than combat did. The same applied to civilians. Sieges usually resulted in more deaths from disease and malnutrition than deaths at the hands of soldiers during the pillaging that often accompanied a city's fall. Armies also spread disease. Their mere movement from one location to another transformed them into vec-tors for transmitting pathogens. Moreover, sexual contact between soldiers and the populations of areas they visited and occupied spread venereal diseases.

Although videogames depicting these periods of history certainly take account of epidemics, they rarely portray the impact of disease to the extent it occurred historically. Writing for *PCGamer* magazine, reviewer T. J. Hafer complains about the presence of plague (or lack thereof) in Paradox's Medieval grand-strategy game *Crusader Kings II*:

> The plague is a blip on the economic radar, reducing tax income by 80% in affected regions … and causing troops stationed there to take moderate casualties. A handful of named characters at my court might keel over. If I'm really unlucky, someone who matters might be among them. After it's passed, the world remains almost indistinguishable from when it came, as if an uncomfortable El Niño had passed over it.
>
> *(Hafer, "Stop Nerfing the Plague")*

In *Medieval II: Total War* cities occasionally suffer from plague, which armies can spread between regions. Most important, the Black Death arrives on schedule in the mid-fourteenth century. Nevertheless, the population reduction is more an annoyance than a catastrophe, and the game does not demonstrate a clear connection between the plague and the transformation of Western Europe's economy with the decline of serfdom. In *Anno 1404* plague accompanies an increase in the population of beggars. While the association of poverty and disease is fair enough, *Anno 1404* appears to mix up cause and effect. In reality, poverty provides a fertile ground for disease, but it was armies, and people involved in commerce, who spread pathogens the quickest, not beggars, unless they were refugees from war. As for epidemics associated with the Columbian Exchange, *Empire: Total War* ignores them, although they were still a significant issue in the depopulation of indigenous North Americans in the eighteenth century, when the game takes place (*Disease & Disaster*).

Hafer attributes the relatively mild impact of disease in many historical video-games to "nerfing," the practice of reducing the power of a feature in order to maintain balance in gameplay. He argues that the problem of fully accounting for the impact of disease boils down to historical determinism versus player agency:

> As Sid Meier says, a strategy game is a series of interesting choices. Realism doesn't universally translate to fun, and the reality of diseases like the Black Death is that there was no decision anyone at the time could have made to significantly dampen the chaos.
>
> *(Hafer, "Stop Nerfing the Plague")*

He goes on, however, to disagree with the assumption, common among designers, that gamers are invested in winning. With games such as *Crusader Kings II*, he argues that the fun is in the story rather than a victory, and that the "post-apocalyptic" aspect of catastrophic epidemics, in which one must rebuild society, is entertaining in itself. Indeed, *Crusader Kings II*'s developers took heed of criticisms such as these and highlighted disease in their purchasable update to the game, titled *Reaper's Due*. This expansion includes a map that shows the spread of disease geographically (see Image 5.4). Therefore, much as merchants in Medieval Eurasia, the player hears news of the plague before it actually arrives. The game also provides players with the option at the outset of determining how devastating and frequent epidemics will be.

Paradox Interactive published *Crusader Kings II*, and significantly one of this company's most popular titles, *Europa Universalis IV*, does a better job than most games in simulating the impact of disease, particularly following contact between an indigenous American and a European faction. The effects are a 25-percent reduction of local manpower, taxes, and production for one to three years depending on the disease. Each disease can happen only once, the assumption being that the population has built up immunities thereafter. Three distinct epidemics can hit a region, each diminishing the population by 25 percent (*European Diseases Events*). As significant as this effect is, it may not thoroughly simulate the full magnitude of the impact of disease in the Americas. The game is unusual in not attempting to create a balance among the factions.

IMAGE 5.4   *Crusader Kings II: The Reaper's Due*, spread of the Black Death. Copyright © 2019 Paradox Interactive AB. www.paradoxplaza.com

Rather, in the introductory screen in which the player chooses a faction, the game rates the difficulty level of playing that faction. Spain, for instance, is one of the easier factions to play. The Aztec Empire is decidedly more difficult, mainly for its lack of technology, but also because of disease. Players who choose factions indigenous to the Americas do so knowing the deck will be stacked against them. No doubt, the design team for *Europa Universalis IV* would argue that so too was the deck stacked against indigenous Americans in reality.

Hafer's reference to the fun associated with rebuilding a society that has collapsed because of disease points to an assumption that appears to be common among game designers. Although they shy away from representing the full impact of disease in most historical strategy games, they are happy to use disease as a central premise for dystopian societies in action games. Many of the plotlines are fantastic, in which disease destroys society and transforms humans into mutants or zombies. *Bioshock, Day Z, Dying Light, The Last of Us,* and *Resident Evil* all fall into this category. However, less fantastic scenarios include Tom Clancy's *Division*, in which a smallpox outbreak causes panic in New York, and *Plague Inc*, in which players try to infect the world (Donnelly). Because all these games have players guiding the protagonists through their virtual worlds, players have a sense of their characters' agencies given the post-apocalyptic circumstances surrounding them.

It is with this post-apocalyptic model in mind that Creative Assembly developed *Total War: Attila*. This strategy game focuses on the collapse of the Western Roman Empire in the fourth and fifth centuries CE. The game designers clearly see this historical event as a type of apocalypse. The game's official website declares:

Against a darkening background of famine, disease and war, a new power is rising in the great steppes of the East ... A time of apocalyptic turmoil at the very dawn of the Dark Ages. How far will you go to survive? Will you sweep oppression from the world and carve out a barbarian or Eastern kingdom of your own? Or will you brace against the coming storm as the last remnants of the Roman Empire, in the ultimate survival-strategy challenge?

That *Total War: Attila's* marketers present it as "the ultimate survival-strategy challenge" warns customers before they buy the game that there will be little if any "nerfing" of catastrophic circumstances surrounding the period. In this case, disease is not an annoying event interfering with player agency, it is part of the virtual environment that the designers are advertising as one of the game's attractions.

While the *Total War* and Paradox series both incorporate disease into their simulations of the past to varying extents, *Civilization* does so only in a very abstract manner. Cities can become unhealthy if their population grows too large and if they lack facilities that reduce disease. However, the game series does not clearly connect the spread of disease to either trade or the movement of armies. This is a shame, since *Civilization V: Brave New World* and *Civilization VI: Rise and Fall* in particular do so well explaining exactly how much religious and cultural influence, as well as wealth from commodities, spreads along trade routes. One could easily imagine plague spreading along these routes as well, diminishing the population of cities and eroding the effectiveness of armies. Given the historical impact of disease on isolated populations suddenly encountering one another, the absence of disease in the game is a significant omission in its modeling of world history.

Of course, disease is an aspect of history that action games can portray as well as strategy games. The constant fear of epidemics shaped public policy and haunted societies throughout most of recorded history. These dramatic events could provide a backdrop of tension against which to play out a story in the past. However, epidemic disease seems curiously absent in some of the most popular action games. *Assassin's Creed* is the most popular action videogame series focusing on periods before the age of modern medicine, yet disease only occasionally enters into it. For instance, the third "sequence" of *Assassin's Creed II* occurs in and around Florence during the period 1478–80, during which a severe epidemic hit the city (Morrison et al. 530). Yet the game doesn't highlight it. Certainly, "plague doctors" abound, clearly identifiable by their masks, in the shape of bird's beaks, which contained aromatic substances thought to deter the spread of disease. In the game, however, these doctors don't cure diseases. Their sole function in gameplay is to provide the protagonist with elixirs that magically heal him of injuries from falls and wounds from combat. This is not to say that disease is totally absent from the *Assassin's Creed*. It appears in later titles incidentally, but the most effective presentation in the series so far is in *Assassin's Creed: Odyssey*. Early in the game, the player has the protagonist choose whether or not to prevent the execution of infected villagers in a desperate measure to stop the spread of plague. If the player decides to have the protagonist rescue them, then plague spreads across Greece later in the game. Nevertheless, throughout most of the series, disease appears as an incidental occurrence, rather than the community-disrupting and family-devastating catastrophe it often was.

The relative absence of disease in relationship to the historical record is a missed opportunity to present a graphic depiction of life and death before the age of modern medicine, when life was much more tenuous than it is today. Designers could make disease a compelling element in the storylines of action games. It could become a complicating factor in opening up trade routes and developing large cities in strategy games. In either game genre, it would help to complicate a narrative common in historical videogames, that the greater commerce and urban culture of civilizations was superior to the more isolated, village communities of less highly organized societies. Civilization came at a cost, and epidemic disease was one of the greatest prices to pay. Games that understate the presence of disease, and most games do, distort one of the most basic aspects of history.

Climate change and geological events

We can properly regard pandemics as catastrophes, but the environment has had an equally profound effect on past societies. Scientific research shows that climate change and natural catastrophes, such as floods, earthquakes, and volcanic eruptions have caused social and political turmoil. For instance, historians have long noted the unusual number of wars, political upheaval, and human mortality during the seventeenth century. These included the Thirty Years' War in central Europe, the English Civil War, civil wars in India's Mughal Empire, and the collapse of China's Ming Dynasty followed by the brutal suppression of coastal communities under the Qing Dynasty. Historians have suggested many human causes for these apparently unconnected events. For example, the conventional list of causes for the English Civil War (1642–49) include dissent against the Church of England's hierarchy and theology, lesser gentry and businessmen objecting to customary laws and taxes favoring the rural elite and aristocracy, and growing ideological opposition to a monarchy that was increasingly seeking to aggrandize and centralize its power in Britain. Historians also might note the growing importance of British trade with Asia and settlement of North America. However, only since the beginning of the twenty-first century have some historians argued that an extraordinary episode of cool weather in the seventeenth century brought drought, floods, and other localized disasters that inspired resentment, rebellion, and war.

Historian Geoffrey Parker identifies two archives, "human" and "natural," that enable him and his colleagues to reach these conclusions. The "human archive" includes written records (correspondence, diaries, government records, and newspapers), numerical data about harvests and weather gained from these records, images (such as paintings depicting iced-over rivers that never are today), and arch-aeological evidence such as inscriptions referring to floods, and excavations of aban-doned settlements. Most of these sources had long been available to historians, but required them to change the type of written sources they read and the way they analyzed them. This change began to occur in the mid-twentieth century, with the shift toward an emphasis on social history. The "natural archive" draws on several techniques for detecting past climates. One is boring into ice sheets, which tells us the composition of the atmosphere at the last point that different layers froze. Another is examining debris left by retreating glaciers, pollen and spore deposits, which often remain in sediment at the bottom of lakes, bogs, and estuaries. Yet another is measuring tree rings, which record not only the age of the tree according to the number of rings, but also the amount of each year's growth depending on the thickness of the ring (Parker, "Crisis and Catastrophe" 1065–66, Parker, *Global Crisis*). Most of this information relies on scientific equipment and techniques that have only become available since the mid-twentieth century. As a result, it has only recently become possible to make confident connections between geological and climatic events of the past and events in human societies of the same period.

This intersection of environmental science and history has become more urgent as human influence over climate change has gained nearly unanimous acceptance among scientists. Understanding the relationship between society and natural events helps us with the current climate change crisis in a couple of ways. First, it reminds us how devastating climate change can be. Scholars now attribute a variety of political upheavals at least partly to episodes of climate change. Among them are: the desiccation of the Sahara from the sixth through the fourth millennia BCE, which gave rise to Egyptian civilization; a protracted period of severe drought in the twenty-second century BCE that contributed to the collapse of the Akkadian Empire of Iraq and the beginning of the collapse of the Indus Valley Civilization; another dry spell during the thirteenth to twelfth centuries BCE that caused the collapse of several Bronze Age societies from Greece and Egypt to Persia; a major drought (accompanied by plague) during the years 536–539 CE, which may have intensified (although certainly didn't cause) migrations across Eurasia; and the "Little Ice Age" (1250–1850 CE) of which the seventeenth-century crises noted above were part of the most extreme phase.

At the margins of civilization, the relationship is more apparent. Norse Settle-ment of Greenland and Newfoundland occurred during a warm period (800–1250). Conflicts with Native Americans probably led to the abandonment of the colony in Newfoundland (possibly the "Vinland" of the Norse sagas), but it was almost certainly the onset of the "Little Ice Age" that caused the Norse settlers of Greenland to abandon their two settlements there by the mid-fifteenth century. Although even in the case of Greenland, the Norse settlers' reluctance to adapt to climate change as the Inuit had done was a major cause of the settlements' collapse (Seaver; Diamond, *Collapse* 178–276).

Scientists have identified a number of factors leading to climate change, depending on the episode. For instance, there have been attempts to connect some volcanic eruptions with droughts resulting from diminished sunlight. In some cases, geological activity may have had direct effects on societies. For instance, the gradual natural damming of Himalayan tributaries may have added to the effects of the twenty-second-century BCE droughts to dry up one of the major rivers supplying the Indus Valley Civilization. The explosion of the volcanic island Thera (modern Santorini), and the resulting tsunami around 1600 BCE, probably contributed significantly to the collapse of the Minoan Civilization centered on Crete. All these events show the fragility of civilization, a fragility which is perhaps less pronounced in an age when food can be shipped rapidly across the planet, but is nevertheless still present. Inadequate government response to Hurricane Katrina in 2005 may have magnified the size of the Democratic Party's victory in the US midterm elections the following year.

If one role of historical climatology has been to remind us of the susceptibility of civilization to climate change, another has been to establish human causes for many of the most recent changes in climate and topography (the latter mainly through melting ice and rising oceans). The knowledge that human activity is causing the current phase of global warming has led to a debate about how long. Certainly, the last two centuries of industrialization are primarily responsible, but the mere presence of human farming over the last 10,000 years may also have played a role. Agriculture includes deforestation, and the domestication and raising of livestock, both of which add to greenhouse gases. Because plants consume carbon dioxide, deforestation reduces the amount locked up in plant life. Because animals consume oxygen and eliminate carbon dioxide through exhaling, and methane through excretion, they too alter the atmospheric balance in favor of more greenhouse gases. More recently, of course, the use of fossil fuels to power modern industries has created the spike in temperatures we know as "global warming." Because fossil fuels consist of former life, and are therefore based on carbon, their burning releases greenhouse gases into the atmosphere.

Since climatologists, archaeologists, and historians have now determined that climate had a major impact on past societies, as well as present ones, climate change should be a consideration for anyone designing a historical videogame. And indeed, it has been. Obvious differences in past climates from today's appear in many virtual worlds that form the settings for action games. Ubisoft's *Far Cry: Primal*, set around 10,000 BCE, ranges from temperate to frozen environments in Europe before the retreat of the glaciers soon after. Gameplay involves hunting (and being hunted by) extinct species, such as woolly mammoths, woolly rhinos, dire wolves, and saber-toothed cats. In order to make for a more compelling environment, however, the game compresses both space and time. Concerning the former, the player can wander from temperate zones to glacial walls, which were in reality hundreds of miles apart, in less than half-an-hour.

The larger problem, however, is the conflation of time, because doing so is essential to the game's storyline, in which the protagonist, Takkar, a member of a hunter-gatherer clan of modern humans, must defeat rival clans of Neanderthals (to the north – see Image 5.5) and herder-farmers (to the south). The story is supposed to highlight the extinction of the Neanderthals (not finally accomplished in the game but certainly helped along) by modern humans and the displacement of hunter-gatherers by herder-farmers. Since climate change probably played a significant role in both these developments, one might argue that the game is in fact highlighting environmental issues. The problem is that these two developments occurred at least 20,000 years apart. The latest date for which there is evidence of Neanderthals is around 26,000 BCE, whereas cultivators migrated into central Europe around 6,000 BCE. Many physical anthropologists consider the date of Neanderthal extinction to be much earlier, perhaps around 37,000 BCE. So the Neanderthals of *Far Cry: Primal* should have disappeared at least 18,000 years earlier, and the cultivators from the Middle East shouldn't show up for another 4000 years. Furthermore, *Primal* takes liberties with some of the fauna. The saber-tooth cat, for instance, resembles the more terrifying North American subspecies rather than anything that inhabited Europe at the time. Finally, in order to create the aura of authenticity and full immersion in the prehistoric setting, *Primal*'s designers developed a language based on the actual pre-historic Proto-Indo-European (PIE). PIE was the common ancestor of most European and many southern Asian languages. Unfortunately, PIE existed around 4000 BCE, 6000 years after the setting of the game, and at least 1000 miles east, probably on the western Eurasian steppe.

IMAGE 5.5 *Far Cry: Primal*, hunter-gatherers and recently killed Neanderthal. © 2016 Ubisoft Entertainment. All Rights Reserved. Far Cry, Ubisoft and the Ubisoft logo are registered or unregistered trademarks of Ubisoft Entertainment in the US and/or other countries. Based on Crytek's original Far Cry directed by Cevat Yerli. Powered by Crytek's technology "CryEngine."

Acknowledging these anachronisms and inaccuracies, however, is not to condemn the educational utility of *Far Cry: Primal*. The game invites players to consider the forces at work in prehistoric Europe. Certainly, it conflates the displacement of people and the introduction of new ways of life, but in addressing them at all, it gives gamers an idea of what these forces were. Although climate change does not obviously occur during the story, it forms an unspoken backdrop. The player surely knows that the Neanderthals will die out, although some interbred with modern humans. The player also knows that agriculture and herding replaced hunting and gathering. The game encourages the player to reflect on these changes through what amounts to an interactive work of art.

At the opposite end of the chronological spectrum, *Assassin's Creed: Syndicate*, set in 1860s London, features coal-burning pollution prominently, including belching factory chimney stacks, steam locomotives, and smog. Indeed, steam is everywhere, but perhaps more to appeal to the gamers attracted to the technological innovations of the era. Unlike *Primal*, climate is not a central issue in the game.

By contrast, environmental change is essential to the plot line of some postapocalyptic games, such as the *Fallout* series. In this case, the trigger is clearly human-made. In the backstory, starting in the 1950s, the world follows an alternate timeline in which culture stagnates while technology advances. The result is a midtwenty-first century that looks more like a 1950s vision of the future. This alternate timeline is necessary in order to evoke a setting reminiscent of the early Cold War, even though the game occurs centuries later. As part of the backstory, the world experiences a series of wars from 2052 to 2077 over the dwindling supply of oil and uranium. (This is an obvious critique of our current reliance on non-renewable energy sources.) These wars culminate in a brief nuclear war that wipes out most of the world's cities and forces survivors into shelters. Those exposed to too much radiation breed "mutants," genetically altered humans who appear in the series as zombie-like enemies. The games are set during the two centuries following, when much of what was the United States is a ruined wasteland. The artifacts of a Disney-style Tomorrowland surround the player, but the inability to break free of dependence on dangerous sources of energy has turned the environment into a macabre distortion of that vision. A post-apocalyptic dystopia replaces the optimism of this mid-twentieth century-style society, while simultaneously evoking the fears over technology that played out in many of the horror and science-fiction films of the period. The *Fallout* series is therefore both futuristic science-fiction and historical, since many of its virtual world trappings are reminiscent of the midtwentieth century and the storyline relies on a well-developed alternative history.

The problem with portraying climate change in historical action games is that their plots usually cover too short a period to see it occur in the virtual world. This is less of an issue with strategy games since they often cover a century or more. For instance, *Total War: Attila* simulates the period of global cooling in the fifth century CE that accompanied the collapse of the Western Roman Empire. According to lead designer Janos Gaspar:

> As you begin the game, the seasons will be normal and the campaign map
> will be the one you know from Total War: Rome 2, but as you go fur-
> ther and further into the campaign, the snowline begins moving more and
> more to the south. In the north, there'll be multiple turns that behave like
> winter. It's going to change food production and economic output.
>
> *(Dumitrescu)*

And food production affects gameplay, particularly the areas that "barbarians"
are likely to settle. The assumption built into this game, based at least indirectly
on scholarship, is that the cooling trend across northern Eurasia encouraged
nomadic tribes to move south and west, putting pressure in turn on agrarian
tribes in central Europe, who then attacked the Roman Empire.

If *Total War: Attila* can show the impact of climate change in the mere fifty-five-
year time frame of its grand campaign, then *Civilization*, which covers more than
6000 years, should be able to do so even more obviously. Unfortunately, this most
famous of strategy videogames disappoints in this regard. Earlier versions of the
game did experiment with environmental issues. Deforestation and pollution could
negatively affect population growth and could even lead to rebellion. However,
Civilization V and *VI* don't obviously connect over-farming or industrialization to
negative consequences for the environment. This is all the more remarkable since
Civilization VI encourages the preservation of land in order to build national parks.
However, these parks generate tourism. Over-farming has no long-term environmental consequences. Nor does industrialization. One can play through the ages of
fossil-fuel burning without generating pollution, much less global warming. Unhap-
piness can result from coal-burning power plants, but the connection is less explicit
than it could be. Certainly, building renewable-energy power plants, such as a solar
farm, increases productivity and happiness, but this is all rather abstract, unlike *Civilization II*, in which coastal areas flooded if players didn't control their pollution.
Little wonder that reviewers have called for the designers of *Civilization VI* to
include climate change in any major expansions they develop (Hafer, "3 Things";
Capps). At the time of writing, the game's designers appear poised to address these
criticisms in its second major expansion, *Gathering Storm*. By contrast, *Civilization
V*'s futuristic spin-off *Civilization: Beyond Earth* connects human activity to the
environment much more clearly. In fact, the game encourages players to choose at
the outset whether they intend to choose an environmentally friendly strategy or
one of hostile domination. Both can lead to victory, but in very different ways.

Conclusion

Because environmental issues are usually about long-term trends, it has been difficult for people in the past to understand why they were occurring or what effect
they had on long-term historical developments. Contemporary observers might
record droughts and epidemics or even remember better or worse times in their
childhood. However, in the absence of systematic statistical data and scientific

observations it was impossible to attribute major events directly to climate change or truly appreciate the origins and long-term impact of diseases. Many people blamed gods, or their disobedience to them, instead. Only very recently have scientists and historians had access to sufficient data to identify clear connections between past climate changes and epidemics, and major political and societal events. Some game designers have brought elements of the environment into their virtual worlds. Yet it's surprising how little such events feature in historical videogames. In strategy games, floods, diseases, and droughts are all dramatic events that could serve as consequences of players' activities or at least wild cards to inject some uncertainty and realism into their calculations. In action games, these forces could serve more than they do as settings that pose challenges for players. However, game designers have been reluctant to give environmental issues the impact in their historical games that they actually had in the past. The reason appears to be mainly concerns over the role of agency in playability. Disease and climate change were beyond the knowledge and control of past societies, and players tend to dislike major, seemingly capricious setbacks suddenly befalling them during gameplay. By contrast, the reason for not modeling the impact of the Columbian Exchange of plants and animals more fully appears simply to be the complexity involved. Nevertheless, as noted above, there are some good examples of games that do deal with the environmental and ecological issues. Other designers might learn from them.

Works cited

Anno (game series), Max Design/Related Designs/Blue Byte, 1998–2018.
Anno 1404, Related Designs/Blue Byte, 2009.
Assassin's Creed II, Ubisoft Montreal, 2009.
Assassin's Creed: Odyssey, Ubisoft Montreal, 2018.
Assassin's Creed: Syndicate, Ubisoft Quebec, 2015.
Bioshock, 2K Boston/Australia, 2007.
Blaut, James M., "Environmentalism and Eurocentrism." *Geographical Review*, vol. 89, no. 3 (July 1999), 391.
Braudel, Fernand, *The Mediterranean and the Mediterranean World in the Age of Philip II*, translated by Sian Reynolds. University of California Press, 1995.
Brooke, John L., *Climate Change and the Course of Global History: A Rough Journey*. Cambridge University Press, 2014.
Capps, Kriston, "'Civilization VI' Has a Problem (As Does Civilization)." *CityLab*, www.citylab.com/work/2016/10/what-civilization-vi-gets-wrong-about-civilization/504653/.
Crosby, Alfred W., *The Columbian Exchange: Biological and Cultural Consequences of 1492*. Greenwood, 1973.
DayZ, Bohemia Interactive, 2018.
Diamond, Jared M., *Guns, Germs, and Steel: The Fates of Human Societies*. W. W. Norton & Company, 1999.
Diamond, Jared M., *Collapse: How Societies Choose to Fail or Succeed*. Viking, 2005.
Disease & Disaster. www.twcenter.net/forums/showthread.php?300522-Disease-amp-Disaster.
Donnelly, Joe, "10 Most Devastating Virus Outbreaks in Games." *IGN*, 12 April 2016, www.ign.com/articles/2016/04/12/10-most-devastating-virus-outbreaks-in-games.

Dumitrescu, Andrei, "Climate and Disease Are Central to Total War: Attila, Say Developers." *Softpedia*, http://news.softpedia.com/news/limate-and-Disease-Are-Central-to-Total-War-Attila-Say-Developers-460717.shtml.

Dying Light, Techland, 2015.

The Epic of Gilgamesh, translated by Morris Jastrow, Jr. and Albert T. Clay, Yale University Press, 1920. Available at *Project Gutenberg*, www.gutenberg.org/files/11000/11000-h/11000-h.htm.

Europa Universalis (game series), Paradox Development Studio, 2000–18.

Europa Universalis III, Paradox Development Studio, 2007.

Europa Universalis IV, Paradox Development Studio, 2013.

Europa Universalis IV - Paradox Interactive. www.paradoxplaza.com/europa-universalis-4.

European Diseases Events – Europa Universalis IV Wiki., www.eu4wiki.com/European_diseases_events.

Fallout (game series), Interplay et al., 1997–2017.

Far Cry: Primal, Ubisoft Montreal, 2016.

Hafer, T. J., "3 Things That Civilization 6's Expansions Must Improve." *PCGamer*, 1 November 2016a, www.pcgamer.com/civ-6-expansion/.

Hafer, T. J., "Stop Nerfing the Plague, Strategy Games." *PCGamer*, 17 April 2016b, www.pcgamer.com/stop-nerfing-the-plague-strategy-games/.

Hughes, Donald J. *What Is Environmental History?* Polity, 2015.

Jones, David S., "Virgin Soils Revisited." *The William and Mary Quarterly*, vol. 60, no. 4 (October 2003), 703–42.

Kelly, John, *The Great Mortality: An Intimate History of the Black Death, the Most Devastating Plague of All Time*, reprint edn. Harper Perennial, 2006.

Ladurie, Emmanuel Le Roy, *Times of Feast, Times of Famine: A History of Climate Since the Year 1000*, translated by Barbara Bray. Doubleday, 1971.

The Last of Us, Naughty Dog, 2015.

Morrison, A. S. et al., "Epidemics in Renaissance Florence." *American Journal of Public Health*, vol. 75, no. 5 (May 1985), 528–35.

Parker, Geoffrey, "Crisis and Catastrophe: The Global Crisis of the Seventeenth Century Reconsidered." *American Historical Review*, vol. 113, no. 4 (October 2008), 1053–79.

Parker, Geoffrey, *Global Crisis: War, Climate Change and Catastrophe in the Seventeenth Century*. Yale University Press, 2013.

Plague, Inc., Ndemic Creations, 2012.

Pomeranz, Kenneth, *The World That Trade Created: Society, Culture, and the World Economy, 1400-the Present*. M.E. Sharpe, 1999.

Resident Evil (game series), Capcom, 1996–2017.

Seaver, Kirsten A., *The Frozen Echo: Greenland and the Exploration of North America, ca. A.D. 1000-1500*. Stanford University Press, 1996.

Sid Meier's Civilization: Beyond Earth, Firaxis, 2014.

Sid Meier's Civilization V: Brave New World, Firaxis, 2013.

Sid Meier's Civilization VI: Rise and Fall, Firaxis, 2018.

Tom Clancy's The Division, Massive Entertainment, 2016.

Tomlinson, Tom, "Guns, Germs and Steel: The Fates of Human Societies." *Reviews in History*, no. 51 (May 1998), www.history.ac.uk/reviews/review/51.

Total War: Attila, Creative Assembly, 2015.

"Total War: ATTILA." *Total War*, www.totalwar.com/total_war_attila/.

Turner, Frederick Jackson, "The Significance of the Frontier in American History." *American Historical Association Annual Report for the Year* 1893.

6
CULTURE AND ETHNICITY

Introduction

"Welcome to Tropico, Presidente! I am your loyal advisor and number one fan, Penultimo, and I am here to remind you of the joys of dictatorship." So begins the tutorial for *Tropico 5*, a game that has the player, "El Presidente," guide a stereotypical Caribbean dictatorship, all the while embezzling from the national treasury into a Swiss bank account. Of course, "El Presidente" can't steal too much money from the people, because a "ruler that doesn't pay attention to his subjects may end up on the wrong side of a coup d'état." While Latin-Caribbean music plays in the background, Penultimo informs the player of the country's achievements. Many of these occur through the assistance of foreign-"educated workers," whom the player has paid to lend their expertise. The player will need them, because it's fairly obvious that the island's population could use some enlightenment. For instance, it takes the island's soldiers quite a while to learn that in order to fire the "muskets" sent to them by the island's imperial overlord at the game's beginning, they should "not look into the barrel when pulling the trigger." Perhaps this is because Tropicans seem naturally dishonest and lazy. After all, their constitution declares their desire to "maintain the traditional universal Tropican values of liberty, peace, love, understanding, siesta and hidden Swiss bank accounts."

If the player is a corrupt dictator and the island's citizens lazy imbeciles, the major powers the player deals with are not much better: according to Penultimo, "Foreign powers are important because they provide foreign aid and because if we piss them off too much, they may invade us." The, obviously British, overlords at the game's beginning appear uncaring, exploitive, and decadent. If, after independence, players pursue policies that conflict with those of the United States, they can expect an American invasion. If they repel it, they receive a "Bay of Pigs trophy." In *Tropico 5*, the US president is Ruddy Thompson, a composite of Teddy Roosevelt and Franklin Roosevelt. In *Tropico 4*, he is the less friendly Nick Richards, who looks like Richard Nixon. His liaison with the island's regime is "Ambassador Crane," whose image is based on Nixon's CIA director of operations in Latin America. Crane treats Tropico as an American satellite, insisting it pay a "freedom tax" to the United States and threatening to invade the player's island when it doesn't cooperate. In one exchange, Crane agrees to send $20,000 to Tropico on the condition that the player embezzle "only some" of the money ("Ambassador Crane"). *Tropico 4* also features a cast of Soviet characters, one of whom looks like Joseph Stalin. Cartoonish figures, often based on actual participants in the Cold War, form the images of all the characters in the *Tropico* series.

The designers and marketers of *Tropico* obviously intend to lampoon twentieth-century Latin American dictatorships and their relationships with the superpowers, as well as declining colonial powers. In his production notes for the original version of the game, released in 2001, lead designer and Pop Top Software studio founder Phil Steinmeyer writes that his team wanted to produce a city-building game that was different from *SimCity* or *Sid Meier's Civilization*. They considered a game focusing on the colonization of the Americas, but settled on the idea of a "Banana Republic" theme because it was more original.

> And so the decision became easy. The artists were dispatched to the library to get books on Latin American architecture. We started cracking Juan Valdez jokes and shouting Cuban revolutionary slogans. And I tried to come up with a better working title than Banana Republic – after all, there's a clothing store by that name with more trademark attorneys than we've got total employees.
>
> *(Steinmeyer)*

Ironically, Steinmeyer's team, who had taken over Sid Meier's *Railroad Tycoon* franchise, arrived at the Latin American city-builder games partly because they had rejected fan proposals for a "Drug Tycoon"-themed game "as poor taste."

Not surprisingly, some critics thought *Tropico* was in poor taste too. Media scholar Gonzalo Frasco deemed the original game "insulting" and "disgusting" for its "extreme use of clichés and simplification" (Quoted in Penix–Tadsen 224). Gender-studies scholar Shoshana Magnet pointed to the game's "stereotypical scenes representing Spanish Caribbean street life."

> From the sex worker to the fruit seller to the revolutionaries unloading explosives out of the back of a military truck, the characters that inhabit this game are fully recognizable cardboard cutouts – each of whom signifies a different form of essentialized Latina/o identity.
>
> *(Magnet 143)*

Magnet also criticized Kurt Squire, a pioneer in the use of videogames as a learning tool, for suggesting that *Tropico* could be used to educate students about the Cold War and Latin American politics (143, 157).

However, other scholars have pushed back. Latin-America specialist Phillip Penix-Tadsen observes that Magnet failed to take note of Squire's insistence that such games required instructors to mediate their use in the classroom. He objects to her and Frasca's criticisms as "built on the normative assumption of a 'naïve' player, uninformed and incapable of interpreting irony, satire, or parody." He argues that such approaches "equate theme" (autocratic imperialism) "to thesis" (support for autocratic imperialism) (224–25).

The general public seems to have largely ignored this academic debate and has bought the *Tropico* series in sufficient numbers to ensure plenty of sequels. *Tropico 6* followed in 2018. The current development team, Haemimont Games, is Bulgarian. The lead designer likens the cynical comedy of *Tropico* to the way fellow Bulgarians regarded their government during the Cold War:

> Living in Bulgaria, most of our writers have first-hand childhood experience with the real-life totalitarian regimes, and political jokes come easily to us. We decided to capitalize on the series' sense of humor as much as we can in *Tropico 5* and to joke with everything that we can get away with, researching important technologies like "Hot Water" and "Sliced Bread" and settling international diplomacy with dance-off competitions between presidents. Bearing in mind that the game touches several sensitive subjects, we try to keep the tone lighthearted and goofy, staying away from anything offensive.
>
> *(Spasov 2)*

The *Tropico* series is a problematic focus for criticism, because its original and current designers intended their audience to treat it as parody; on the basis of fan sites and blogs, there is every indication that most of the series' audience does. Considering the issues discussed in Chapter 1, one could argue that the entire series is an act of opposition to the pretensions of all the Cold War participants. On the other hand, Magnet makes a valid point regarding the dangers of misunderstanding this intent. Much as audiences can subvert the meaning that media transmits, whatever the ideological perspective of its authors, so could some uninformed consumers. After all, many viewers of Comedy Central's *Colbert Report* regarded host Stephen Colbert as serious when he parodied right-wing commentators (LaMarre et al.). The same could potentially occur with *Tropico*. Nevertheless, *Tropico* is exceptional among historical videogames because it so obviously presents itself as parody.

The problem is more serious with games that may be less overtly offensive but in fact embody cultural stereotypes that go unacknowledged as such. For over a generation historians, particularly those focusing on non-Western societies, have wrestled with these issues. This chapter focuses on cultural bias and the presentation of culture and ethnicity in videogames' portrayal of the past. It places these presentations in the context of what scholars have argued about representing these aspects of the past generally. The stress here is on "argued," because this is an academically divisive and controversial subject, which has spilled over into politics.

The cultural turn in history

We learned in Chapter 1 that the study of history began to move in a different direction in the late twentieth century, one that forced historians to regard all knowledge as influenced by the context in which scholars gathered and interpreted it. Although many facts are indisputable, the cultural, social, and political contexts in which scholars examine them determine how they "construct" the resulting body of knowledge. Michel Foucault applied this theory initially to the history of insanity in France. How people defined insanity had as much to do with their own prejudices about what constituted abnormal behavior as it relied on any dispassionate knowledge of what was actually occurring in peoples' brains.

Foucault's ideas reinforced those of another thinker whose writings were gaining popularity among scholars in the 1970s. This was Antonio Gramsci, an Italian Communist Party leader in the 1920s. Like many Marxists, Gramsci was puzzled and frustrated by the inability of communism to take hold in the industrialized countries where Marx had predicted it would. According to Marx's dialectic (discussed in Chapter 3), the industrial working class would overthrow the managerial class, bringing about a classless society whose citizens would have equal access to economic resources. However, by the mid-1920s no industrialized country had experienced a successful communist revolution. Rather, it was Russia, the least industrial of the major powers, which was experimenting with Marx's ideology. Doing so had required the Bolsheviks to adopt a revisionist view of Marx's dialectic, one which allowed the Communist Party to create the industrial working class rather than the other way round.

By contrast, in industrialized countries, politics seemed to be veering to the right. Pro-business governments dominated the politics of Britain, France, and the United States for most of the 1920s. Germany was in economic disarray with right- and left-wing groups vying for control, and in Italy, Benito Mussolini had become dictator, espousing a virulent nationalist ideology while throwing socialists and communists into prison. Gramsci was one of his victims, imprisoned for his opposition to fascism, and dying in confinement in 1937. While in prison, however, he was able to write his reflections in notebooks, published after his death. Gramsci modified Marx's economic determinism. For him, culture more than material well-being motivated the masses and interfered with the development of a working-class consciousness. Socialism had not taken over in industrial countries because the ruling class was able to persuade the working class that socialism would destroy their culture, overturning all of their traditions. Moreover, the ruling class was able to manipulate popular culture to inhibit the development of a class consciousness among workers. Gramsci called this ability to control the message and the terms in which the working class understood what was best for it "cultural hegemony."

Propaganda and appeals to traditional values perpetuated a culture in which socialism appeared to many to be immoral.

Edward Said applied both Gramsci and Foucault's methods of examining the
past to the body of knowledge that Europeans, and their descendants overseas,
acquired about non-Western societies. His landmark book *Orientalism* (published
in 1978) examined the ideas of "orientalists," Europeans and Americans who
presented themselves as experts on non-Western cultures. The core group of
orientalists were academics who traveled to Asia and the Middle East and
learned about their cultures – although occasionally these scholars based their
knowledge on books without ever visiting the areas they studied. Sometimes
orientalists were colonial or diplomatic administrators, who based their knowledge on governing these societies or negotiating with their leaders. From the
mid-eighteenth to the mid-twentieth centuries, orientalists were highly respected
in Western countries for their detailed knowledge of societies that seemed
incomprehensible to the average European or American. The views of these
experts spread, particularly among the upper and middle classes, and influenced
presentations of the "Orient" in art, music, literature, and popular culture.
Many of these themes primarily served as a means of escape for audiences, much
as science-fiction does today. Said, however, argued that, far from transmitting
accurate views of these societies to Western audiences, orientalists distorted their
cultures and histories. This occurred partly out of the intention of some orientalists to belittle the societies they studied, but more generally because even well-
intentioned ones acquired their knowledge in the context of Western global
dominance. Similarly, much of the artistic presentation of the "Orient" provided
escapism while presenting negative stereotypes of its people and practices. In
other words, orientalists created a global cultural hegemony, which perpetuated
assumptions of Western superiority over the rest of the world.

Said's argument has many layers to it: first, because orientalists developed their
theories about non-Western societies at a time of European global dominance, the
relationship between them and the objects of their study was never neutral. Rather,
it reflected the power that Western countries exerted over non-Western societies.
Therefore, however fascinating they found the societies they studied, orientalists
usually presented them to their Western audiences as culturally inferior to those of
the West. Second, orientalists were able to persuade many non-Western intellectuals
in the lands they dominated that Western culture was superior. Third, by contrasting non-Western societies with Western societies, orientalists helped to strengthen
a common sense of identity in the West. This process is known as "othering." Said
argued that the idea of Western civilization had begun mainly as European Christian
societies contrasting themselves with those of the nearby Islamic world. However,
starting in the eighteenth century, Western Europeans highlighted their growing
technological superiority as a manifestation of their cultural superiority over the rest
of the world (Adas 69–128). Fourth, orientalists tended to identify the supposed
flaws in other region's cultures as originating deep in the past. They argued that
although China, India, and the Middle East may all have had great civilizations in

the past, essential aspects of their societies, such as the Confucian emphasis on bureaucracy, the caste system in India, or Muslim tolerance of polygamy, had stifled innovation. Said argued that in making these assertions, European scholars "essentialized" societies, reducing their long and varied histories, full of change, to a few essential features that determined the rest of their histories onward. Of course, such claims generally ignored these societies' contributions of commodities, technology, and ideas to Europe (discussed in Chapter 4), which profoundly shaped Europe's development over the centuries.

Finally, and most controversially, Said claimed that this pro-Western bias continued in modern Western universities and across much of Western culture. Modern scholars still focused on the areas of difference between Western and non-Western societies, and still identified ancient characteristics of those societies as explaining why Western ones were supposedly more dynamic. Said argued that in doing so, Western thinkers and artists perpetuated a cultural hegemony that helped the United States to dominate non-Western societies.

Said's ideas raised considerable opposition, partly because they implicated fellow scholars, but also because they were difficult to prove empirically. Nevertheless, his approach to history gained favor with a new generation of scholars focusing on the encounter between Western and non-Western cultures. "Orientalist" went from being a positive term of respect for Westerners knowledgeable about the East, to a negative term describing Westerners who disparaged non-Western cultures or any oppressed ethnic group. At the same time the term "orientalist" expanded in geographic scope to include any portrayal of non-Western cultures in negative terms, especially when they misrepresented non-Westerners through stereotypes.

Said was not the only scholar to argue that cultural, social, and political contexts shaped the way people viewed the past. In 1983 some already-prominent historians co-authored *The Invention of Tradition*. In this book, each author contributed a chapter describing a tradition that most people regarded as very old, but that in reality was of much more recent origin. For instance, one chapter explained the origin of the Scottish kilt in the eighteenth century, not in the Middle Ages, as most people supposed. Another chapter focused on the pomp surrounding British coronations and royal weddings, pointing out that they were relatively mundane and poorly organized affairs until Queen Victoria's Golden Jubilee in 1887. Two chapters showed how European powers tried to invent traditions in their colonies, such as grand assemblies of princes, in order to coopt local elites and reinforce the permanence of European occupation. Since ethnic groups and nation-states rely on shared traditions to establish and maintain the shared identity of their members, the idea that timeless traditions were actually recent inventions serving political purposes challenged nationalist ideologies and the notions of national identity on which they depended.

The concept of "invented traditions" complemented another academic phrase based on the title of a book published the same year: *Imagined Communities*. In it, author Benedict Anderson argued that nations are not communities in the traditional sense, since they are too large for every member to know every other member, as might have been common in village communities. Rather, they arose from the needs of the middle classes to carve out common identities that also helped them achieve political changes that served their economic interests. The widespread literacy of the middle classes meant that language often served as their principal internal bond. Anderson's argument arose in the context of other writers who had already argued that modern national identities were mainly products of the previous two centuries rather than dating back to time immemorial.

Finally, a new field of "World History" emerged. It didn't focus on the essential qualities of discrete regional civilizations as the areas studies programs had. Rather, this field drew on the "world systems" histories (discussed in Chapters 1 and 4) to emphasize the "interstices" (areas between) where goods and ideas transferred among civilizations. Examples include the Mediterranean Sea, the Indian Ocean, and the Eurasian steppe during ancient and Medieval times, and the Atlantic, Pacific, and Indian Oceans in modern times. Historians also focused on "contact zones," where different cultures intermingled. Cosmopolitan cities such as ancient Alexandria, Medieval Baghdad, and modern London and New York are examples of such zones. But so are territories such as Punjab (a border area between majority-Muslim and majority-Hindu areas), the east African coast (where Arabs and sub-Saharan Africans met), and the Caribbean (where Europeans intermingled with Native Americans and Africans). World historians examine how the interactions among cultures in these areas often create new cultures and generate new ideas. The message underlying this approach is clear: societies constantly evolve and borrow from one another, and none of them exists intact as it was centuries or millennia ago. For instance, historians who would have focused on American colonial history a generation ago might today concentrate instead on the "Atlantic economy" or the frontier as "interstices" and "contact zones." By taking this approach, they are more likely to emphasize ways in which non-white cultures contributed to America's heritage from the start.

These arguments, all highlighting the transient nature of supposedly fixed cultural and national identities, have transformed the way historians since the 1980s have interpreted past interactions between societies and the way people view their own cultures. As noted in Chapter 1 their focus has shifted from bottom-up, often statistically-based social history toward identity issues: how people perceived themselves and others. Historians have shown a great interest in tracing the origins of supposedly timeless institutions to find out when they really became the way that people assume they always were.

Yet not all scholars agree with this view of societal values and identities as transient and evolving. A few think this process will not persist. Soon after the collapse of the Soviet Union, political scientist Francis Fukuyama argued that Western democracy had triumphed over rival political ideologies and the world was moving toward a period in which there would be no autocracies. Opposing this view was another political scientist, Samuel Huntington, who argued that ideological rivalries had not ended with the Cold War. Rather, the end of the rivalry between capitalism and communism had merely made room for more ancient rivalries to take its place. These, he predicted, would be a "clash of civilizations," in which major regions, organized around markedly different ancient traditions, would compete against one another. In Huntington's view Western civilization remained the most dynamic, inventive, and productive, but could expect significant competition from East Asia and the Indian subcontinent, whose Confucian and Hindu origins he highlighted respectively. Most problematic for Huntington was the "Islamic" civilization, whose disproportionately young population was suffering in what he considered stagnant societies and was lashing out violently at neighboring civilizations.

Not surprisingly, these arguments met with strong objections from other scholars. Said accused Huntington of essentializing civilizations ("Clash of Ignorance"), while Indian economist Amartya Sen objected to the notion that democracy was solely an invention of the West. Sen argued that, unusual among developing nations, India's democracy has thrived because its pre-colonial traditions of intellectual pluralism made it fertile ground for political pluralism (3). The debate shows little sign of ending, particularly because the "clash of civilizations" view is popular with much of the public and many political parties across much of the Western world. Even if they have never heard Huntington's name and are unaware of the nuances of his arguments, much of the public perceives the West to be in a clash of civilizations. A major question to consider in this chapter is whether historical videogames encourage or discourage such a view.

Characterizing cultures in action videogames

In the opening scene of Rockstar Games' *Red Dead Redemption*, protagonist John Marston boards a train heading for the fictitious town of New Austin in the American Southwest. As the train moves across the sagebrush-dotted countryside Marston overhears conversations around him. One woman declares to another: "Well, I for one am grateful Mrs. Bush, that they are finally bringing civilization to this savage land!" Mrs. Bush replies: "I could not agree with you more, my dear. My daddy settled this land and I know he'll be looking down on us, pleased at how *we* helped the natives." To which the first woman agrees: "Yes they've lost their land, but they've gained access to heaven." Meanwhile, another conversation nearby between a preacher and his daughter focuses on the same theme. Protests the daughter to her father: "[D]o you mean unless an innocent receives communion, they're destined to go to Hell? That hardly seems fair." The preacher responds: "What I mean to say, Jenny, is that there is a great deal of difference between an innocent and a savage." To which the first woman interjects: "Yes, they live like animals. But they're happier now. Aren't they?" Later, on the train, Jenny, obviously troubled by what she has heard, tells her father: "It's so confusing, Father. Sometimes, I find it impossible to make the distinction between a loving act and a hateful one. I mean, they often seem to be the same thing." The preacher reassures her: "Yes, Jenny, it is confusing, but you only have to ask me if you need help" ("Exodus in America/ Dialogues").

This exchange, filled with ethnic stereotypes about Native Americans, is difficult for the modern ear. One rarely hears such open contempt expressed today, although there is certainly plenty of veiled racist rhetoric in modern politics. Indeed, at the time of writing, more public forms of racist expression seem to be on the rise. Nevertheless, it's important to understand the role of this type of conversation in historical videogames, and distinguish between bigotry that informs players about the past and subconscious ethnic assumptions that inform us about the game's designers and the current societal values from which these assumptions come. The scene described above is an example of the former. It has three apparent purposes. First, it establishes the social setting of religiously informed ethnocentrism in which the story occurs. Second, it explains how the current setting is significantly different from what it was only a generation earlier. By 1911, the year in which the game is set, the US government had effectively subdued indigenous resistance to its rule and secured the region for white settlers and mining corporations. Finally, Jenny's almost comically innocent remark at the end of the conversation, a question that might also have a ring of sarcasm, foreshadows the many hateful acts the player will witness and take part in during the game.

John Marston is a flawed hero, albeit one who reflects a time-honored trope in movie Westerns. He is a former gunslinger who wants to settle down with his wife and son, but has to help out the Bureau of Investigation (predecessor to the FBI) root out the gang he belonged to before the government will exonerate him of his former crimes. Nevertheless, this ex-gunfighter continues to participate in morally dubious behavior. Although he spurns the advances of prostitutes, because he is "a married man," he temporarily allies with a sadistic Mexican officer who supervises massacres of civilians and kidnaps women to serve his commanding officer's sexual desires. Eventually, Marston sides with the more sympathetic but equally violent rebels, modeled on the historical Mexican revolutionaries led by Pancho Villa.

Red Dead Redemption's storyline does not follow up consistently on the awareness it indicates in the first scene. Most of the characters appear to be stock stereotypes from the mid-twentieth-century heyday of Western movies. A reviewer for the online Irish newspaper *Herald.ie* criticized the game for its portrayal of a drunk Irishman on the frontier (Byrne), and several players discussed the game's stereotyping of Mexicans on fan blogs ("Poll"). One fan, an educational technology graduate student at the University of Arizona, thought the game had some serious messages, but he also criticized it for the scenes set in the fictitious Mexican state of Neuvo Paraiso:

> The Nuevo Paraiso missions are badly paced and full of silly stereotypes. They're also full of rapists and misogynists, and these scenes don't add up

to either a meaningful satirical indictment, or to a realistic portrait of life –
two avenues that would tend to justify such material.

(Lieberman)

This observation relates well to the issues of stereotyping in *Tropico*. If game designers intend their characters to satirize a genre, in *Red Dead Redemption*'s case, movies
about the old West, rather than simulating the old West itself, they must make it
clear that this is satire. *Tropico*'s distributing company, Kalypso, markets the game as
satire. *Red Dead Redemption*'s distributor, Rockstar, does not.

However, another set of ethnic groups receives better (although inadequate)
treatment in the storyline. Nastas, a Native American informant for the Bureau
of Investigation, is the main representative of this group. He serves as
a confidante to Marston. Writing from the perspective of an English literature
professor and a Cherokee, Phill Alexander argues that "Nastas shows some classic Native American traits (he's generally quiet, he tends to not be combative,
he has a deep tie to nature and the environment), but he is not presented to the
gamer as a cartoon."

Rather, the game reserves the stereotyping of Native Americans to fictitious
Yale professor Harold McDougal. Typical of anthropologists of the early twentieth century, McDougal studies humans as a zoologist might study animals. He
connects their apparent physical differences and essential cultural traits. He
thinks certain ethnic groups are naturally more "savage" and wonders whether
Marston is of "Norse stock" because he exhibits a "savage spirit ... Natural
nobility, but also simple." McDougal has traveled west with preconceived con-
victions that Native Americans are savages too, and professes astonishment after
conducting a comparison of European-American and Native-American blood
samples that "[t]hey're exactly the same! It's remarkable!" When Nastas enters
the room, McDougal interprets everything in terms of Native Americans' supposed savage behavior. He begins speaking to Nastas slowly, in metaphors,
which he assures Marston is necessary when dealing with Native Americans.
Nastas confounds McDougal's assumptions by responding in fluent English,
informing him that he attended school on a reservation. However, the educated
response of a Native American, and the discovery that white and Native American blood are indistinguishable, does not prevent McDougal from continuing to
make everything he hears fit his racial theory. When he finds out that a white
antagonist has recruited some members of a reservation to fight, he declares:
"The savage heart cannot be conventionally civilized! I was right all along!"("At
Home with Dutch/Dialogues").

This comic exchange not only reveals some of the underlying assumptions of
the period that the game portrays. It also demonstrates that the game designers
knew the issues surrounding ethnic stereotypes well enough to comment on
them as part of the storyline. Rockstar Games' most famous title is *Grand Theft
Auto*, which has received a barrage of criticism, not only for its violence, but
also for it portrayal of women and ethnic minorities. Much of *Red Dead*

Redemption's design team had worked on *Grand Theft Auto*. As with *Grand Theft Auto*, they intended the new game to be a gritty and violent view of America ("Interview"). Yet, they also had to wrestle with their portrayal of diverse cultures in this borderland. *Red Dead Redemption* demonstrates sensitivity to these concerns, but, as the game's portrayal of Mexicans indicates, still not enough.

A series that has proclaimed from the outset its sensitivity to issues of cultural diversity is *Assassin's Creed*. Its first game contains the following disclaimer in an introductory screen every time a player begins a session: "Inspired by historical events and characters. This work of fiction was designed, developed and produced by a multicultural team of various religious faiths and beliefs." Starting in 2015, Ubisoft added "sexual orientation and gender identities" to the disclaimer (Totilo). Since the series often visits areas of contact between different cultures, such a disclaimer is understandable. However, cultural diversity generally rather than religious diversity specifically is a more common theme in the games. Table 6.1 shows the twelve 3D-standalone installments of *Assassin's Creed* released for PC, PS, and X-Box. It also includes the *Freedom Cry* expansion for *Assassin's Creed IV: Black Flag*, which was subsequently released as a standalone version. The original game, *Revelations, III, Liberation, Black Flag, Freedom Cry, Syndicate*, and *Origins* all have cross-cultural encounters as significant themes. *Assassin's Creed II, Brotherhood, Unity*, and *Odyssey* don't.

The *Assassin's Creed* series tries to steer clear of any judgments about culture by assigning protagonists and antagonists on the basis of its science-fiction backstory of an Assassin's conflict with the Templars. Historically, these organizations identified with religious factions, although the established leaders of their respective religions ultimately rejected both of them. In the game the precise details of each group's ideology are vague, but the Templars clearly seek to impose order (and autocracy) on the world, and the Assassins try to thwart them. Although a "clash of civilizations" (the Crusades) forms the backdrop to the original *Assassin's Creed* game, it doesn't invite the player to take sides in the conflict. Islamic culture, in the form of the Ottoman court and Muslims living in Istanbul, receives respectful treatment in *Revelations*, as do Native American cultures in *Assassin's Creed III*; people of African descent in *Liberation, Black Flag*, and *Freedom Cry*; and Asian Indians in *Syndicate*. The absence of degrading stereotypes of these groups, however, doesn't prevent them from falling into stereotypes regarding religion, as we shall discuss later. Nevertheless, Ubisoft has obviously taken care to present sympathetic portraits of people of color. Most significantly, people of non-European or mixed heritage are the playable protagonists in four games: *Assassin's Creed III, Liberation, Freedom Cry*, and *Origins*. Ubisoft therefore requires the gamer to adopt the persona of a person of color in the virtual world, who at least in the first three of these games operates in a society and storyline in which racial oppression plays a major role.

For most of *Assassin's Creed III*, the gamer plays Ratonhnhaké:ton (aka Connor), the son of an Englishman and a Mohawk woman. Since Connor grew up in a Mohawk village, he identifies himself as Mohawk. Moreover, whereas

TABLE 6.1 *Assassin's Creed* Reference Chart. Includes the thirteen stand-alone 3D games for console and PC. *Freedom Cry* originated as a DLC, and Liberation was first released for Vita. Religions and ideologies are those that receive significant representation

Game	Location	Context	Cultures	Religions/Ideologies
I	Levant	Crusades	Arab, English, French,	Christianity, Islam
II	Italy	Renaissance	Italian, French	Catholicism
Brotherhood	Rome	Renaissance	Italian	Catholicism
Revelations	Istanbul	Early Ottoman Empire	Turkish, Italian	Islam
III	New York, New England	American Revolution	English, Native American	Native American, Enlightenment
Liberation	Louisiana, Yucatan	Slavery	African, French, Mayan	Voodoo
IV: Black Flag	Caribbean	Eighteenth-Century Piracy	African, British, French, Spanish, Mayan	None
Freedom Cry	Caribbean	Slavery	African, European	None
Rogue	New York, New England, French and British Canada	Eighteenth-Century Piracy	British, French, Native American	None
Unity	Paris	French Revolution	French	Enlightenment, Catholicism
Syndicate	London	Victorian Society	British, Asian Indian	Scientific method
Origins	Egypt	Roman Conquest of Egypt	Ancient Egyptian, Greek, Roman	Egyptian pantheon, Greco-Roman pantheon, Hellenism
Odyssey	Greece	Peloponnesian War	Ancient Greek	Greek pantheon, Greek philosophy

Mohawk society appears to have accepted him, colonial British America does not. He is therefore an outsider. *Assassin's Creed III* indulges in stereotypes about Native Americans, albeit positive ones. Connor is an excellent tracker and hunter, who travels swiftly through backwoods New England and New York. He can also call on animals to do his bidding, a bit of fantasy in which the series repeatedly indulges. Connor is not particularly dependent on white people for his knowledge of their society. Rather, Achilles, a free African-American, serves as his mentor after Connor loses his family during a British Templar raid on his village. The game treads carefully around the character of George Washington, with whom Connor interacts. It portrays the American Revolution as a positive development, but acknowledges that Washington is willing to order the destruction of native villages that oppose him.

If Connor must navigate the boundaries between European and Native American societies, often looking from the outside, Adéwalé must work to free himself from oppression within a highly racially stratified colonial system. We first meet Adéwalé, an Afro-Trinidadian who escaped slavery and became a pirate, when he and *Black Flag* protagonist Edward Kenway hijack the *Jackdaw*. They agree that Kenway will be the captain and Adéwalé the quartermaster, because as Edward puts it: "It's true, most of these men wouldn't accept you as a captain. So what fair role would complement such unfairness?" In spite of this racial barrier, however, *Black Flag* portrays the pirate communities as accepting of racial diversity. As outlaws, these men and women are not bound by the more prejudiced conventions of the European-dominated plantation colonies against which they have rebelled. In the *Freedom Cry* expansion to *Black Flag* the playable protagonist is now Adéwalé, who, using his Assassin's stealth, single-handedly attacks Caribbean plantations, killing their European guards and owners, and freeing enslaved Africans, who then join his crew. He even takes part in the Second Maroon War in Jamaica (1731–39) in which enslaved Africans escaped their bondage and ultimately received British acquiescence in the self-government of five towns on the island. For historical advice, the design team relied on journalist Colin Woodard, author of *Republic of Pirates* (2008). His emphasis on piracy as rebellion against class-ridden, racist authority of the European powers is evident, albeit in simplified form, in the storylines of *Black Flag* and *Freedom Cry*.

Perhaps the *Assassin's Creed* series' most fascinating presentation so far of a playable protagonist who is also a person of color is *Liberation*'s Aveline de Grandpré, the daughter of a white French merchant and his enslaved African mistress. Because Aveline, as a creole woman, is an example of intersectionality (two or more categories of identity overlapping), we will return to her in the next chapter, to focus on the presentation of her as a woman. Perhaps the most significant criticism leveled against Ubisoft regarding *Liberation* is that the company didn't invest sufficient resources in the concept. Ubisoft let the title languish on a small console, Nintendo Vista, for two years before releasing it for PC and PlayStation. Partly because of the modest capabilities of its original platform, the missions are often overly simple and repetitive. The game's otherwise-favorable *New York Times* review made the obvious connection between the marginalizing of this theme and the similar marginalizing generally of people of African descent in the gaming market. Until recently, Ubisoft confined ethnically African playable protagonists to the periphery of its gaming world, with the minor stand-alone game of *Liberation* and a couple of expansion packs to *Black Flag*.

This changed with the release of *Assassin's Creed: Origins* in 2017. The game's protagonist, Bayek, is a dark-skinned Egyptian of Nubian descent. However, the storyline itself echoes some aspects of "the clash of civilizations" thesis. The game is set during the reign of Cleopatra VII. A descendant of Alexander the Great's general Ptolemy, her dynasty had long prided itself on its Greek bloodline even as it had increasingly adopted the trappings of Egyptian culture. This fusion of the two cultures was typical of Hellenism, the spread of Greek culture across the lands that Alexander had conquered three centuries before Cleopatra. *Origins* portrays this melding of the two cultures, particularly in the form of the Greco-Egyptian god Serapis (see Image 6.1) as something the Ptolemaic Dynasty encourages but many Egyptians oppose. Bayek, a proponent of traditional Egyptian civilization, nevertheless opposes violent resistance to the incursion of Greek culture. In showing how the two cultures interacted, *Origins* accurately depicts Ptolemaic Egypt as a contact zone. However, if one views Greece and Rome as the beginnings of Western society, and ancient Egypt as essentially African, then the "clash of civilizations" between Europe and Africa is apparent even though the game invites the player to identify with Bayek's African culture.

Having a non-white playable protagonist is important for conveying historians' understanding of the past, because it demonstrates that people of color in the past had "agency," that is, some level of control over their lives and the events unfolding around them. As historians have focused on "bottom-up" history, they have discovered the many ways in which people who apparently had little power were nevertheless able to exert influence over events. This concern has arisen in a variety of subfields of history. "Resistance studies" (mentioned in Chapter 1) has expanded our concept of resistance to include minor forms of disobedience. Similarly, "subaltern studies" has focused on the influence that the colonized were able to exert on colonizers during the period of European

IMAGE 6.1 *Assassin's Creed: Origins*, Bayek at the Serapion. © 2017 Ubisoft Entertainment. All Rights Reserved. Assassin's Creed, Ubisoft and the Ubisoft logo are registered or unregistered trademarks of Ubisoft Entertainment in the US and/or other countries.

occupation of their lands. In some cases, even collaboration can mask various forms of resistance. If, by reducing a ruler's options or persuading a ruler to avoid or adopt a particular course of action, an apparent collaborator subverts the intent of an oppressive government, this too can serve as resistance. Both the African National Congress and the Indian National Congress began as lobbying groups seeking to work entirely within the law of their colonial occupiers. Only later did their activities transform to boycotts, civil disobedience, and sometimes violent rebellion.

Characterizing cultures in strategy videogames

Because action videogames usually focus on interactions among individuals, their challenges are in dealing with the cultural contexts of these encounters. By contrast, strategy games usually deal with interactions among factions, often at the sovereign state (i.e., political power) level. Gaming at this level is no less susceptible to cultural bias than at levels that focus on individual characters. Sometimes the culturally based assumptions built into strategy games are more subtle, and sometimes more obvious.

Scholars have tended to focus on the more subtle manifestations of cultural bias, particularly with the *Civilization* series. Writing in 2002 historian and anthropologist Matthew Kapell argued that the series, which was in its third version at that point, presented the viewpoint of Frederick Jackson Turner, mentioned in the previous chapter. Turner saw the purpose of American society as pushing back and taming the frontier, which he regarded as the "meeting point between savagery and civilization" (8). Kapell argued that, in its juxtaposition of the expansion of civilization against "barbarians," early in the game, *Civilization* behaves in a similar manner: "Success for Turner's America, and *Civilization*'s players, is determined by moving that frontier ever more outward." Furthermore, Kapell points out that the game's measurement of progress through "technology, territorial expansion, and, usually, a move toward more representative (albeit simulated) government" indicates a very American perspective of history (131). Focusing on a different aspect of both the *Civilization* and the *Age of Empires* series, Sybille Lammes argues that "such games entail nostalgia for being a colonial military strategist and/or new world explorer that marks out 'new' territory" (Lammes 4). Inasmuch as "discovery" of already inhabited lands is a Western concept, one can see this process as extolling a Western approach to the interactions of civilizations.

The more obvious examples of cultural bias in strategy videogames, however, exist in the cultural stereotypes that some of the most popular games use to depict variations between societies and explain their historical behavior. To use a technical term discussed in Chapter 1, does the game present culture as an affordance? The answer in the case of two major historical series is "yes," and this section will focus on them as examples: *Civilization* and *Europa Universalis*.

All versions of *Civilization* distinguish each civilization by innate qualities. In the original version this was mainly a function of how civilizations controlled by the artificial intelligence (AI) responded to the player. For instance, according to the Fandom Wiki for the first game, America is "generally more concerned with building and growing, rather than continual expansion," whereas, although the French are "[p]erhaps not as dangerous as the Aztecs or Greeks, they are still a threat that must be watched." Table 6.2 shows a list of the civilizations in *Civilization III* (which Kappell critiqued) with descriptions of their innate characteristics.

TABLE 6.2 *Sid Meier's Civilization III*, Faction Strengths and Starting Techs Adapted from "List of Civilizations in Civ3," *Fandom Civilization Wiki*, http://civilization.wikia.com/wiki/List_of_civilizations_in_Civ3

Civilization	Leader	Strengths	Starting Techs
American	Abraham Lincoln	Industrious, Expansionist	Pottery, Masonry
Aztec	Montezuma II	Religious, Militaristic	Warrior Code, Ceremonial Burial
Babylonian	Hammurabi	Scientific, Religious	Bronze Working, Ceremonial Burial
Chinese	Mao ZeDong	Industrious, Militaristic	Warrior Code, Masonry
Egyptian	Cleopatra VII	Religious, Industrious	Masonry, Ceremonial Burial
English	Elizabeth I	Seafaring, Commercial	Alphabet, Pottery
French	Joan of Arc	Industrious, Commercial	Masonry, Alphabet
German	Otto von Bismarck	Militaristic, Scientific	Masonry, Alphabet
Greek	Alexander the Great	Scientific, Commercial	Bronze Working, Alphabet
Indian	Mohandas Gandhi	Religious, Commercial	Ceremonial Burial, Alphabet
Iroquois	Hiawatha	Expansionist, Religious	Ceremonial Burial, Pottery
Japanese	Tokugawa	Militaristic, Religious	Ceremonial Burial, Wheel
Persian	Xerxes	Scientific, Industrious	Masonry, Bronze Working
Roman	Julius Caesar	Commercial, Militaristic	Warrior Code, Alphabet
Russian	Catherine the Great	Scientific, Expansionist	Bronze Working, Pottery
Zulu	Shaka	Militaristic, Expansionist	Warrior Code, Pottery

Description of Strengths

Agricultural	Extra food produced from river squares and aqueducts are cheaper.
Commercial	The center city squares of all cities and metros produce extra commerce, and less corruption is experienced.
Expansionist	The civilization starts the game with a Scout and can build more later, and passive minor barbarians are friendlier.
Industrious	Workers complete tasks faster and the center city square of all cities produces extra shields in cities and metros.
Militaristic	It is easier to build military improvements (barracks, for example), and combat experience is gained more quickly.
Religious	Religious civilizations do not experience periods of anarchy during revolutions, and religious city improvements (temples, for instance) are easier to build.
Scientific	Scientific city improvements (like research labs) are easier to build and the civilization receives a free Civilization Advance at the start of every era.
Seafaring	Naval units get +1 movement, harbors are cheaper, extra commerce in coastal cities.

The selection and strengths of the civilizations reflect the American perspective of the design team. America is industrious and expansionist. As the "Description of Strengths" in Table 6.2 indicates, the former boosts production and the latter makes discovering and settling new territory easier early in the game. By contrast, Germany is militaristic and scientific with appropriate boosts to units and buildings in those areas. Other militaristic factions are the Aztecs, Chinese, Japanese, Romans, and the Zulus. There are justifications historically to consider all these factions militaristic. The problem is that this negative label could apply to all the other factions too. For instance, England's strengths are seafaring and commercial. Obviously, the designers were thinking of Britain's commercial empire and domination of the ocean in the nineteenth century. No doubt, many Britons would like to remember this aspect of their history. However, from the reign of Elizabeth I to the aftermath of World War I, Britain was possibly the world's most aggressive and expansionist power, almost perpetually at war across the globe and eventually controlling a quarter of its population and land surface. Similarly, the United States launched wars against other peoples – Native Americans, Mexicans, Central Americans, and most recently Iraq – often with the flimsiest of justifications. Britain and the United States only appear relatively benign if viewed in the context of European politics, because they did not seek to build formal empires on the European mainland. Eurocentric (particularly British and American) perspectives, therefore, tinge the attribution of different strengths to these societies. If this perspective is geographically limited, so it is also chronologically. In British and American popular memory, Germany is militaristic, mainly because of the two world wars, as is Japan for its behavior in World War II.

One might argue that the game's designers base these traits on the leaders representing the factions over their entire 6000-year existence. Bismarck was not responsible for World War II, but he effectively used the Prussian military to unite Germany. Tokugawa lived hundreds of years ago, but he is emblematic of the shogunate and the Samurai military ethos. However, this merely shifts the question to the choice of leaders. Why Lincoln, "the Great Emancipator," and not Andrew Jackson who launched the infamous "Trail of Tears?" Why Tokugawa, who established a 350-year military oligarchy, and not the nineteenth-century Meiji Emperor, in whose reign Japan embarked on a remarkable period of modernization? Table 6.2 suggests that many of these choices occur for game balance, since no two factions have the same combination of strengths. However, the choices also adhere to the popular late twentieth-century American view of many of these societies. It is therefore possible to argue that the game perpetuates American "cultural hegemony," even if the designers had no intention to.

Nevertheless, it was not professional historians who caused the designers of subsequent versions of *Civilization* to address these issues so much as it was the fan base and the historical knowledge of the designers themselves. Meier, who designed the first game, but became less involved in subsequent versions, might be described as a "history buff," an educated person with an enthusiasm for history, but little to no formal training. Later designers sometimes held bachelor's degrees in the subject. While this did not make them professional historians, it did mean that they were familiar with some of the modern objections to popular historical narratives and assumptions. For instance, Soren Johnson, who had studied with some of the world's most prominent historians at Stanford University, led the design team for *Civilization IV*. In its last expansion package, *Beyond the Sword*, the game included thirty-four civilizations, including multiple representatives from East Asia, the Middle East, Africa, and the Americas. Moreover, although each civilization had unique beginning traits that lasted throughout the game, the ability to change back and forth between "civics" during the game allowed players to fine-tune their civilizations as contingency demanded. Furthermore, several civilizations allowed players to choose at the beginning of the game among rulers. For instance, a player could choose either Elizabeth I, Victoria, or Winston Churchill for England. Although the player then had to stick with the choice of ruler throughout the game, it provided some level of variation to the supposed essential traits connected with each civilization.

This tendency to make original traits less important in the later game continued with *Civilization V*. After a rocky start in its vanilla version, the designers responded to many complaints and suggestions from the game series' fan base on its official blog. They introduced several variables that allowed for the gradual evolution of a faction's culture in a wide variety of directions depending on the players choice, which random events would also often shape. Among players' choices were social policies, permanent sets of traits that replaced *Civilization*

IV's civics options, but were permanent features that players chose to add as the game progressed. Another was religion, which allowed the addition of traits and even special buildings during the middle of the game. *Civilization VI* combines the civics options of *Civilization IV* with the evolving religion of *Civilization V*. While the basic characteristics, unique units, and special buildings of each civilization continued to be set at the beginning of the game, a given civilization's strengths and weaknesses might look very different in the middle to later stages of two different games.

Of course, none of these improvements alter the fact that the *Civilization* series continues to assign permanent, distinctive core traits and unique units and buildings to each civilization at the outset of the game. Some of these traits make little sense if the civilization does not exist in the same ecological or geographical context in the game as it did in reality. For instance, all versions of *Civilization* ensure that on a standard map with continents, England has a starting location near to the sea. This is just as well, since the last two versions of the game have endowed it with unusually strong early modern naval units. However, the series also allows players to choose various types of world on which to play, including one without large bodies of water. Clearly, it makes no sense to play a power with uniquely maritime strengths in such a scenario. Much of the criticism surrounding the attribution of varying characteristics to factions would disappear if the civilizations weren't named, or if their initial characteristics were unpredictable. The series designers' insistence on sticking with popular stereotypes of the civilizations they feature continues to place them at odds with most professional historians even as they mitigate these stereotypes with changeable attributes later in the game.

Civilization is so abstract, allowing all civilizations to exist throughout history, that it might be feasible to abstract it further by simply assigning fictional names to them, or better still, allowing players to. The same can't be said for another game dealing with the interaction of different cultures across the world: *Europa Universalis*. With the exception of the *Conquest of Paradise* expansion for *Europa Universalis IV*, the series has consistently had players explore a map based on the actual world of the fifteenth through eighteenth centuries. Each territory has a name bearing relation to its historical existence. Thus, the numerical values that the game assigns to aspects of each territory, such as population, ethnic characteristics, primary product, and level of productivity, are easily prone to comparison with the actual past. Nowhere has this fact been more controversial than in the assignment of technological values to different cultures. It's not just that different areas of the world start the game in the fifteenth century with different levels of technology. One can hardly deny that, for instance, Aztecs were not as advanced in a variety of technological aspects as Europeans were. It's rather the handicapping of European culture to allow its more rapid acquisition of technology, and even the will to explore, that has caused the most comment among game players. Table 6.3 shows *Europa Universalis III*'s cultural groups with their starting technology level and the speed with which they acquire new knowledge.

TABLE 6.3 Starting Levels and Research Speeds for Cultures in *Europa Universalis III*

Culture	Starting Level	Research Speed
Latin (Western European)	3	100 percent
Eastern (Eastern European)	3	90 percent
Muslim	4	80 percent
Indian (Non-Muslim South Asian)	3	50 percent
Chinese	3	40 percent
African (Sub-Saharan African)	1	20 percent
New World (Pre-Columbian American)	0	10 percent

Some aspects of this chart are astonishing given what we know about the transmission of knowledge between Asia and Europe during the Middle Ages. The start date for *Europa Universalis III* is 1399, and it may be appropriate to rate the knowledge of the Islamic world as more advanced than that of Western Christendom. However, many of the technological innovations that most influenced early modern Europe – for instance: gunpowder, printing, paper, and the compass – arrived from China during the late Middle Ages. Surely, at the end of the fourteenth century, China was just as advanced technologically as the Islamic World. Even India presents a problem, since Indians developed the concept of zero, which ultimately enabled the Islamic world to develop algebra, and Western Europe, calculus.

If technological starting levels are a problem, so are research rates. The designers at Paradox Interactive might argue that whatever the relative levels of technology in 1399, there is little doubt that Europeans (and their overseas settler descendants) acquired knowledge more rapidly during the following four centuries than did any other major cultural grouping. But, it's precisely this assumption that historians have challenged in recent decades. In Chapter 4, we saw that historians comparing data from Western Europe and China have argued that China was close to industrializing when Europe did, but then stalled when Europeans used their superior *military* technology to force China to lower its protective tariffs. Then there are the "discoveries" supposedly made by Westerners since the Renaissance that were in fact already known to non-Europeans. Among these are fingerprints, used in China since the third century BCE, and an early form of smallpox inoculation (known as variolation) that came into Europe from Turkey in the eighteenth century, but probably originated in China in the sixteenth century. This last example is further evidence that Europe was not the only area of groundbreaking research since the Middle Ages.

The only way around the handicaps built into *Europa Universalis III* is to "Westernize." This process involves allowing a faction from the Latin technology group to acquire neighboring territory and then have the non-Western faction adopt a policy of Westernization in a manner similar to that of Peter the Great in Russia in the early eighteenth century or the Meiji government of Japan in the late nineteenth century. Westernization comes at a short-term cost, because it causes unrest among the population and raises the risk of rebellion from traditionalists. However, it's the only way to prevail against Western powers. Of course, this approach assumes that the only way to modernize is to Westernize.

Perhaps the most objectionable aspect of *Europa Universalis III*'s technological groups, however, is their obvious connection with culture. Although the designers don't say so explicitly, the message that culture determines the rate of discovery and innovation is implicit in the very terms used to describe the groups. This is particularly the case with "Muslim," a term normally used to identify an adherent to Islam, a religion. Why being a follower of Islam would lead to greater knowledge in 1399 followed by relative stagnation thereafter, the game designers leave unexplained. However, for players raised on triumphalist notions of Western progress in school, the cultural connection need not be justified. Even the designers probably assumed that causal connections between culture and technological development were uncontroversial, apparently unaware that it has been a central concern of many historical analyses for decades. Indeed, as we have seen with *Civilization*, the very notion that we should measure "progress" mainly in terms of technological prowess was born in the European Enlightenment. Just as Meier's approach to *Civilization* reflected a very American mindset, so did the Paradox development team's understanding of the reasons for European expansion and growing global dominance from the fifteenth through the nineteenth centuries come from a decidedly European perspective. In fact, the very title of the game belies its original Eurocentric conception. The developers at Paradox intended the original *Europa Universalis* to be a game about early modern European exploration and expansion, as well as the wars of the Protestant Reformation.

However, starting with the original game, released in 2000, many fans of the series called for more attention to non-European playable factions, and acknowledgment of their potential to compete with Europe. A typical exchange occurred on a Paradox discussion board topic titled "Historical Plausibility vs. Determinism," following the release of *Europa Universalis IV* in 2013. Most of the discussion had centered around events occurring in the game that were specific to Europe. Then "Mcmanusaur" weighed in:

Mcmanusaur: One of the most egregious instances of Europa Universalis taking an arbitrarily deterministic approach is the concept of tech groups. For me, most of the dynamic historical events (which already tend to give Western nations enough advantages) are much more excusable than the flagrant, politically incorrect "Eurocentric vs. third world" categorization of tech groups. Does anyone else feel this way? I definitely agree with what a lot of people have said in this thread about simulating historical mechanisms over simulating historical outcomes, and this seems an obvious case of the latter ...

Zodium: It's a fair point, to some extent, but the game is called *Europa* [italics in original] Universalis, so that's where the bulk of development time goes. I'm sure given infinite money and time, P[aradox] D[esign] S[tudio] would love to drop the Europa, though.

Mcmanusaur: This is true. That said, I don't see how we can nitpick the finer details of historical determinism between European powers when the game so deterministically favors Western European countries over all others. ("Historical Plausibility vs Determinism").

A standard response from players defending the *Europa Universalis* series' Eurocentrism is that the game is about European expansion, thus its title. However, such responses raise two major objections. First, any game focusing on European encounters with non-European lands should pay as much attention to the latter as the former, or fail to present a balanced simulation of what such encounters involved. Second, even if the game were just about Europe, developments on that continent can't be understood in isolation from the rest of the world. Europe wouldn't have prospered as it did without access to raw materials from other parts of the world. To ignore this fact is to distort the presentation of the past.

To Paradox's credit, it has responded to criticism. *Europa Universalis IV*, the most recent major release in the series, abandoned simple culturally based research handicaps for a more nuanced mix of influences. The main distinction among regions' abilities to innovate is now between the band of civilizations extending from the Mediterranean to East Asia (including East Africa) on the one hand, and the rest of the world on the other. All of the first set of cultures begin with the same levels of technology (though not necessarily the same specific technologies) and full ability to adopt or create new technologies, whereas Sub-Saharan Africa (apart from East Africa) and Pre-Columbian America both suffer from considerable handicaps in their innovative abilities, albeit with Sub-Saharan Africa starting ahead of the Americas. Aboriginal Australian areas are not playable, and are suitable only for colonization. All the favored cultures (across Eurasia and North and East Africa) start with the "institution" of "Feudalism." Medievalists no doubt recoil at this inaccurate use of the term, not only as an economic system (a better term is "manorialism") but also for its application to all the societies across Eurasia, which in fact had significantly different land systems and societal relations from one another. Depending on their proximity to factions that have other institutions or political and social events occurring in their realms, players can nudge their faction toward adopting six other institutions: Renaissance, Colonialism, Printing Press, Global Trade, Manufactories, and Enlightenment.

Perhaps the greatest changes in *Europa Universalis IV* involve East Asia. Not only does the game's initial release pay close attention to internecine warfare in Japan, it also models a completely different form of government, "Celestial Empire," for China than for the rest of the world. This system involves bonuses for maintaining the "Mandate of Heaven," i.e., social and political stability, and equally harsh penalties for failure to do so. However, operating within this system an emperor can choose to favor one of three court factions: Temple, Bureaucratic, and Eunuch. The first is mainly concerned with maintaining religious tradition; the second, internal stability; and the third, trade and diplomacy. A player wanting to reverse China's tendency toward isolation should empower the Eunuch faction through decisions responding to various events. Doing so opens possibilities for exploration and colonization.

These efforts have caused much comment and criticism, among them that *Europa Universalis* continues to reveal the Eurocentric bias of its designers. Nevertheless, the development over time of both the *Civilization* and *Europa Universalis* series shows that designers have responded to criticisms of their fans, whose sometimes sophisticated historical knowledge has played no small role in improving both series. The more recent abandonment of the overly stereotypical view of the functioning of the Chinese "Celestial Court" is further evidence of Paradox's willingness to heed criticism.

Religion

Smite, released in 2014, is one of the world's most popular MOBA (multi-player online battle arena) games. It requires five players on a team, each choosing one from a list of contestants to fight against a rival team. Typically, MOBAs involve fantasy heroes, often with supernatural powers. *Smite* differs from other titles in this genre by drawing on actual polytheistic traditions to provide its heroes. For instance, Medusa, famous from Homer's *Odyssey*, can bite opponents with vipers that serve as locks of her hair. More important, she can petrify opponents by her stare. (In *The Odyssey*, her stare turned victims to stone.) By contrast, Anubis, Egyptian god of the dead, can release a plague of locusts, while Norse trickster god Loki can vanish instantly and dispatch decoys of himself to distract opponents.

As part of their effort to represent a wide array of traditions around the world, *Smite*'s designers at Hi Rez studio outside Atlanta included gods from India, China, and Japan. The difference between these gods and those of Europe and the Middle East, however, is that monotheism has not displaced them. Rather, most of Asia experienced philosophical overlays to their polytheistic cultures that either marginalized the traditional deities or incorporated them into more transcendent systems of understanding the universe. Taoism developed as an understanding of humanity's place in nature without actually denying the existence of Chinese gods or forbidding their worship. The same occurred with Confucian philosophy, which is more concerned with societal behavior and good governance than the supernatural.

Hindu philosophy developed a sophisticated system of understanding its gods, and all creation, as manifestations of the all-encompassing pantheistic Brahman. This did not mean, however, that the average Hindu stopped worshipping the rich pantheon of Indian deities. For instance, elephant-headed Ganesh, traditionally described as the god of fortune and the remover of obstacles, but styled as the "god of success" in *Smite*, adorns the dashboard or exterior paintwork of many an Indian cab, truck, or auto-rickshaw. His image serves as a talisman protecting travelers, much as Hermes used to for the ancient Greeks, and St. Christopher still does in Catholicism. Indeed, one of Ganesh's attributes in *Smite* is "remover of obstacles," which enables him to hold an enemy back while team members pass by. Similarly, Kali, the goddess of death and destruction, is the patron deity of Kolkata (formerly Calcutta), whose city name refers to the steps to her shrine, *kali-ghat* in Sanskrit. Her shrine still draws thousands of devotees every year offering ritual sacrificial sweets and burning incense as they pray to her. Kali is a fearsome goddess, wearing a necklace of skulls and standing on a man's corpse. Yet Kali's portrayal in Hindu art is also overtly feminine, emphasizing her curvaceous figure. This tradition must have seemed a gift to *Smite*'s developers, who have the game play up her female sexuality in ways reminiscent of many videogame heroines.

Nevertheless, *Smite*'s inclusion of Kali soon turned out to be problematic. Rajan Zed, president of the Universal Society of Hinduism, a California-based Hindu-advocacy society founded in 2011, objected to the portrayal of any Hindu gods in videogames. He had already opposed the presence of a playable god in the first totally Indian-designed videogame, *Hanuman: Boy Warrior*. In that game the playable protagonist is the monkey god Hanuman, who features prominently in the ancient Hindu epic the *Ramayana*. The predominantly Hindu designers of the game depicted Hanuman positively and aligned the game's narrative closely to traditional stories about him. Nevertheless, Zed objected: "Controlling and manipulating Lord Hanuman with a joystick/button/keyboard/mouse was denigration ... Lord Hanuman was not meant to be reduced to just a 'character' in a videogame to solidify company/products base in the growing economy of India" ("Universal Society"; Zeiler). Zed argued that player control over actively worshipped deities was offensive even when some of the designers came from that religious tradition. In *Smite*'s case, he regarded it as blatant cultural appropriation and trivialization of the beliefs of over a billion people. "Goddess Kali and other Hindu deities were meant to be worshiped in temples and home shrines and not meant to be reduced to just a 'character' in a videogame to be used in combat in the virtual battleground" ("Hindus"). Several critics described the sexualized depiction of Kali as her "pornification." For instance, one wrote: "This is truly disgusting. Not only is a faith appropriated, but it is done so in a way which turns a widely revered deity into a male sexual fantasy" ("SMITE").

Compounding the offense was the absence of any gods or heroes from the Abrahamic religions: Judaism, Christianity, and Islam. No prophet appears, much less the single deity of the Abrahamic religions or (from a Christian perspective, his divine son) Jesus Christ. Compounding the problem was the ethnicity of the design studio's leaders, white men located in the United States' "Bible Belt." Some critics argued that they had not afforded Hinduism the same respect or protection they did Christianity and Judaism. This inconsistency led critics to claim that Hi Rez was simply pandering to the American market, and exploiting a religion whose adherents had less influence locally while carefully respecting religions that had more (Sheridan). Hi Rez responded to these criticisms by redesigning Kali's appearance, although not to critics' satisfaction. However, far from eliminating Hindu gods from *Smite*'s cast of characters, the designers subsequently incorporated more into the game. Zed responded by calling for a boycott of *Smite* and imploring gaming conventions to shun Hi Rez. So far, this call has largely gone unheeded.

The controversy over *Smite* demonstrates the dangers of including religion in videogames. First, designers must take great care not to presume to speak for religions that they know little about. *Smite*'s producers were neither Hindu themselves, nor is there any evidence that they consulted experts on the religion, whether academic specialists on Hinduism or Hindu community leaders, before objections arose. Second, designers need to understand that adherents of a living religion may hold views about its past that vary significantly from that of academic scholars of the religion. For instance, many academically trained biblical scholars today question whether the Exodus recounted in the Bible ever occurred, because archaeologists have not uncovered evidence supporting it. However, the vast majority of Jews, Christians, and Muslims believe it did occur.

Anyone producing a game featuring a religion must expect opposition from some of its adherents, even if the designers follow academic knowledge on the subject closely. This is not a problem when dealing with religions such as Greco-Roman or Norse polytheism, whose practitioners have long since died. Finally, if designers are dealing with multiple religions, they need to take care not to favor one over the other, even by including some and omitting others. Players often feel slighted by the decision not to include their culture in a game. With *Smite* the opposite was the case. By treating Hinduism on a par with long-dead polytheistic religions (through inclusion) rather than current living monotheistic faiths (through omission), the Hi Rez team appeared to denigrate Hinduism in comparison to the Abrahamic religions.

Given these pitfalls, many designers understandably steer clear of religion altogether. For instance, in spite of the disclaimer at the beginning of its games, the *Assassin's Creed* series devotes very little space to the subject matter of religions. Rather, religion forms a backdrop to the cultural setting. Nowhere is this clearer than in the first title in the series. The original *Assassin's Creed* game is set during the Crusades, a time of brutal massacres and warfare between Christendom and Islam. Yet, apart from determining which groups are guarding the cities in which the hero, Altair, operates, the Crusades have little relevance to the game's plot. Rather, the conflict in which the protagonist takes sides is between the fictional versions of Assassins and Templars.

These two groups actually existed during the period in which the game takes place. Founded in 1119, the Knights Templar was a monastic order devoted to Christendom's military reconquest of Jerusalem from Islam. (Muslim armies had conquered Palestine in the seventh century.) After the Crusaders' failure to establish a permanent presence in the Middle East, France's King Philip IV, who was in debt to the Templars but also controlled the pope, arrested many of the organization's leaders and in 1312 had the pope disband the order. Whereas the Templars emerged from Christian society, the Assassins did so from the Islamic world. Unlike the Templars their targets were from the outset fellow practitioners of their religion, but of a different sect within Islam. The Assassins were a Shi'ite order that practiced asymmetrical warfare against the ruling Sunni elite. Most notably, some of its agents killed political leaders, thus lending the name of their organization (in Westernized form) to the practice. This practice extended to non-Muslim invaders of Muslim-controlled territory, including Crusaders and Mongols. Indeed, the Mongols ultimately wiped out the Assassins in the fourteenth century. It's in the context of the religious and political rivalry between Christianity and Islam, therefore, that there is a historical basis for the rivalry between the Templars and the Assassins.

However, the game designers have largely stripped both groups of their religious associations. Instead, they have created a fantastic backstory about an advanced humanoid species that died out during a solar storm thousands of years before modern humans developed agriculture and civilizations. This prehistoric society has left behind powerful spherical artifacts, "Apples of Eden," that the Templars want to find in order to dominate the world. The Assassins oppose them. Far from existing only for a couple of centuries during the Middle Ages, both organizations have operated since ancient times and continue to do so, albeit secretly, today.

In the world of *Assassin's Creed*, the Templars sometimes use religion as a tool for world domination. For instance, in *Assassin's Creed II* and its spinoff, *Brotherhood*, Pope Alexander V (originally Rodrigo Borgia) is a Templar, using Catholicism as part of his cynical plot for world domination. By contrast, the Assassins usually appear as secular individualists. At the end of *Assassin's Creed II*, after the brief reign of the radical priest Savonarola has ended with his execution, protagonist Ezio Auditore declares to the citizens of Florence:

> We don't need anyone to tell us what to do; not Savonarola, not the Medici. We are free to follow our own path. There are those who will take that freedom from us, and too many of you gladly give it … Choose your own way! Do not follow me, or anyone else.
>
> *("Bonfire of the Vanities")*

This sentiment could easily come from the lips of a modern liberal or libertarian, but it seems odd in an age when, even though many intellectuals were criticizing the Church's behavior, the idea of allowing everybody simply to develop their own individual worldviews was almost unknown in Europe. For instance, when Protestant reformers Martin Luther and John Calvin broke with Rome, neither advocated individual freedom of belief. Rather, they sought to impose their distinct views of Christianity on society. Calvin even had a dissident priest, Servetus, burned at the stake for questioning the Doctrine of the Trinity. Only in the seventeenth century, after decades of bloody sectarian conflict, did Europeans start discussing the merits of allowing individuals to choose how they worshipped. Ezio's statement, therefore, better represents the perspective of the twenty-first-century game designers than of even the most rebellious fifteenth-century Italian.

The problem for designers of historical games, however, is that religion was a defining feature of most societies until very recently, and continues to fulfill that role across much of the world today. Designers can lessen the potential for controversy if they don't highlight the differences between religions or assign them special individual characteristics that adherents may regard as stereotyping. For instance, games dealing with the Middle Ages may differentiate between Roman Catholicism, Eastern Orthodoxy, Sunni Islam, and Shi'a Islam, but not in ways that assign specific advantages or disadvantages to any particular faith. Thus both Paradox Interactive's *Crusader Kings II* and Creative Assembly's *Medieval II: Total War* take account of religious differences among Christians and Muslims, and even provide different mechanisms for launching a crusade from launching a jihad. However, the most important feature of religious difference in these games involves the likelihood of developing alliances or arranging royal marriages. The games do not have to speculate on, for instance, whether one religion is more pacifist than another in order to model the diplomatic obstacles present between religiously dissimilar factions.

Another way to lessen the potential for controversy is to focus on the mechanics of religious institutions and their effects on politics. *Medieval II: Total War* does this regarding the papacy (see Image 6.2). In the game, as in Medieval Western Christendom, it's important to keep on the right side of the pope. Players can improve their faction's standing with the Vatican in the following ways:

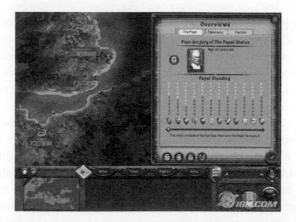

IMAGE 6.2 *Medieval II: Total War*, papal standing. Images from *Total War* videogames developed by Creative Games and published by SEGA, published with kind permission of SEGA.

- build churches and cathedrals
- train priests and send them on missions to convert non-Catholic populations to Catholicism, including solidifying its presence in the faction's home territories
- have clergy "debate" witches and heretics, leading (if successful) to their executions
- participate in crusades, which involve building armies and leading them to cities (usually in Muslim-controlled territory) that the pope has identified as targets for Catholic conquest.

Such piety in the long run may pay off in getting the College of Cardinals to elect one of the player's clergymen to be pope himself, in which case the player can get the pope to warn other factions against military campaigns targeting the player's faction's territories.

By contrast, antagonizing the pope in *Medieval II: Total War* can bring severe consequences for Catholic powers. In particular, if the pope forbids a player's faction from attacking a particular city or AI-controlled faction and the player ignores the edict, the pope might excommunicate the player's faction. When this occurs, the player's faction becomes a target of attack from other factions. Excommunication also raises the likelihood of armed uprisings in the offending faction's territory. These provisions in the game represent the real power of the Papacy during the twelfth and thirteenth centuries, when popes forced an English king and a Holy Roman emperor to give up their attempts to determine who received appointments to Church offices in their realms.

Yet another way to bring religion into history, without passing judgments on any actual current belief systems, is to have players invent their own religions. The two most recent versions of *Civilization* feature this solution. The first three versions of *Civilization* barely mentioned religion. Players could build temples, then cathedrals, both of which improved happiness and stability, but religion had no further presence in the games. *Civilization IV* broke this mold by making religions available by name, when players were the first to discover the "technology" that triggered their creation. For instance, Mysticism triggered Buddhism, and Monotheism, Judaism. Once players adopted a religion, they could dispatch missionaries to other cities converting them to their faction's specific faith. Having all one's cities under a single state religion provided certain production benefits and spread cultural influence. Factions that followed the same religion got along better with one another than those that didn't.

Civilization V adopted a dramatically different system of presenting religion, one that *Civilization VI* retained. In these games, a faction begins building up faith points almost immediately, leading early on to the founding of a "pantheon" focusing on some aspect of society or nature. The player chooses this aspect from among several options available – those not already taken by another faction. For instance, choosing the "god of the open skies" provides a culture bonus for each pasture resource the faction controls. Similarly, the desert god provides a faith bonus for each desert tile controlled, and a pantheon focusing on "idols" provides additional science and gold for each precious metal or gem resource the player mines. Later, when the faction has built up enough faith to generate a prophet, the player can found a religion. Although players choose the names of actual religions, the religion's characteristics are not predetermined. Rather, the player chooses two distinctive characteristics the religion will have from a new list of features (see Image 6.3). These may include bonuses for proselytizing, military advantage when fighting near a city following the player's religion, or the ability to build sacred structures, such as cathedrals, mosques, or pagodas, that generate extra faith, culture, or gold. Players get another shot at this list further into the game, when they generate enough faith to enable religious reform.

The strength of this system is the contingency it embodies. If one's faction is landlocked next to a jungle at the time the pantheon becomes available, it makes little sense to focus on the god of the sea to generate extra resources from fisheries. Rather, a focus on oral tradition (providing benefits from plantations) or the god of the rainforest (providing benefits from rainforest tiles) are the logical choices. Similarly, if at the time a player founds a religion, the player's faction is running out of gold, then it makes immediate sense to choose a religious benefit that will provide greater wealth. In this way a combination of political, economic, social, and ecological contingencies at a specific point in a civilization's development influences the player's choices in shaping the characteristics of a religion. The chance confluence of these circumstances, rather than any supposed essential historical features of a religion, shapes its characteristics.

The main criticism that could be leveled against this system is that it focuses too heavily on ecological determinism. However, these are not the only characteristics players can choose for their religions. In any case, this system more closely aligns with

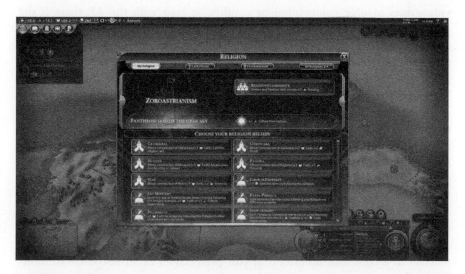

IMAGE 6.3 *Sid Meier's Civilization VI*, religion design screen. Licensed Asset Courtesy of Firaxis Games, Inc. and 2K Games, Inc.

a modern anthropological and historical understanding of the development of religions than does the assigning of supposed essential features belonging to a particular set of beliefs and practices. By allowing players to design their own religions without being locked into any essential features, rightly or wrongly, associated with a particular belief system, the designers of the two most recent versions of *Civilization* have shown remarkable sophistication while avoiding controversy.

Religion is one of the most sensitive issues to simulate in historical videogames, because so many people consider it the core of their worldview. However, simply avoiding it is hardly a viable option for games portraying societies in which it played a central role. Game designers have wrestled with a variety of solutions to the dilemma of presenting religion without offense. Sometimes doing so results in injecting a modern critique of religion into societies where it does not apply. Sometimes it involves simply accounting for the fact that religious difference has often been an obstacle to cooperation between factions in the past. At its most ambitious, it involves having players design their own religions. So far, no game has delved deeply into the actual doctrinal differences among religious groups. Such differences often arise in history courses, in which students can discuss and qualify the role these doctrines have played in the past. Trying to simulate such a complicated issue in a videogame would be difficult and potentially offend some religious groups. It is, therefore, no surprise that no major game producer has tried it so far.

Conclusion

If videogame designers were unwilling to deal with the interaction of different cultures, historical videogames would be poorer for it. Cultural diversity enriches the world and makes history more interesting. However, since most videogames involve competition or conflict, at least with the AI, there is the temptation to focus on cultural interactions as a "clash of civilizations." That cultures have clashed often in the past is indisputable. Less well-known are the many ways in which they have cooperated and, through interaction, given birth to new cultures. The videogame industry has evolved from simplistic stereotyping in the 1990s to more sophisticated and sensitive portrayals of different societies and the contacts between them in recent years. Regarding religion, some major videogame designers have gone from almost ignoring its role in history to making it an integral part of the historical process. Nevertheless, when presenting religion in action videogames, producers have sometimes projected the secular values of modernity anachronistically into their games' historical settings.

Issues relating to culture often occur in conjunction with other themes in videogames. The next two chapters analyze first gender, then violence, in videogames, but both these themes often involve cultural stereotyping and "othering," whether as a conscious simulation of past perspectives or an unconscious, unintentional expression of game designers' own culturally based assumptions. Issues of cultural identity can intersect with all other aspects of history, and often do so in videogames. In fact, "intersectionality" of identities (that is the point at which, for instance, ethnic and gender identity intersect) is a major concern of scholars working in the social sciences and the humanities. Not surprisingly, it also arises in historical videogames. We shall therefore revisit cultural issues often as we consider other themes in digital representations of the past.

Works cited

Adas, Michael, *Machines as the Measure of Men: Science, Technology, and Ideologies of Western Dominance*. Cornell University Press, 1989.

Alexander, Phill, "Red Dead Redemption and the Myth of the Noble Savage." *Not Your Mama's Gamer*, 17 April 2014, www.nymgamer.com/?p=4937.

"Ambassador Crane." *Tropico Wiki*, http://tropico.wikia.com/wiki/Ambassador_Crane.

Anderson, Benedict R., *Imagined Communities: Reflections on the Origin and Spread of Nationalism*. Verso, 1983.

Assassin's Creed, Ubisoft Montreal, 2007.

Assassin's Creed (game series), Ubisoft, 2007–18.

Assassin's Creed III, Ubisoft Montreal, 2012.

Assassin's Creed IV: Black Flag, Ubisoft Montreal, 2013.

Assassin's Creed: Origins, Ubisoft Montreal, 2017.

Assassin's Creed: Freedom Cry, Ubisoft Montreal, 2014.

Assassin's Creed: Liberation, Ubisoft Sofia, 2012.

Assassin's Creed: Syndicate, Ubisoft Quebec, 2015.

"At Home with Dutch/Dialogues." *Red Dead Wiki*, http://reddead.wikia.com/wiki/At_Home_with_Dutch/dialogues.

Bayly, C. A., *Origins of Nationality in South Asia: Patriotism and Ethical Government in the Making of Modern India*. Oxford University Press, 1998.

"Bonfire of the Vanities." *Assassin's Creed Wiki*, http://assassinscreed.wikia.com/wiki/Bonfire_of_the_Vanities

Byrne, Cormac, "Irish 'drunk' Sours Launch of Hit Game." *Herald.ie*, 20 May 2010, www.herald.ie/news/irish-drunk-sours-launch-of-hit-game-27952064.html.

Europa Universalis (game series), Paradox Development Studio, 2000–18.

Europa Universalis III, Paradox Development Studio, 2007.

Europa Universalis IV, Paradox Development Studio, 2013.

"Exodus in America/Dialogues." *Red Dead Wiki*, http://reddead.wikia.com/wiki/Exodus_in_America/dialogues.

Fukuyama, Francis, *The End of History and the Last Man*. Free Press; Maxwell Macmillan Canada; Maxwell Macmillan International, 1992.

Gramsci, Antonio, *Prison Notebooks*. Columbia University Press, 1992.

Grand Theft Auto (game series), Rockstar, 1997.

"Hindus Ask PAX To Drop Smite." *The Escapist*, 30 August 2012, www.escapistmagazine.com/forums/read/7.386785-Hindus-Ask-PAX-To-Drop-Smite.

"Historical Plausibility vs Determinism." *Paradox Interactive Forums*, https://forum.paradoxplaza.com/forum/index.php?threads/historical-plausibility-vs-determinism.727571/.

Huntington, Samuel P., *The Clash of Civilizations and the Remaking of World Order*. Simon & Schuster, 1996.

"Interview: Dan Houser Talks Red Dead Redemption." *NowGamer*, 19 May 2010, www.nowgamer.com/interview-dan-houser-talks-red-dead-redemption/.

Kapell, Matthew, "Civilization and Its Discontents: American Monomythic Structure as Historical Simulcrum." *Popular Culture Review*, vol. 13, no. 2 (Summer 2002), 129–36.

LaMarre, Heather L. et al., "The Irony of Satire: Political Ideology and the Motivation to See What You Want to See in The Colbert Report." *The International Journal of Press/ Politics*, vol. 14, no. 2 (April 2009), 212–31.

Lammes, Sybille, "Postcolonial Playgrounds: Games and Postcolonial Culture." *Eludamos. Journal for Computer Game Culture*, vol. 4, no. 1 (April 2010), 1–6.

Lieberman, Max, "History, Genre and Conflicting Narratives in Red Dead Redemption." *Luderacy*, 20 May 2011, http://luderacy.com/old-blog/history-genre-and-conflicting-narratives-in-red-dead-redemption/.

Magnet, Shoshana, "Playing at Colonization: Interpreting Imaginary Landscapes in the Video Game Tropico." *Journal of Communication Inquiry*, vol. 30, no. 2 (April 2006), 142–62.

Penix-Tadsen, Phillip, *Cultural Code: Video Games and Latin America*. MIT Press, 2016.

"Poll: Red Dead Redemption: No Controversy?" *The Escapist*, www.escapistmagazine.com/ forums/read/9.266429-Poll-Red-Dead-Redemption-No-Controversy.

Ranger, Terence et al., *The Invention of Tradition*. Cambridge University Press, 1983.

Red Dead Redemption, Rockstar San Diego, 2010.

Said, Edward W., *Orientalism*. Vintage, 1978.

Said, Edward W., "The Clash of Ignorance." *Nation*, vol. 273, no. 12 (October 2001), 11–13.

Sen, Amartya, "Democracy as a Universal Value." *Journal of Democracy*, vol. 10, no. 3 (July 1999), 3.

Sheridan, Connor, "Deity-Based MOBA SMITE Will Not Use Jewish, Christian, Islamic Figures." *GameSpot*, 16:20, www.gamespot.com/articles/deity-based-moba-smite-will-not-use-jewish-christian-islamic-figures/1100-6384974/.

Sid Meier's Civilization (game series), Microprose/Firaxis Games, 1991–2018.

Sid Meier's Civilization III, Firaxis, 2002.

Sid Meier's Civilization IV, Firaxis Games, 2005.

Sid Meier's Civilization V: Brave New World, Firaxis Games, 2013.

Sid Meier's Civilization VI, Firaxis Games, 2017.

Smite, Hi Rez Studios, 2014.

"SMITE: 'I Know Your Religion Better than You!' And the Pornification of Kali." *Archive. Is*, 24 March 2015, http://archive.is/4Iv8o.

Spasov, Boian, "Starting from Scratch: Haemimont Games' Tropico 5 Postmortem." *Gamasutra: The Art and Business of Making Games*, 17 March 2015, www.gamasutra.com/view/ news/237667/Starting_From_Scratch_Haemimont_Games_Tropico_5_postmortem.php.

Squire, Kurt, "Cultural Framing of Computer/Video Games. By Kurt Squire." *Game Studies: The International Journal of Computer Game Research*, vol. 2, no. 1 (July 2002), www.gamestudies.org/0102/squire/.

Steinmeyer, Phil, "A Dime a Dozen." *Inside the Sausage Factory*, 9 June 1999, web.archive. org/web/20060505215709/www.philsteinmeyer.com/xoops/modules/wfchannel/index. php?pagenum=7.

Subaltern Studies: Writings on South Asian History and Society Vol 1., ed. Ranajit Guha. Oxford University Press, 1982.

Totilo, Stephen, "New Assassin's Creed Changes Series' Signature Message About Diversity." *Kotaku*, 23 October 2015, http://kotaku.com/new-assassins-creed-changes-series-signature-message-ab-1738263702.

Tropico (game series), PopTop Software/Haemimont Games, 2001–18.

Tropico 4, Haemimont Games, 2011.

Tropico 5, Haemimont Games, 2014.

Turner, Frederick Jackson, "The Significance of the Frontier in American History." *American Historical Association Annual Report for the Year 1893*, American Historical Association, 1893, 199–227.

"Universal Society of Hinduism Wants Sony to Pull Hanuman: Boy Warrior." *VG247. Com*, www.vg247.com/2009/04/18/universal-society-of-hinduism-wants-sony-to-pull-hanuman-boy-warrior/

Zeiler, Xenia, "The Global Mediatization of Hinduism through Digital Games: Representation versus Simulation in Hanuman: Boy Warrior." *Playing with Religion in Digital Games*, ed. Heidi Campbell and Gregory P. Grieve. Indiana University Press, 2014.

7

GENDER

Introduction

Brothers in Arms 3: Sons of War is a third-person shooter for mobile platforms. Players can team up with other players to fight as a company of soldiers, or a single player can play the campaign with artificial intelligence (AI) partners. Combat occurs during the period following the Allied landing in Normandy in World War II, and the campaign has the player serving as US Army Sergeant Cole Wright, alongside his comrades. As with so many first- or third-person shooters, players must achieve objectives in a sequential series of scenes. In order to advance past the first few missions, players must upgrade their own character's weapons by expending dog tags or medals. (The game's business model almost requires players to expend real money in order to get enough dog tags or medals to purchase the necessary upgrades.)

However, in order to advance, players must also attend to other soldiers in their unit. Each of these "brothers" has a backstory and specific strengths in combat. The player's character doesn't do all the combat, relying instead on comrades to help finish off the German soldiers they are all fighting. *Brothers in Arms 3* highlights this camaraderie, not only through the interdependence of successful combat, but also through the sense of loss the central character expresses when one of his "brothers" dies. In the game, Sergeant Wright has promised a comrade, Jacob Hall, that if Hall dies, he'll return his dog tags to "his mama." When Hall dies in combat, however, Wright has to flee the area to save his own life. As the player proceeds from one mission to the next, Wright adds entries to his diary. In the second one following Hall's death, Wright describes his "mind as a dark cave," writing that he will remember Jacob Hall: "Fresh-faced and eager to serve. His is a face I'll never forget … nor can I forget the promise I broke." The close bonds that soldiers in combat formed with comrades in their units has long been a theme of historical scholarship. In his analysis of soldiers' reminiscences of World War II and their correspondence from the war, Paul Fussell notes that for soldiers engaged in combat,

> if you embraced the right attitude, you could persuade yourself that in the absence of any pressing ideological sanction, the war was about your military unit and your loyalty to it … And to kill effectively and go on living, you had to believe in your comrades.
>
> *(140)*

Observed one soldier of his decimated platoon, "When there might be 15 left out of 30 or more, you got an awful strong feeling about those 15 guys" (quoted in Fussell 141).

If the main focus of the game (besides killing the enemy) is the brotherhood and courage of men in combat, it also gives brief recognition to the role of men as protectors of women. In the game Wright goes on to rescue Rachelle Dubois, a member of the French resistance. She is the only significant female character in the game. A cut scene immediately following the rescue shows Wright writing to Dubois and voiceovers of the two expressing their love for one another. Other than these brief scenes the game focuses solely on Wright and his comrades engaging in combat, and dying. Other "brothers in arms" give their lives for allied victory, including ultimately Wright himself in the game's final mission.

In spite of (and partly because of) the almost complete absence of women in *Brothers in Arms 3: Sons of War*, the game serves as a useful example with which to begin an analysis of gender in videogames. Most important, it underscores the point that gender studies is not simply another term for women's studies. Just as whiteness in North America and Europe often stands as the norm against which society measures other ethnicities, heterosexual masculinity serves as the standard by which society measures other constructions of gender, whether heterosexual-feminine or various other sexual orientations and identities. Like so many other combat videogames, *Brothers in Arms 3* doesn't have much of a plot. Nevertheless, to the extent there is one, it emphasizes a traditional view of masculinity that would have been socially acceptable during the period it portrays. The "brothers" are heroic. They look out for one another, kill the enemy, and rescue women in distress. They rarely show emotion, but the death of one of their own causes obvious grief. These ancient values of masculine behavior went largely unquestioned until the 1960s. It was changes in contemporary society that caused historians to re-examine the past in the light of new understandings of gender identities. This chapter focuses on how historians' understanding of gender's role in the past has changed, what we now know about the roles of gender in past societies, and how well videogames portray these roles. It also considers the importance of gender in the videogame industry and the effect it has on the presentation of gender history in videogames.

Gender in the study of history

Gender history arose out of social history during the late twentieth century. Famous women had occasionally been the subject of biographies. However, as long as historians focused on political and military history, their studies of the past tended to ignore women, because men had overwhelmingly wielded formal power. British author Virginia Woolf described the invisibility of most women in history aptly in her 1929 extended essay *A Room of One's Own*:

> [T]he majority of women are neither harlots nor courtesans; nor do they sit clasping pug dogs to dusty velvet all through the summer afternoon. But what do they do then? ... For all the dinners are cooked; the plates and cups washed; the children sent to school and gone out into the world. Nothing remains of it all. All has vanished. No biography or history has a word to say about it. And the novels, without meaning to, inevitably lie. All these infinitely obscure lives remain to be recorded.
>
> *(Chapter 4)*

Indeed, a few veterans of the women's suffrage and labor movements had already published histories focusing on the effect of women upon major social changes. For instance, Alice Clark's *Working Life of Women in the Seventeenth Century* (published in 1919) highlighted the role of women in Britain's early industrialization. Nevertheless, these histories were rare. It took the growing importance of social history after World War II and the rise of second-wave feminism in the 1960s to create the circumstances in which many historians would apply a "bottom-up" focus to the largest group of voiceless and disenfranchised people of the past: females. Nevertheless, until the 1980s "women's history" formed a niche among historical fields. Its existence may have ironically, in one respect, perpetuated the central problem that gender studies would eventually critique. This problem, as noted above in connection with many videogames, is that in Western societies white heterosexual maleness tends to be seen (at least subconsciously) as the norm from which all other identities deviate. Although women make up roughly half of the population, only in the last decades of the twentieth century did academic writing abandon the use of "man" to describe all human beings and male pronouns to describe (depending on the context) all people when both men and women were involved. To create a niche field for the history of women could imply that they were not an integral part of mainstream history, even though they were present throughout all history in all societies.

The shift toward "gender history" accompanied the new focus on the importance of the use of language in the past to exert control over society. Previously "gender" was either synonymous with "sex" as a supposed biological category or referred to the cultural manifestations of the sexes. However, in *The Second Sex* (first published in 1949) philosopher Simone de Beauvoir argued that gender is a social construct rather than a manifestation of underlying biological differences between the sexes. We know that this is certainly the case for many aspects of gender, because the definition of masculine and feminine behaviors varies among societies and changes over time. For instance, the assumption that blue is inherently male and pink inherently female dates back no further than the period between the two world wars (Paoletti 108–22). De Beauvoir also argued that gender norms delineated power relationships that served as forms of control. Men had defined the female gender by what it was not: male. In 1986, historian Joan Wallach Scott drew on this concept that gender is a social rather than a biological distinction to argue that gender was a category of analysis that should concern all historians no matter what the focus of their research. Just as societies couldn't understand femininity without contrasting it with masculinity, neither could they understand masculinity without contrasting it with femininity. The two cultural concepts existed as a dichotomy, two sets of social expectations that existed only inasmuch as they were different from their supposed opposite. Women's history therefore became a subset of gender history, the latter also including the history of masculinity and alternative sexual orientations.

The scope of gender history has expanded rapidly over the last few decades as it has included new applications crossing into other fields of history and taking account of new understandings of sexuality. Philosopher Judith Butler responded to these changes by developing the concept of "gender performativity," in which a set of behaviors, rather than one's sex, determines gender. She does not claim that these behaviors are conscious performances. Rather, they are a set of cultural expectations drummed into children, depending on their sex. These expectations shape an individual's personality along masculine or feminine lines.

Since everyone has a gender identity, that identity exists alongside others, such as race, ethnicity, class, nationality, and religion. The intersection of these identities creates different experiences among groups who do not benefit from the dominant heterosexual white male discourse, and often pits one group that has suffered discrimination against another. Arguing that "the intersectional experience is greater than the sum of racism and sexism" (140), legal scholar Kimberlé Crenshaw observed that the experience of black women in America was historically different from that of white women, who defined the feminist movement in the United States. As an example, she pointed out that for a white man to rape a black woman was an act of both sexual and racial oppression: "Their femaleness made them sexually vulnerable to racist domination, while their Blackness effectively denied them any protection" under the law. By contrast, false accusations that black men had raped white women often led to lynchings of black men. Therefore: "Black women are caught between a Black community that, perhaps understandably, views with suspicion attempts to litigate questions of sexual violence, and a feminist community that reinforces those suspicions by focusing on white female sexuality" (158–59).

Historians have similarly explored the intersection of gender and race in areas where white men dominated non-white societies. Ann Stoler, for instance, has focused on the interplay of sex, class, and race among Dutch colonists and the indigenous population of the East Indies. Of particular concern, as in the American South, was the prevention of miscegenation (the sexual mixing of races) by protecting white female chastity. This of course went in only one direction, because white men felt entitled to force sex on black and brown female slaves and servants, thus producing "mixed-race" offspring. What they couldn't tolerate was black and brown men producing such offspring with white women. White men therefore asserted white power over people of color by determining which men could exercise power over which women.

Some scholars have focused on the intersection between feminism and orientalism. For instance, Antoinette Burton has shown that nineteenth-century British feminists (most of whom were middle class) argued that Indian men kept their female relatives in a state of oppression compared to their British "sisters" by denying them educations and uplifting social outlets. This argument helped to further the interests of British feminists at home, by reminding British men of the respect and agency that they should accord women. However, it also reinforced orientalist stereotypes about the oppression of women in Asia, and served as another justification for Britain's occupation of India. Other scholars point out that Europeans used gendered language to denigrate societies that they considered inferior to their own. For instance, Mrinalini Sinha has shown that British imperialists used feminine terms to describe Bengalis as weak and incapable of governing themselves. They did so because they correctly perceived Bengal's rising middle class as a major threat to British rule over India.

Along with historical studies of masculine and feminine identities has arisen a whole subfield devoted to departures from these accepted norms. Foucault's History of Sexuality addressed homosexuality at a time when the American lesbian-gay-bisexual-transgender-queer/questioning-intersex-asexual (LGBTQIA+) population was just beginning to gain political acceptance. Historians had previously mentioned homosexuality mainly in passing and assumed it was a feature of social "decadence," but during the 1970s and 1980s they began to examine it as a valid alternative form of sexual intimacy and as the basis of a set of social communities deserving of analysis in their own right. Most significant was John D'Emilio's assertion that gays and lesbians constituted a "minority" community, that this community was a social construction, and that it had a distinctive history of its own. Equally important, however, is the tendency of many historians to integrate consideration of LGBTQIA+ relations and identity in their examination of the past, just as they do with heterosexual gender identities.

It's now rare for historians to publish on any facet of society without taking gender into account. For this reason, games deserve analysis in terms of how they portray gender in the past, even when the storyline involves only one biological sex. However, gender is a major consideration in historical videogames for another reason: the biases of their designers and the climate of sexism in the videogame industry generally. It is to this issue that we must turn next, before analyzing games themselves for aspects of their content relevant to gender.

Sexism and the female market for historical videogames

Producers of the original *Assassin's Creed* game in 2007 anticipated controversy. After all, the game is set during the Crusades, one of the most divisive events between religious communities in history, and one that still perpetuates hostility between some Muslims and Christians. In order to diminish concerns about the game's content, its designers created a disclaimer introducing the game, assuring potential players that "This game was developed by a multicultural team of various faiths and beliefs."

However, the biggest controversy arose not over the game's content but over its producer, the second-ranking team member after executive producer Patrice Désilet. For many fans producer Jade Raymond suffered from an incurable problem: she was a woman, and attractive. Blogging on the issue five years later, a fan included a photograph showing her with the predominantly male design team membership standing behind her. Underneath was the caption: "Beauty: Because hard work is for the losers behind you." The assertion that Raymond held her position only because of her physical appearance, rather than her abilities as a game designer, was evident in the discussion board topic's title: "Is Jade Raymond just an industry Pin-Up girl used to drive sales?" Such sentiments had already reached fever-pitch following the release of the original *Assassin's Creed* when an anonymous critic of Ubisoft posted a pornographic cartoon making the same point, albeit with even less taste.

The incident, and the attitudes represented years later in the blogger's post, reveal some of the many problems that gaming culture has exhibited regarding women. First, since at least the mid-1980s, the fan base for action games has consisted predominantly of teenage boys and young men, who have often projected sexist attitudes onto the entire industry. Second, the videogame industry itself is overwhelmingly male, and consciously or subconsciously indulges in sexist stereotyping that caters to its predominantly male consumer base. Third, the combination of the two has led some in the gaming community to assume that women involved in designing videogames are there for their appearance rather than their expertise. Thus the assumptions regarding Raymond.

In fact, Raymond was well-qualified to hold the position she did. After earning her bachelor's degree in Computer Science from McGill University, she worked for Electronic Arts as a producer of *The Sims Online*. With this experience, she moved to Ubisoft Montreal in 2004. After serving as producer on the original *Assassin's Creed*, she became executive producer of *Assassin's Creed II* and *Assassin's Creed: Brotherhood*. Not surprisingly, other contributors to the discussion knew Raymond's qualifications and set the record straight in their rebuttals (Crecente).

In 2014 the Gamergate controversy drew international attention in part because the treatment of its victims was even more serious. The controversy began when the former boyfriend of game developer Zoë Quinn published private e-mails and claimed she was in a relationship with a journalist from Kotaku gaming magazine. The boyfriend claimed that the journalist was publishing favorable reviews of Quinn's games without acknowledging the potential conflict of interest. She soon became a victim of doxing (publishing personal information, such as her address and phone number online), and received rape and death threats from gamers mainly operating under the Twitter hashtag "Gamergate." People using the hashtag then attacked other prominent women connected with the videogame industry, most notably feminist media critic Anita Sakeesian, who had posted critical analyses of sexism in the videogame industry on YouTube, and Brianna Wu, independent developer of an anime action game focusing on four female protagonists. They too received rape and death threats, causing Sakeesian to cancel a speaking engagement and Wu and her husband to leave their home. Quinn went temporarily into hiding too (Todd).

The Gamergate controversy and the one surrounding Raymond underscore a final point: the gender composition of the industry is changing, and this development makes some male gamers uncomfortable. As videogames have become as important as films in the entertainment industry, more and more women and girls have embraced them. The Entertainment Software Association's (ESA) most recent annual report on the industry highlights some striking statistics. Among them:

- gamers age 18 or older represent 72 percent of the videogame-playing population, and the average gamer is 35 years old
- adult women represent a greater portion of the videogame-playing population (31 percent) than boys under age 18 (18 percent)
- sixty-seven percent of parents play videogames with their children at least once a week ("Essential Facts").

Moreover, ESA has the ratio of males to females playing videogames as 63:37. These numbers suggest that videogame designers need to cater more to a female market than they have done so far.

However, these statistics mask an important difference between male and female gamers: they play different genres of games. Gaming analytics firm deltaDNA released a survey in 2015 showing gender breakdown by game genre (Table 7.1). These are broken down further. For instance, females account for only 10 percent of gamers playing first-person shooters (FPSs), a subset of the

TABLE 7.1 Gender Breakdown by Genre of Games Played

Game Genre	Male	Female
Action	75 percent	25 percent
Strategy	68 percent	32 percent
Puzzle	18 percent	82 percent
Social Casino	39 percent	61 percent

action genre ("Gender Split in F2P Games"). These figures have important implications for designers of historical videogames. The best-selling historical games, and the ones that are able to deal with history in the greatest depth, tend to be in the action and strategy genres, both of which are male-dominated.

The deltaDNA study's authors caution that their statistics do not mean that action and strategy games can't appeal to female gamers. They point out that "While some may blindly argue this reflects an innate preference, it is quite clear that many games have been purposively tailored to appeal to one gender" ("Gender Split"). Explanations other than the biological abound. Among them that men perform fewer household chores and therefore have more time to immerse themselves in lengthy, complex games than women do (Prescott and Boggs 77). A 2007 study of women playing the massive multi-player online role-playing game *Everquest* supports this caution. Women made up 20–30 percent of the players, and many of those interviewed expressed enjoyment at taking part in combat as a means of taking "aggressions out." Young girls playing the game declared that they "would rather play violent games any day," than games oriented specifically toward the young female market, such as *Barbie Fashion Designer* (Taylor). It's also worth noting that a quarter of action gamers and a third of strategy gamers are women. Given the overall size of the markets for these genres, developers should not ignore these significant minorities of market share. The trick is to include content that appeals to females without alienating males.

Complicating this goal, however, is the disproportionate number of males responsible for videogame production. A 2008 study found that only 6.9 percent of people directly responsible for game development in the United Kingdom were women (Prescott and Boggs 130). The Gamergate controversy and the hostility to Raymond reveal misogyny among players, but female programmers and producers also encounter obstacles in the predominantly male workplace. Many of these obstacles – long hours, inflexibility for childcare, and general assumptions that women are not in the job for the long haul – are typical of many high-powered workplace environments. Others simply arise from the general assumption that women aren't technologically adept, whether for biological or cultural reasons. This assumption has meant that women have had to make an extra effort to break into the male-dominated culture of videogame production. Elspeth Tory, who worked on animation first for Microids then Ubisoft, recalls that when she first entered the industry "people were generally surprised if I could technically problem-solve" (John). However, once she demonstrated her ability, she gained acceptance. The presence of women in videogame development is important because they challenge male assumptions. A female developer recalls that the men on her team were basing their female characters' appearances on *Tomb Raider*'s Lara Croft.

> It's not until I came onto the characters team, I sort of made the women a little bit less stereotypical … they are looking more like a woman now than Lara Croft, whose proportions were all wrong and I think that's where you see men being quite sexist and stuff.
>
> *(Quoted in Prescott and Boggs 138)*

Indeed, more than any other game series, *Tomb Raider* has come simultaneously to symbolize both the empowerment and objectification of women. Although this game occurs in a modern setting, it involves a female protagonist searching for historical artifacts and, therefore, can be considered a historical videogame. Ever since its heroine, Lara Croft, first hit consoles and computers in 1996, her character has been the subject of controversy. On the one hand, she can take care of herself. Croft is both fit and brave, and possesses an impressive array of fighting and survival skills. She easily disposes of physically more formidable (and usually male) opponents. She is also well educated, possessing an extensive knowledge of history and languages. On the other hand, particularly in the early versions of *Tomb Raider*, her body appears as a hypersexual fantasy of the female form, with improbable breast size, and shorts and tight-fitting tank top that show off her legs, midriff, and cleavage. As media scholar Maja Mikula observes: "Lara is everything that is bad about representations of women in culture, and everything good" (Mikula 79–80). With seventeen games in the franchise and over 45 million units sold as of 2015 (Square Enix 18), *Tomb Raider*'s success is remarkable given that its audience has been mainly male. Indeed, the male, British-based developers of the original game assumed a male market aged 15 to 26 (Pretzsch 6).

But why would boys and young men want to take on the role of a female protagonist? First, the *Tomb Raider* series is third-person action, so players see the body of the character they are playing, rather than seeing through the character's eyes as in a first-person action game. As a result, players are constantly viewing Lara Croft as they guide her through the story line. For heterosexual male players, the constant viewing of a sexy female character is an attractive feature of the game. Moreover, anecdotal evidence suggests that some male players approach Lara as a beautiful woman whom they control and care for. They may not so much personally identify with Lara themselves, as treat her as a virtual lover. Female players are drawn to Lara Croft, less ambiguously, as a role model with whom they identify. Mikula observes that "[b]y and large, women enjoy 'being' Lara, rather than controlling her" (Mikula 81).

Nevertheless, women no more insist on playing a female character than men insist on playing as males. The gender of the playable protagonist may be less important than other aspects of games in determining their appeal to female gamers. An important feature of both the *Assassin's Creed* series and *Red Dead Redemption* is their complex story lines, relative to many FPSs, and the social interaction they depict. Studies of female gaming preferences indicate that girls and women prefer games that involve social interaction, either among the characters on screen or among players. Like their male counterparts, females enjoy controlling characters, but they prefer them to engage in less violence and more strategy and puzzle-solving. Female players also tend to value open story lines where one can choose to go in multiple directions and create characters and aspects of the environment. If, as social science suggests, these preferences are culturally constructed, then videogame corporations are simply perpetuating an endless feedback loop of gender stereotyping. A 2000 American Association of

University Women Educational Foundation study of early adolescent girls pointed out that "[f]or the most part, the girls described characteristics that converge with some qualities that boys value in games, and challenge the notion that software should be designed and marketed to girls and boys as distinct market 'niches'" (AAUW 32).

Noting how popular *The Sims* is among women, one adult female player half-jokingly suggested that an ideal historical game for women might bear the title *The Sims: Jane Austen*.[1] Perhaps game designers should treat the idea seriously. *The Sims* franchise's only foray into the past is *The Sims: Medieval*, which purports, in tongue-in-cheek fashion, to simulate life on a Medieval manor. Regarding historical accuracy, producer Rachel Bernstein admitted that

> we're not a group of historians about to crack open history books we've never looked at before. We all have a picture in our mind of what medieval times looked like, and that picture is from movies, it's from books that we read as a kid, all sorts of, you know, beautifully published story books.
>
> *(GameSpot)*

The Sims: Medieval has fantasy elements, with wizards operating alongside clergy. It has quests, most of which don't focus on combat. It also allows players to choose which characters in its virtual world they want to control. This last feature seems to be an important one for the female gaming market. Women and girls generally prefer games in which they can build their own characters and virtual worlds, which probably explains why *The Sims* franchise is most popular among women (Lockwood).

Considering the importance of social history in the historical profession and the focus of so much scholarship on the dynamic surrounding social interactions in the past, it's surprising that major design studios have not focused more on creating *Sims*-type games set in the past. Doing so might tap on a large market of female players who are interested in history but not in killing virtual opponents. Games such as *Assassin's Creed* and *Red Dead Redemption* hint at the daily routines and social aspects of the past, but such tasks are simply backdrop and interlude to the action-adventure side of the games.

A franchise that focused more on daily life in the past was the survival game *The Oregon Trail*. Originally a creation of the Minnesota Educational Computing Consortium (MECC) and subsequently marketed through the Learning Company, *The Oregon Trail* became one of the best-selling educational games of the 1980s and 1990s. However, financial problems associated with Mattel's purchase of the Learning Company ended production of the franchise after *The Oregon Trail V*'s release in 2001 (Lussenhop). Surprisingly, no major corporation has combined a *Sims*-style emphasis on social relations and daily life with a setting on the American frontier. One could easily imagine such a game having broad appeal across genders. This absence may reflect the continued male dominance of the videogame industry and the assumption that all popular games about the past must involve violence-oriented action. As recently as 2015 women constituted 40 percent of *The Sims*'s development team, which a woman also heads. On the one hand, this figure shows how far the gender gap in game design has come, and holds out the promise of greater equity and consideration of the female market in future videogame design. On the other hand, the continued male-majority composition of the design team for a game so popular with women shows how far the industry still must go (Gaudiosi).

Female characters in the virtual past

The Oregon Trail franchise was not just about pioneers. It was also pioneering, particularly in the sense that it featured so many female characters. After all, men did not cross the prairie alone, nor did they set up the modern towns of the American West without women. Indeed some of the earliest extensions of the voting franchise to women occurred in Western territories and states trying to attract women to the frontier in order to build families and settle the land for white Americans. (This is yet another example of the intersection of gender and race in history.) *The Oregon Trail* allows players to assume the personas of female characters as they make the arduous journey west. Nevertheless, the series came under criticism for gender bias. High school teacher and education author Bill Bigelow argues:

> Without acknowledging it, *The Oregon Trail* maneuvers students into thinking and acting as if they were all males. The game highlights a male lifestyle and poses problems that historically fell within the male domain, such as whether and where to hunt, which route to take, whether and what to trade, and whether to caulk a wagon or ford a river … It's clear from reading women's diaries of the period that women played little or no role to deciding whether to embark on the trip, where to camp, which routes to take, and the like. In real life women's decision revolved around how to maintain a semblance of community under great stress … Women decided where to look for firewood or buffalo chips, how and what to cook using hot rocks, how to care for the children, and how to resolve conflicts between travelers, especially between the men. These were real-life decisions, but, with the exception of treating illness, they're missing from *The Oregon Trail*.
>
> *(Bigelow 85)*

Moreover, Bigelow points out:

> In *The Oregon Trail* people don't talk to each other; they all talk to you, the player … An *Oregon Trail* more alert to feminist insights and women's experiences would highlight relationships between people, would focus on how the experience affects our feelings for each other and would feature how women worked with one another to create and maintain a community, as women's diary entries clearly reveal.
>
> *(Bigelow 86)*

For his ideal game, Bigelow might almost be describing a *The Sims: Oregon Trail*. Yet designers of major videogame franchises set in the past have not gone in this direction. Rather, they have adopted a supposed solution more along the lines of *Tomb Raider*. Yet doing so is not only a less effective way to appeal to the female market, as Bigelow's remarks indicate, it is also a less accurate depiction of the experiences of most women in the past.

Simply put, historical action game designers face a dilemma. In order to have playable female characters, or even non-playable female partners in action sequences, designers must make them behave like men in the past. Yet social constraints in the past made such characters historically rare. The evolution of female characters in the *Assassin's Creed* series provides an excellent illustration of the problem. Certainly, *Assassin's Creed*'s designers have sought to appeal to the female market. The presence of women, already noted, in leading positions on these teams has no doubt helped to encourage this desire. Women are almost invisible in the original *Assassin's Creed*. Apart from one scene, they serve only as backdrop to action among male characters. This changes significantly in *Assassin's Creed II, Assassin's Creed: Brotherhood*, and *Assassin's Creed: Revelations*, the trilogy of games focusing on the adventures of the fictional character Ezio Auditore. In the first game, Ezio escorts his mother, Maria, and sister, Claudia, from Florence to his uncle's estate after the family nemesis has executed his father and brothers early in the story. The game portrays both women as educated and competent, albeit relying on Ezio's protection. It shows Maria procuring paintings from Leonardo da Vinci early in the narrative, and Claudia keeping the financial ledger at the Auditore estate later on. However, Ezio also relies on women elsewhere, particularly the "courtesans" of Florence, who train him how to lead the life of a wanted man, picking pockets and disappearing into crowds. He also has sexual relations with a young fictional woman in the game's opening scenes, and later with the historical figure Caterina Sforza. The activities of Maria and Claudia are quite plausible in the first game of the trilogy. More surprising is their decision to open a bordello in *Brotherhood*, an act that would have likely ruined their family's reputation in Italian Renaissance polite society. Although the family members are temporarily outlaws in *Assassin's Creed II*, they gain the support of the influential (and historical) Medici family by the end of the game, so they have much to lose by sullying their reputations.

Perhaps the most obvious criticism of the Ezio trilogy's portrayal of Italian Renaissance women is that they seem to occur in only two types, ladies and prostitutes. This follows a pattern common not only in entertainment (particularly before the sexual revolution of the 1960s), but observed in psychology. What is commonly known as the "Madonna-Whore Complex" describes men and societies who divide women into two categories, either virtuous virgins and chaste mothers or depraved prostitutes and adulteresses. Certainly, this manner of thinking was common among wealthy Italian Renaissance men, who ideally expected the women in their family only to venture out of their homes in the company of male relatives. The Ezio trilogy reflects this dichotomy. However, it also subverts it in *Brotherhood* through the actions of Maria and Claudia. More-over, the games portray prostitutes sympathetically, supporting Ezio against the forces of evil. In a recurring, laughable sequence, Ezio hires prostitutes to gyrate in front of guards, distracting them while he sneaks past. In these sequences, the guards behave as if trained dogs mesmerized by a treat. They make exclamations at the prostitutes, such as "Bella ragazza!" ("Beautiful girl!"), while completely abandoning their posts. Therefore, although the Ezio trilogy's portrayal of gender in Renaissance Italy is grossly oversimplified, it does not accept the simple dichotomy between ladies and prostitutes uncritically.

Indeed, in their zeal to present strong female characters *Assassin's Creed*'s develop-ment teams have gone out of their way to feature women who bucked the social norms of their eras. The historical pirates Anne Bonny and Mary Reed serve as major supporting characters in *Assassin's Creed IV: Black Flag*. However, they were highly unusual women, who gained notoriety during the early eighteenth century precisely because it was so unusual for women to engage in combat. Similarly, in *Assassin's Creed: Unity*, the protagonist's girlfriend, the fictional Elise, is a sword-and pistol-wielding French revolutionary. Certainly, women did sometimes engage in combat, particularly when enemies overran their supporting positions behind the lines. It would, however, be inaccurate to assume this situation as anything close to normal. But, of course, very little about the *Assassin's Creed* series is close to normal. Most men were not constantly in combat, and almost none left the trail of enemy bodies behind that the heroes and heroines of the series do.

Probably more than any other game in the franchise, *Assassin's Creed: Liberation* attempts to deal with the historical problem of portraying women of action in the past. To recap from Chapter 6, this game, which appeared as a standalone spinoff from *Assassin's Creed III*, has the player guiding Aveline de Grandpré, the daughter of a white French New Orleans businessman and his formerly enslaved African mis-tress during the 1760s. The game begins with the mother having long ago vanished and Aveline living with her father and white stepmother. This setting provides an interesting opportunity to explore the intersection of gender, race, and class. In order to reconcile the dress of an eighteenth-century upper-class "lady" with the activities required of an Assassin, *Liberation*'s design team created three outfits for Aveline to wear: those of a lady, a slave, and an Assassin (see Image 7.1). Each outfit has different strengths and weaknesses. In the lady outfit, Aveline can "charm" male characters to obtain information. However, she can't run or climb. In the slave outfit, she can infiltrate plantations unobserved and interact with other slaves. She can also run and climb, although not as effectively as an Assassin. However, she can't gain access to areas that the lady might in high society. Finally, in the Assassin outfit Aveline can run and climb with ease, but her dress is so outlandish that she easily attracts attention and suspicion. Particularly the difference between other characters' reception of Aveline, in her lady and slave outfits, gives a sense of the social chasm between wealthy slave-owners and slaves. Moreover, the fact that in her lady persona she is nevertheless creole adds nuance to the game. Although Anglo-Southern society would later impose "one drop" laws effectively

IMAGE 7.1 *Assassin's Creed: Liberation*, Aveline de Grandpré's three personas. © 2012 Ubisoft Entertainment. All Rights Reserved. Assassin's Creed, Ubisoft and the Ubisoft logo are trademarks of Ubisoft Entertainment in the US and/or other countries.

delegitimizing mixed-race offspring, French Louisiana was more tolerant of creoles operating in high society. The design team makes some attempt to explore the resulting social and racial ambiguities. For instance, early in the game Aveline goes shopping, with her own slave dutifully following her and carrying her purchases (see Image 7.2). This casual interlude reminds us of how natural slavery appeared to the slave-owning classes, even on those relatively rare occasions in the New World when clothes were the most obvious difference between master and slave.

Ubisoft didn't make the marketing of *Liberation* a priority, and a playable female protagonist didn't appear until two major titles later, when gamers could choose to (and sometimes had to) play Evie Frye, the female half of the fictional brother-sister assassin duo in the Victorian London of *Assassin's Creed: Syndicate*. In this game, however, the designers made no attempt to have Evie change personas through changes in dress. Only during one scene at Buckingham Palace does she show up in women's evening dress. Rather, she wears a long coat covering leggings that allow her to run around as an assassin while appearing, sort of, to wear a dress. *Assassin's Creed: Origins* has some scenes that require gamers to play the fictional character of Aya, the wife of the male protagonist, Bayek. As in colonial Lousiana, women dressed differently according to class in Egypt at the time of Cleopatra. Women working in the fields would wear clothes that allowed for greater mobility than the fashions worn by their wealthy counterparts. While *Origins* notes these differences in its street scenes of

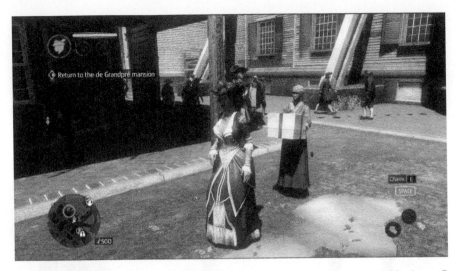

IMAGE 7.2 *Assassin's Creed: Liberation*, Aveline de Grandpré shopping with slave. © 2012 Ubisoft Entertainment. All Rights Reserved. Assassin's Creed, Ubisoft and the Ubisoft logo are trademarks of Ubisoft Entertainment in the US and/or other countries.

ancient Egypt, it doesn't dwell on the restrictions that the long dresses of wealthy women placed on their ability to move and climb, both essential activities for protagonists in the series. Rather, as in *Syndicate, Origins* dresses Aya in an outfit that may look plausibly Egyptian to a modern gamer, but would have brought stares from people at the time. This is important, because what women wore was a constant reminder of their social roles. A woman wearing clothing that restricted her mobility could not perform certain tasks that men could. By ignoring this issue, except in *Liberation, Assassin's Creed* features women by having them behave more like men.

If the women of the past behave more like men, they certainly don't look like them. All protagonists in *Assassin's Creed*, male or female, are very attractive and the physical features denoting their sexes are highlighted. In this sense the videogame industry is similar to the film industry. The audiences for both like to look at sexy main characters, and the creators of the games and films oblige. However, when games depict characters who actually existed, it's possible to compare these portrayals to what we really know. In most cases, historical videogames over-sexualize the appearance of historical female characters and perpetuate sensational depictions of their behavior. For instance, *Black Flag* portrays Anne Bonnie in a low-cut dress with ample cleavage. Both she and Mary Reed are physically very attractive by modern standards. However, the few, albeit unreliable, contemporary depictions of these two pirates provide no indication that they looked as the game portrays them.

Similarly, the designers of *Velvet Assassin*, a non-Ubisoft game, based their protagonist, Violette Summer, loosely on the actual World War II spy Violette Szabo. But it is probably safe to assume that Szabo did not conduct her missions in a body-hugging catsuit worthy of a James Bond movie. The design team also could not resist the opportunity to use the protagonist's recovery in a hospital to indulge in "dream sequences" in which she conducts missions in a flimsy negligée. Such attempts to sex up the career of an inspiring woman, presumably for the benefit of a primarily male audience, arguably has the unfortunate effect of trivializing the important role of women in the allied intelligence services and resistance movements during World War II.

An excellent example of videogames perpetuating sexualized portrayals of powerful women of the past is the industry's treatment of Cleopatra VII of Egypt. She first appears in *Assassin's Creed: Origins* at a party, declaring: "I will sleep with anyone as long as they agree to be executed in the morning." In fairness, *Origins* also shows her planning military campaigns (see Image 7.3). Similarly, as the ruler of Egypt in *Civilization VI*, she appears sexy and seductive. Although she doesn't offer to sleep with anyone, she provides visual cues of sexual interest as she offers to conduct diplomatic relations. However, Cleopatra's reputation for her beauty and sexual appetite is more the product of negative Roman propaganda than of historians' analyses of her life. In the centuries immediately following her death, Roman authors blamed her for causing a civil war between Mark Antony and Octavian (later Emperor Augustus) and subverting Roman values with her foreign influence and feminine wiles. Orientalist artists and twentieth-century filmmakers focused on her role as a *femme fatale* in Roman politics and a romantic, tragic figure in Egyptian history. Perhaps her appearance today is most identified with Elizabeth Taylor, the British actress who played her in the 1963 movie *Cleopatra*. Because she had affairs

First Siwa, now Faiyum. It is the most oppressed region in all of Egypt

IMAGE 7.3 *Assassin's Creed: Origins*, Cleopatra planning with advisors. © 2017 Ubisoft Entertainment. All Rights Reserved. Assassin's Creed, Ubisoft and the Ubisoft logo are registered or unregistered trademarks of Ubisoft Entertainment in the US and/or other countries.

with two of Rome's most powerful politicians, Julius Caesar and Mark Antony, her reputation as a sexual temptress lives on.

Nevertheless, historical analysis paints a far less sensational portrait of Egypt's last pharaoh. Contemporary evidence suggests that Cleopatra was not the stunning beauty of painting and film, either by ancient or modern standards. Rather, her dynamic personality and the prospect of a powerful military alliance attracted the sexual attention of Caesar and Antony. Moreover, these two men may have been the only ones with whom she had sexual relations. She met Caesar at the age of eighteen after three years of marriage to her prepubescent brother who was trying to depose her. As her biographer Stacy Schiff points out: "What that 'harlot queen' was unlikely to have had when she materialized before Caesar in October 48 [BCE] was any sexual experience whatsoever" (18–19).

Removing some of the sexual glamor from Cleopatra, however, does not alter the fact that she was remarkable as a ruler and survivor in a brutal, male-dominated world. In political terms, she was adept at fending off Roman occupation for eighteen years. That she did so by transforming the contemporary disadvantage of her gender into an advantage through her personal alliances with two powerful Roman men does not make her less remarkable. She used the resources she had, including sexual attraction, to advance her own interests in an age that did not easily accept the legitimacy of female rule. Creative Assembly, the design studio for *Total War: Rome II*, acknowledges as much in one of its trailers by having Cleopatra declare: "And have we not built the impossible. And for what? To share our bed with a Roman! Our alliance was born of necessity not love" (GameNewsOfficial). However, Cleopatra's only appearance in *Rome II* is as Antony's wife, adding a bonus in food supply from Egypt, barely a presence at all compared to *Origins* and *Civilization VI*. Both of the latter recognize Cleopatra's political abilities considerably more than *Rome II* does. Their designers just couldn't resist perpetuating the time-honored, inaccurate emphasis on her supposed sexual attributes. After all, sex sells.

Much of the problem that game designers encounter as they attempt to include historical female characters in their creations results from the types of games they are making. The current state of historical videogames is akin to that of the historical profession a century ago. They focus on the public sphere – war, politics, and macro-economics – rather than the private – homemaking, community service, and micro-economics. The former was the domain of men, and the latter one in which women exerted considerable influence. This is why until World War II, historians tended to focus on narratives about great white men, while ignoring all but the handful of politically influential women. The same bias in focus also explains why historical videogames have mainly been about men and male activities.

As a result, attempts to include women in action and strategy games sometimes appear forced. As we have seen, action games usually have women behave as men, even as these games often exaggerate their feminine appearance. Strategy games, which focus less on interactions between individuals, fall into the trap of over-representing women in matters of state. By featuring a significant number of female leaders, *Civilization* represents women in a far larger proportion than men than was historically the case, or is even the case today. Similarly, a common practice in both the *Civilization* and *Total War* series is to emulate the historic division between men's presence in the public sphere and women's in the private by having the in-game advisors on military affairs be male and those on domestic affairs, women. But this hardly represents the reality of the past. Advisors to monarchs whether on military and foreign affairs, or on domestic and financial matters, were almost always male. Only in informal, personal ways did women usually reach the levels of senior advisors to rulers.

Less sexualized depictions of women in the past occur in more casual games that, at least individually, command a lesser share of the market than *Assassin's Creed* or *Civilization*. Seattle-based Big Fish, "the world's largest producer of casual games," markets a line of games titled *Hidden Mysteries*, in which players move from location to location (in still frames) uncovering objects and clues. Some of these games have supernatural elements; some occur in the present, but all focus on issues in the past, and some occur in the historical periods of their focus. About half of the twelve titles require the player to take on the character of a woman, and in all but one, women play major roles in the mysteries to be uncovered. For instance, in *Royal Family Secrets*, the player takes on the character of a handmaiden to English Queen Elizabeth I, who is sentenced to death for the theft of a magical broach, which has actually been stolen by another servant. The use of the broach unleashes the spirits of historical figures from London. The handmaiden must escape her own fate in the Tower of London, while also visiting several other historic locations, including Westminster Abbey and the Globe Theatre in order to lay the spirits back to rest. Meanwhile, the player learns about the social interactions, particularly romantic entanglements, of famous people in England's past.

A more compelling social setting surrounds *The Fateful Voyage – Titanic*. The sinking of the *R.M.S. Titanic* is an ideal setting to explore early twentieth-century British and American society. The ship constituted a self-contained, isolated microcosm of society suddenly faced with a disaster in which choices occurred as to who would live and who would die. The crew of the *Titanic* privileged the upper-classes (those with first-class tickets) over the lower (those in "steerage"). They also privileged women and children over men. Pre-World War I upper-class masculinity was on full display with well-heeled gentlemen toasting one another as the ship went down, assured in their conviction that they were doing the decent thing as their wives and daughters evacuated, even though the wives and daughters of the "steerage" section did not. *Fateful Voyage* explores these issues within the limited structure of a casual game. The playable character, Margaret, is an educated Englishwoman of working-class origin who embarks on her honeymoon with her wealthy husband. Unbeknown to her, her mother books a passage in the steerage section. As an upper-class woman, Margaret is clearly favored to board a lifeboat. At a crucial juncture in the game, the player must decide whether she will accompany her mother to the boats or remain with her husband on the sinking ship.

A more detailed window into past societies is available in other mystery series, particularly *Sherlock Holmes*. The playable character, Holmes, is male. Yet his interactions with women and their importance to his cases present a more accurate picture of the lives of women of various classes in 1890s Britain than do the attempts of action games to provide playable heroines engaging in combat. For instance, in *Sherlock Holmes: The Silver Earring*, the most obvious immediate subject is the upper-class eighteen-year-old heiress, Lavinia. Holmes interviews her, her housekeeper, maids, relatives, a suitor, and stable hands, among others. The accumulation of details gives the player plenty of information about life in 1890s England, and in doing so reveals the importance of both class and gender roles. Indeed, since a woman is the main suspect in *The Silver Earring*, the story revolves around her, revealing interesting details of the behavior of upper-class women of the period. Similar comments could be made of Agatha Christie mysteries rendered in videogame format. Christie wrote her novels from the 1920s to the 1970s. Although the settings are far from typical of English life (since they tend to occur among the rural elite), the details of her cases reveal much about evolving social assumptions of the period. One of Christie's two most famous detectives is Miss Marple, who could provide an interesting, and because of her age less sexy, playable female character than appears in action videogames. However, so far videogames have only recreated the cases pursued by Christie's main male detective, Hercule Poirot. Mysteries also present the possibility of videogames exploring daily life in past societies in ways that depict women with greater accuracy than action games do. They therefore deserve greater attention than they tend to receive among the videogaming community, and among historians evaluating the presentation of the past in virtual form.

A popular and informal way of assessing the amount of sexual bias in a work of entertainment is the Bechdel Test. Virginia Woolf anticipated the test by nearly sixty years in her reflection on the portrayal of female characters in literature:

> I tried to remember any case in the course of my reading where two women are represented as friends … They are now and then mothers and daughters. But almost without exception they are shown in their relation to men. It was strange to think that all the great women of fiction were, until Jane Austen's day, not only seen by the other sex, but seen only in relation to the other sex. And how small a part of a woman's life is that.
>
> *(Chapter 5)*

Inspired by this passage, Alison Bechdel had a character in a 1985 segment of her comic strip *Dykes to Watch Out For* declare: "I only go to a movie if it satisfies three basic requirements. One, it has to have at least two women in it … who two, talk to each other about, three, something besides a man" (Bechdel). The point in both Woolf's essay and Bechdel's comic is that in most creative art, whether literature or film, women's characters are defined by their relationships to men. They are mothers, wives, girlfriends, and daughters. Moreover, their interactions with one another tend to be about men, as fathers, husbands, boyfriends, and sons. Rarely does one find two female characters who discuss a topic with each other that isn't about men. By contrast literature and film often portray men discussing issues that do not obviously involve women, for instance, sports, war, business, education, and religion. Some movies, particularly war movies, have no females in them at all. When they do, women often form minor characters in the social backdrop to the more important central goals the men are pursuing.

The Bechdel Test began as a joke. (The character in the comic concludes that the last movie she was able to see was *Alien*, because two females discussed the alien rather than men.) Yet the test grew in popularity over the decades following the comic's publication, and is now a regular feature of literary and film analysis. Not surprisingly, scholars and players alike have applied it to videogames as well. However, since the content of videogames might change depending on the character a player chooses and variations in narrative that player decisions may cause, media critics have suggested modifications to create a videogame Bechdel Test. For instance, writing for the feminist gaming blog *Not Your Mama's Gamer*, Sarah Nixon suggests the following modifications to the Bechdel Test.

1. Must have at least two named female characters that are meaningful to the story or gameplay.
2. At least one of the aforementioned characters must be a player character or a playable character or NPC [non-playable character] in the player's party.
3. The female characters must interact with each other in a manner representative of the dialogue/conversational style of the game.
4. The characters' conversation is about something other than a man.

It's surprising how few historical games meet this test of gender inclusivity. Very few combat games do. Given their military settings, these games usually involve men shouting orders or information at other men. Action games are not much better. Some of the *Assassin's Creed* games come close to meeting the test, particularly if they feature women protagonists. For instance, *Syndicate*'s Evie Frye interviews several women during her investigation of the Jack the Ripper murders. However, they are usually talking about men, albeit not as romantic interests. Moreover, the Jack the Ripper mystery is additional downloadable content, not part of the main game itself. The same problem presents itself in the casual mystery games mentioned above. Even when two women discuss events, they are likely to be discussing men.

Given the professional and occupational prominence that men have held in contrast to women through most of recorded history, some of these biases may simply reflect the historical situations they depict. However, it's worth asking whether the reason women are so difficult to include in historical videogames is a result of what actually was, or a result of the topics game designers choose. Perhaps the growing proportion of women on design teams will open up new possibilities in this regard.

Male characters in the virtual past

This chapter began with a videogame's portrayal of male behavior in war. Indeed, *Brothers in Arms 3: Sons of War* hardly includes women at all, focusing instead on male bonding in combat situations. The phrase "band of brothers," often used to describe this type of bonding, comes from Shakespeare's *Henry V* (Act IV, Scene iii, 18–67), in which the English king raises the morale of his soldiers just before they go into battle against the French at Agincourt on St. - Crispin's Day, 1415:

> And Crispin Crispian shall ne'er go by,
> From this day to the ending of the world,
> But we in it shall be remembered-
> We few, we happy few, we band of brothers;
> For he to-day that sheds his blood with me
> Shall be my brother; be he ne'er so vile,
> This day shall gentle his condition;
> And gentlemen in England now a-bed
> Shall think themselves accurs'd they were not here,
> And hold their manhoods cheap whiles any speaks
> That fought with us upon Saint Crispin's day.

Literary historian Herbert Sussman considers the "band of brothers" to be a feature of "warrior identity," which cuts across time and space from Spartan hoplites, to Medieval knights, to Samurai warriors, to modern special-ops units. It arises out of the need of individuals in a combat unit to look out for their comrades in order for any of them to survive. Along with this male bonding comes a code of honor, which bears similarities across societies, but with significant variations. Common features include courage, loyalty, and a willingness to place the good of the unit over one's own, even at the cost of one's life. Variations include the expectation of suicide rather than surrender. On the one hand, Romans and Samurai are famous (perhaps stereotypically so) for impaling themselves with knives or swords rather than suffer the dishonor of capture. By contrast, Islam and Christianity forbid suicide, although not the selling of one's life dearly in combat – which often amounts to nearly the same thing. Some warrior codes, such as chivalry (European) and bushido (Japanese), embodied peacetime activities, such as service to the poor and vulnerable. On the other hand, other codes, such as those of Sparta and Nazi Germany, encouraged brutality toward civilians outside the governing caste or ethnic group (Sussman 11–28). Indeed, as we shall see in the next chapter, although the "band of brothers" mentality can lead to noble acts of heroism on behalf of the unit or the soldiers own society, it can also pressure all members of the unit to participate in atrocities against groups they regard as other.

The "band of brothers" approach to masculinity is not the only one featured in videogames. Another and contrasting model of manhood is the "cowboy," a man who rides into town to solve its problems, usually through force. Frequently a man of action rather than words, he relies very little on others, because he alone is capable of making things right. This ideal is apparent in many films of the Western genre, but also a variety of action movies. Actor Clint Eastwood, already famous as a problematic Western protagonist in the "Spaghetti Westerns" of the 1960s, portrayed a similar character in the *Dirty Harry* contemporary urban crime movies of the 1970s and 1980s. In these movies, he frequently flouts the law in order to bring about rough but effective justice by using unauthorized force.

This self-sufficient form of manhood is ideal for many single-player action videogames because it maximizes the amount of agency in the player's character. It also resonates with libertarian sentiments in the United States that extol independence and individualism. *Call of Duty* titles set on battlefields demand cooperation with either AI- or human-controlled characters. However, *Call of Duty: Black Ops*'s story puts greater emphasis on the actions of the protagonist, Alex Mason, since many of the missions rely mainly on him achieving his Cold War covert objectives. Nevertheless, most of the game's missions, and all its multi-player options, require cooperation with another character.

A more obvious example of self-sufficient manhood is apparent in *Sniper Elite*, a third-person shooter series that follows the career of fictional agent Karl Fairburne of the US Office of Strategic Services (OSS). The first game, released in 2005 and reproduced in altered form in 2012, has Fairburne capturing or killing German scientists working on the V-2 rocket program during the months immediately preceding Germany's collapse at the end of World War II. *Sniper Elite III* occurs three years earlier in North Africa as Fairburne uncovers the secrets about the development of advanced German weaponry. *Sniper Elite 4* (note the change from roman to Arabic numerals) fills in the gap between these two settings as the allied armies advance through Italy. The games involve considerable stealth and plenty of gory violence. However, they mainly occur devoid of the context of Fairburne's life. He acts on orders, but usually alone. Even when he is helping other soldiers, he is usually perched in isolated positions picking off enemy snipers and soldiers who are targeting allied forces. He shows grief in *Sniper Elite III* when an informant dies, but there is little sense of his backstory or of his relationship to anyone back home. The series very much focuses on the mechanics of killing while avoiding detection.

One would expect the most obvious presentation of the cowboy image of masculinity to be in a game set in the American West. Surprisingly few videogames have this setting. The two most popular are the *Call of Juarez* FPS series and *Red Dead Redemption*, a 2010 third-person action game, whose prequel came out in 2018. Polish studio Techland developed *Call of Juarez* and Ubisoft has published the series. Since neither of these companies is American it's not surprising that the series takes a tongue-in-cheek approach to Western stereotypes. This is apparent in the first scene of *Call of Juarez: Gunslinger*, the most recent title in its series, as fictional protagonist Silas Greaves regales saloon patrons in Abilene, Kansas with his increasingly tall tales of his exploits as a young man. These include numerous duels against notorious outlaws, including Butch Cassidy and Jesse James. The tales are so tall that when Greaves's audience catches inconsistencies, the game requires the player to reload scenes in order to play a more plausible version of events. Much of the action involves Greaves taking on the bad guys alone, reinforcing the myth of self-sufficient masculinity in the American West. From a historian's perspective, however, the game's presentation of these events as tall tales has two salutary effects. It shows this model of masculinity to be caricature and an object of humor. It also reminds the player to treat personal accounts of the past with skepticism. The subtext is that this may apply to videogames too.

In contrast to *Call of Juarez*, *Red Dead Redemption* is a product of the modern American West, developed in Rockstar's San Diego, California studio. Its fictional protagonist, John Marston, is a former outlaw released from prison on the condition that he bring fellow gang members to justice. In addition to the missions advancing the storyline, Marston participates in scores of side-missions, mostly alone, in which he often helps locals in distress while attempting to bring outlaws to justice. The player eventually discovers that he is a husband and father. Marston ultimately dies heroically defending his family. *Red Dead Redemption* takes itself more seriously than *Call of Juarez*. With the exception of a few scenes, such as the one with the anthropologist described in the previous chapter, the story is more drama than comedy. Development team leader Christian Cantamessa states: "Our overarching theme is the 'Death of the West' rather than the more conventional 'Myth of the West' that is often seen in the classic John Wayne films." However, he acknowledges, "we also took inspiration from the novels of Cormac McCarthy and from films like Unforgiven, High Plains Drifter and The Proposition." These are more recent Westerns (*The Proposition* is actually set in the Australian Outback) in which the protagonists are much more problematic as heroes, and John Marston is far from a conventional white hat of mid-twentieth-century Westerns. However, he is still the loner typical of the genre, and although some of his female acquaintances can lasso a horse or handle a gun, he still sometimes plays the role of savior to damsels in distress.

Rockstar applied similar stereotypes of American masculinity in *L. A. Noire*, a detective story action game set in post-World War II Los Angeles. Much like *Red Dead Redemption*, this game evokes a style of film from the period rather than the actual reality. Film noir (French for black film, or dark film) was a term that French critics applied to American crime dramas of the mid-twentieth century. Their stories usually occurred in urban settings with low lighting that reflects the pessimism of the plot. Many are based on novels, such as those of Ernest Hemingway, Dashiell Hammett, and Raymond Chandler, noted for their terse dialogue, and in the latter case similes grounded in everyday urban culture. Mid-twentieth-century film noir is also morally ambiguous. The protagonists, while usually pursuing justice, are not always too particular about how they achieve it – and their personal lives are often a mess. The usually male protagonists often begin the films finding life meaningless. They frequently encounter *femmes fatales*, seductive women with the potential to bring calamity on the male protagonist. If the male protagonist survives the story, he often emerges from it just as jaded as he began it. Although different from the cowboy in his urban setting, the film noir protagonist portrays similar qualities. According to film historian Megan E. Abbot,

> The idea of the solitary white man trekking down urban streets has fore-runners in like-minded navigators of Western space or wilderness, but a relocation to the industrialized American city, combined with modernist themes of fragmentation and alienation, created a unique new figure.
>
> *(2)*

L. A. Noire taps on many of these themes in its storyline. Playable protagonist Cole Phelps is a married patrol officer in the Los Angeles Police Department (LAPD), promoted to detective in the vice squad early in the game. In the course of duty, he has an affair with Elsa Lichtmann, a seductive German lounge singer, reminiscent of the roles played by twentieth-century German actress Marlene Dietrich. However, he doesn't realize that his LAPD partner is involved in a scheme to defraud the US government by burning down housing built for World War II veterans in order to claim the insurance. As Phelps uncovers clues pointing to the crime, his partner conspires with the police chief and the district attorney to use Phelps's adultery to demote him, removing him from the investigation and causing the collapse of his marriage. The story goes on as Phelps persists in the investigation, albeit without authorization ("Cole Phelps").

However, the game has already established much about the protagonist's character and his masculine identity. Phelps is a decorated veteran of the Pacific War and the United States Marine Corps, but he knows that the courage that earned him his medal is a sham. This gives him humility and seems to make him all the braver during the events of the game. However, Phelps clearly suffers from post-traumatic stress disorder and moral character flaws, most notably his willingness to enter an adulterous relationship with Elsa, which destroys his marriage and his reputation. Perhaps Phelps's most notable character strength is his open-mindedness regarding women and people of other races, qualities which he holds in stark contrast to those around him. In this way, the creators of *L. A. Noire* allow the protagonist to exhibit flaws that might seem undesirable but forgivable to a modern audience, while shielding him from the far less acceptable failings of sexism and racism. While there were no doubt many men in post-World War II Los Angeles who shared these qualities, it was more common to find white men, in particular, who did not. In the context of the times, it was more acceptable to be a racist and misogynist than an adulterer.

Yet by letting Elsa play the role of *femme fatale*, the game is arguably perpetuating a sexist stereotype of women, particularly regarding their responsibility for exposing and encouraging male character flaws.

Both *Red Dead Redemption* and *L. A. Noire* self-consciously draw as much from film as they do from reality. Their developers frankly acknowledge that they do, so it's important for players to realize that the history they encounter through these games is at least twice removed from the actual past. Nevertheless, in the case of *L. A. Noire*, the films the game draws on were often contemporaneous with the society in which they were set. The ideals of manhood these movies presented were ideals that many men looked up to at the time. Indeed Hollywood often popularized certain ideals making them more pervasive in society. In this sense, perhaps *L. A. Noire* at least comes closer to portraying an ideal of manhood from post–World War II Los Angeles than *Red Dead Redemption* does from the pre–World War I American Southwest. Both games, however, imbue their protagonists with sensibilities about gender and race that are more valued in the society in which they were produced than the societies they portray.

Ironically, one of the most popular series of games to portray the ideal of the lone man delivering extrajudicial retribution is *Assassin's Creed*, even though its historical settings are rarely identified with this model of manhood. One might argue that inasmuch as the series' fictitious Assassins order draws on the historical Medieval Assassins, there is a tenuous historical connection. One might also argue that at least in *Assassin's Creed III*, set on the colonial frontier in New England, the game manifests a level of individualism that would become iconic of white American pioneers pushing the frontier westward. Yet the concept of the lone gunman (or blade-wielder) sits less easily with ideals of masculinity in other societies and other times. This anachronism is particularly obvious in *Assassin's Creed: Origins*, which begins with the male protagonist, Bayek, returning alone from the desert to his hometown oasis of Siwa. He is the last of the Medjay, whom the game portrays as a group of marshals who kept the peace under the old pharaohs. Now he is almost single-handedly cleaning up corruption under the rule of Cleopatra VII's adolescent brother, Ptolemy XIII, while looking back wistfully at Hellenism's encroachment on traditional Egyptian culture. This character is not historical, nor is much of the backstory. The Medjay had disappeared from the historical record long before the time of Cleopatra. However, it is a familiar scenario drawn from the mythology of the American West. Bayek is a combination of the historical federal marshals, enforcing the law on the frontier, and the latter-day cowboy of *Red Dead Redemption*, who sees an old glamorized culture fading around him. Like these characters, Bayek often cooperates with others, mainly rebels against the rule of Ptolemy XIII, but usually delivers justice alone, particularly on side-missions. He avoids killing innocent bystanders, but deals swift death to those who exploit the innocent.

Indeed, although many fans have called for Ubisoft to make the *Assassin's Creed* series more multi-player-friendly, the company has focused mainly on individual gameplay rather than cooperative elements. This decision distinguishes the series from Electronic Arts's *Battlefield*, whose titles often have a sparse story-line, focusing instead on multi-player elements and cooperative play on the battlefield. This is apparent in the series' most recent historical title, *Battlefield 1*, set during World War I. In *Battlefield* collaboration with comrades is usually essential. Ubisoft developers, therefore, do not model their characters as lone assassins out of a lack of historical awareness. Rather they do so for reasons of mechanics, playability, and marketing. Whatever the historical setting, a game focusing on stealth and assassination is likely to have as its protagonist someone who acts alone. Therefore, it will inevitably emphasize the "cowboy" rather than the "band of brothers" model of manhood.

As with the two Rockstar games discussed above, however, *Assassin's Creed* also has its male protagonists interact extensively with female characters – at least after the first installment of the series. Bayek's marriage to Aya falls apart, not because she is completely flouting the norms of ancient Egyptian womanhood, which she is, but because the couple realizes that their lives are going to take them far from each other as they each pursues similar life callings 1000 miles apart. This is a very modern reason for a marriage to fail. Even today, many husbands are reluctant to let their wives' careers take precedence over their own. However, that circumstance almost never arose in ancient Egypt, and Bayek does not raise the litany of gendered assumptions that a man faced with this situation likely would have had back then. Moreover, there are no extended family members on either side of the marriage to pressure Aya to conform to social norms. In other words, although the portrayal of Bayek's behavior toward his wife is not impossible, it's unlikely in the extreme. In this sense *Origins*, by imbuing its male protagonist with modern sensibilities, is parting from the likely behavior of men in the past, even the heroic ones. This may make for a better male role model for modern male players, but it portrays attitudes in the past less accurately.

Portraying non-heteronormative gender roles

If modern sensibilities pervade many historical videogames' portrayal of gender in the past, they have had little effect on the depiction of people who don't fit het-erosexual norms. Homosexual, bisexual, and transgender people are almost invis-ible in these games. In the rare instances that they do occur, they are not playable protagonists. From a marketing perspective, the reasons are obvious. People who don't identify as heterosexual or cisgender make up a significant but relatively small percentage of society. In a 2015 Gallup poll, only 3.8 percent of respondents in the United States identified as gay or transsexual – although a significant per-centage may actually identify with these categories but refuse to acknowledge it to pollsters (Gallup). As discussed above, playable protagonists may appeal to mem-bers of the same sex, who identify with them, or the opposite sex, who enjoy viewing (and in some cases controlling) them. However, the number of players who would identify with an LGBTQIA+ protagonist presumably form a much smaller, niche market. Moreover, game producers assume that some heterosexual players may recoil at the prospect of playing an LGBTQIA+ character. Even gay programmers have been reluctant to include openly gay characters for business reasons. The result is an ethical conundrum in which the industry reinforces the intolerance of a large minority of the market by denying a voice to a smaller minority, primarily for the sake of profit.

One way around this problem has been to allow players to design the identity of their own protagonist at the beginning of the game. *Fallout* and *Elder Scrolls*, to name just two popular series, allow players to choose the race and gender of their character. However, although *Fallout* refers to historical themes, and Medieval lore permeates *Elder Scrolls*, neither game purports to occur in a setting from our world's actual past. Moreover, in order to make the sexual orientation of the protagonist apparent, games would have to actually alter the sexual relationships with other characters in its storyline, a fairly complicated undertaking. In historical games, this is only likely to occur if the non-heteronormative orientation of the protagonist is a significant feature of the story. The most notable case, *Gone Home*, focuses on the adolescent coming-out of the protagonist's sister, Samantha, in the mid-1990s. However, even in this case, the protagonist herself is not lesbian; she discovers that her sister is. More recently, *Assassin's Creed: Odyssey* allows the player to choose the gender of the playable character, and then provides various opportunities for that character to have sexual relations with other characters, regardless of their gender.

There is no reason to believe that the percentage of the population attracted to members of the same sex in the past was different from that percentage today. What certainly differed was whether societies accepted homosexual behavior or suppressed it. (In some cases, such as the Spartan military, homosexual relations among men were even encouraged. However, this did not mean that these men all preferred men to women as sexual partners.) Moreover, we know of many prominent people of the past who were probably gay, no matter how much contemporary society forced them to hide their sexual orientation. Indeed, the whole question of identifying as gay or lesbian may be anachronistic when dealing with past societies, since there is little evidence that people saw it in terms of sexual identity. Rather, they regarded it as sexual behavior. The concept of gay identity is one that emerges fully in the twentieth century.

Even when historical videogames portray actual LGBTQIA+ people from the past, they often choose to ignore this aspect of their character. For instance, in the original *Assassin's Creed*, protagonist Altair meets English King Richard I (aka Richard the Lionheart), and in *Battlefield 1*, T. E. Lawrence (aka Lawrence of Arabia) helps fight a guerilla war against the Turks. In neither instance is there any hint of these historical characters' sexual orientations, although in both cases many historians have argued that they were gay. Indeed the reason for continuing doubt to the contrary lies in part with the condemnation that their societies would have quickly visited on them if they had admitted to homosexual feelings, let alone actual relations. Occasionally, however, a major historical figure's sexual orientation became a matter of public record. This was the case with Leonardo da Vinci, who at age twenty-four stood trial along with three other men for sodomy with a male prostitute. The judge dismissed the case for lack of evidence, perhaps because one of the defendants was a member of the powerful Medici family. Later in life, da Vinci became very close to two of his male students, with whom he may have had sexual relations. *Assassin's Creed: Brotherhood* dwells on his friendship with the first of these, Gian Giacomo Caprotti da Oreno, aka Salaì ("the Devil") to his friends. Salaì studied with da Vinci from age ten to twenty-eight, and served as his model for some paintings, including his portrait of John the Baptist. *Brotherhood* briefly hints at the two being lovers in the following exchange:

LEONARDO: I suppose Salaì is out having fun spending my hard-earned florins?
EZIO: He is safe at home.
LEONARDO: I am relieved … about the florins of course.
EZIO: You do not need to lie to me. Salaì fits you. I approve.
LEONARDO: I …
EZIO: Leonardo da Vinci at a loss for words? That is a first. ("The Temple of Pythagoras").

One might argue that either ignoring a historical figure's sexual orientation or only subtly hinting at it is appropriate, because that person's sexual orientation may be irrelevant to the plot. This argument makes sense if heteronormative behavior is not on display in the game. However, we have already discussed many games in which heteronormative behavior forms a central feature of the story. In action games, male protagonists often have girlfriends or wives, either off-screen or interacting with them. In the much rarer cases of female protagonists, the reverse is often true. The fact that historical videogames rarely acknowledge the sexual orientation of major LGBTQIA+ characters such as da Vinci underscores the criticism that for these games non-heteronormative behavior still hasn't "come out of the closet."

Conclusion

Critics of videogames frequently charge the industry and its products with sexism. They have good reason to do so. Men overwhelmingly dominate the industry and their games' portrayals of females often seem to reflect their creators' sexual fantasies more than anything resembling real girls and women. Even female protagonists, most famously *Tomb Raider*'s Lara Croft, have worn improbable outfits and possessed physically distorted features in order to emphasize their sexual endowments. Publishers have argued that a male-dominated market has driven these preferences. And the sexism of a vocal fraction of this market is beyond doubt, given the behavior of fans toward female developers. Critics of the videogame industry, however, have questioned the extent to which a sexist male market drives these choices, arguing that the choices themselves may be alienating women from buying action games in the first place. After all, women constitute an increasing share of the market, rapidly approaching 50 percent, but they don't command anything like this proportion of action and strategy gamers. These considerations are significant for any analysis of gender in historical videogames, because most of these games fall into the action or strategy categories.

Nevertheless, an additional problem surrounds issues of gender in historical videogames. On the one hand, developers have increasingly included female characters in their games, adding greater depth to their roles in the storylines. On the other hand, in doing so they have often simply had female characters behave identically to their male counterparts. This behavior is particularly jarring in historical settings where social expectations, and even something as everyday as women's clothing, made the type of active aggressive behavior of most videogame protagonists impossible, or at least exceedingly rare. In these cases, developers have exchanged historical accuracy for inclusivity and agency. Moreover, their portrayal of male protagonists, while perhaps more nuanced than in earlier years, continues to focus on combat stereotypes. Videogames that more extensively explore male-female interaction have increasingly made male protagonists less sexist and racist. This development is an improvement if the primary concern is to have the protagonists set better role models of male behavior. However, like the portrayals of women as action heroes, these male behaviors are problematic in historical settings, when the separate roles for women and men were almost universally considered a part of nature, and transgressions of heteronormative behavior, whether across gender lines or through homosexual relations, were considered a violation of natural and divine law. Certainly such social transgressions occurred. Historians often find evidence of them in court records from the resulting prosecutions against them. The apparent ease with which the major characters in these videogames brush off these departures from social norms may make for appealing heroes, but unlikely representatives of the past.

Note

1 My thanks to Dr Janet Donohoe for this insight.

Works cited

AAUW Educational Foundation Commission, *Tech Savvy: Educating Girls in the New Computer Age*. AAUW Educational Foundation Commission on Technology, Gender, and Teacher Education, 2000, https://history.aauw.org/aauw-research/tech-savvy-2000.

Abbott, Megan E., *The Street Was Mine: White Masculinity in Hardboiled Fiction and Film Noir*, 1st edn. Palgrave Macmillan, 2002.

Agatha Christie (game series), Dreamcatcher Interactive, 2005–16.

Alien, directed by Ridley Scott, 20th Century Fox, 1979.

Assassin's Creed (game series), Ubisoft, 2007–18.

Assassin's Creed II, Ubisoft Montreal, 2009.

Assassin's Creed III, Ubisoft Montreal, 2012.

Assassin's Creed IV:Black Flag, Ubisoft Montreal, 2013.

Assassin's Creed, Origins, Ubisoft Montreal, 2017.

Assassin's Creed: Brotherhood, Ubisoft Montreal, 2010.

Assassin's Creed: Freedom Cry, Ubisoft Montreal, 2014.

Assassin's Creed: Liberation, Ubisoft Sofia, 2012.

Assassin's Creed: Revelations, Ubisoft Quebec, 2011.

Assassin's Creed: Syndicate, Ubisoft Quebec, 2015.

Assassin's Creed: Syndicate, "Jack the Ripper" DLC, Ubisoft Quebec, 2015.

Barbie Fashion Designer, Digital Domain, 1996.

Battlefield (game series), EA DICE, 2002–16.

Battlefield 1, EA DICE, 2016.

Bechdel, Alison, "The Rule." *DTWOF: The Blog*, 16 August 2005, http://alisonbechdel. blogspot.com/2005/08/rule.html.

"Big Fish Celebrates 11th Consecutive Year of Record Growth." *Big Fish Games | Media-Room*, 28 January 2014, http://pressroom.bigfishgames.com/2014-01-28-Big-Fish-Celebrates-11th-Consecutive-Year-of-Record-Growth.

Bigelow, Bill, "On the Road to Cultural Bias: A Critique of 'The Oregon Trail' CD-ROM." *Language Arts*, vol. 74, no. 2 (February 1997), 84–93.

Brothers in Arms 3: Sons of War, Gameloft, 2014.

Burton, Antoinette M., *Burdens of History: British Feminists, Indian Women, Andimperial Culture, 1865–1915*. University of North Carolina Press, 1994.

Butler, Judith, *Gender Trouble: Feminism and the Subversion of Identity*. Routledge, 2006.

Call of Duty (game series), Infinity Ward/Treyarch, 2003–18.

Call of Duty: Black Ops, Treyarch, 2010.

Call of Juarez (game series), Techland, 2006–13.

Call of Juarez: Gunslinger, Techland, 2013.

Clark, Alice, *Working Life of Women in the Seventeenth Century*. George Routledge & Sons, 1919.

Cleopatra, produced by Walter Wagner, 20th Century Fox, 1963.

"Cole Phelps." *L.A. Noire Wiki*. http://lanoire.wikia.com/wiki/Cole_Phelps.

Crecente, Brian, "20 Years a Developer, Jade Raymond Weighs Her next Step." *Polygon*, 26 February 2015, www.polygon.com/2015/2/26/8078083/jade-raymond-next-step.

Crenshaw, Kimberlé, "Demarginalizing the Intersection of Race and Sex: A Black Feminist Critique of Antidiscrimination Doctrine, Feminist Theory and Antiracist Politics." *University of Chicago Legal Forum*, vol. 1989, no. 1 (December 2015), http://chicagounbound. uchicago.edu/uclf/vol1989/iss1/8.

D'Emilio, John, *Sexual Politics, Sexual Communities: The Making of a Homosexual Minority in the United States, 1940–1970*. University of Chicago Press, 1983.

De Beauvoir, Simone, *The Second Sex*, translated by H. M. Parshley. Knopf, 1953.

Dirty Harry (film series), Malpaso Productions, Warner Bros., 1971–88.

The Elder Scrolls (game series), Bethesda Game Studios, 1994–2018.

"ESA Muddies Gaming Stats between Male and Female Gaming Demographics." *One Angry Gamer*, 20 April 2017, www.oneangrygamer.net/2017/04/esa-muddies-gaming-stats-between-male-and-female-gaming-demographics/29044/.

"Essential Facts About the Computer and Video Game Industry." *The Entertainment Software Association*,www.theesa.com/about-esa/essential-facts-computer-video-game-industry/.

Everquest, Sony Online Entertainment, 1999.

Fallout (game series), Interplay Entertainment/Bethesda Game Studios, 1997–2017.

Foucault, Michel, *The History of Sexuality*, 3 vols., translated by Robert Hurley. Vintage, 1988–90.

Fussell, Paul, *Wartime: Understanding and Behavior in the Second World War*, revised edn. Oxford University Press, 1990.

Gallup Inc., "Americans Greatly Overestimate Percent Gay, Lesbian in U.S." *Gallup.Com*. http://news.gallup.com/poll/183383/americans-greatly-overestimate-percent-gay-lesbian.aspx.

GameNewsOfficial, *Total War Rome 2 Cleopatra Trailer. YouTube*. www.youtube.com/watch?v=dFs3g1fQQ8Q.

GameSpot, *The Sims Medieval Games.com 2010 Interview: Rachel Bernstein. YouTube*, 2010. www.youtube.com/watch?v=XUlr6eU0U_Y.

Gaudiosi, John, "EA's Biggest Games Are Being Helmed by Female Developers." *Fortune*, September 2015, http://fortune.com/2015/09/04/ea-peter-moore-on-women-in-gaming/.

"Gender Split in F2P Games: Who's Playing What." *Deltadna.Com*, 17 November 2015, https://deltadna.com/blog/gender-split-in-f2p-games/.

Gone Home, The Fullbright Company, 2016.

Hidden Mysteries: Royal Family Secrets, Big Fish Games, 2012.

Hidden Mysteries: The Fateful Voyage – Titanic, Gunnar Games, 2009.

High Plains Drifter, directed by Clint Eastwood, Malpaso Company, Universal Studios, 1973.

"Is Jade Raymond Just an Industry Pin-Up Girl Used to Drive Sales? - General Discussion." *Giant Bomb*, www.giantbomb.com/forums/general-discussion-30/is-jade-raymond-just-an-industry-pin-up-girl-used-527673/?page=1.

John, Tracey, "Women Working In Games: 'Assassin's Creed''s Elspeth Tory On Jade Raymond And Entering The Boys' Club." *MTV News*, 12 December 2007, www.mtv.com/news/2456216/women-working-in-games-assassins-creeds-elspeth-tory-on-jade-raymond-and-entering-the-boys-club/.

L.A. Noire, Team Bondi/Rockstar Games, 2011.

Lockwood, Madison, "The Sims Phenomenon." *EzineArticles*, January 2007, http://ezinearticles.com/?The-Sims-Phenomenon&id=430065.

Lussenhop, Jessica, "Oregon Trail: How Three Minnesotans Forged Its Path." *City Pages*, 23 January 2011, web.archive.org/web/20110123012937/www.citypages.com/content/printVersion/1740595/.

Mikula, Maja, "Gender and Videogames: The Political Valency of Lara Croft." *Continuum: Journal of Media & Cultural Studies*, vol. 17, no. 1 (March 2003), 79.

Nixon, Sarah, "Applying the Bechdel Test to Video Games." *Not Your Mama's Gamer*, 25 July 2013, www.nymgamer.com/?p=3184.

The Oregon Trail (game series), MECC, 1971–2011.

Orwell, George, *1984*. Secker and Warburg, 1949.

Paoletti, Jo Barraclough, *Pink and Blue: Telling the Boys from the Girls in America*. Indiana University Press, 2012. library.uakron.edu library catalog, http://ebookcentral.proquest.com/lib/uakron/detail.action?docID=816833.

Prescott, Julie and Jan Boggs, *Gender Divide and the Computer Game Industry*. Information Science Reference, 2014.

Pretzsch, Birgit, *A Postmodern Analysis of Lara Croft*. Trinity College, 1999, www.cyberpink.de/laracroft/LaraCompleteTextWOPics.html.

The Proposition, directed by John Hillcoat, First Look Pictures, 2005.

Red Dead Redemption, Rockstar San Diego, 2010.

Schiff, Stacy, *Cleopatra: A Life*, reprint edn. Back Bay Books, 2011.

Scott, Joan W., "Gender: A Useful Category of Historical Analysis." *American Historical Review*, vol. 91, no. 5 (December 1986), 1053.

Sherlock Holmes (game series), Frogwares, 2002–16.

Sherlock Holmes: The Silver Earring, Frogwares, 2004.

Sid Meier's Civilization VI, Firaxis Games, 2017.

Sinha, Mrinalini, *Colonial Masculinity: The "Manly Englishman" and the' Effeminate Bengali' in the Late Nineteenth Century*. Manchester University Press; distributed exclusively in the USA and Canada by St. Martin's Press, 1995.

Sniper Elite, Rebellion Developments, 2005.

Sniper Elite (game series), Rebellion Developments, 2005–17.

Sniper Elite 4, Rebellion Developments, 2017.

Sniper Elite III, Rebellion Developments, 2014.

Square Enix 2015 Annual Report, 2015.

Sussman, Herbert, *Masculine Identities: The History and Meanings of Manliness*. Praeger, 2012.

Taylor, T. L. "Multiple Pleasures." *Convergence: The Journal of Research into New Media Technologies*, vol. 9, no. 1 (Spring 2003), 21.

"The Temple of Pythagoras." *Assassin's Creed Wiki*, http://assassinscreed.wikia.com/wiki/The_Temple_of_Pythagoras.

Todd, Cherie, "COMMENTARY: GamerGate and Resistance to the Diversification of Gaming Culture." *Women's Studies Journal*, vol. 29, no. 1 (August 2015), 64–7.

Tomb Raider (game series), Core Design/ Eidos, 1996–2018.

Total War: Rome 2, Creative Assembly, 2013.

Unforgiven, produced and directed by Clint Eastwood, Malpaso Productions, Warner Bros., 1992.

Velvet Assassin, Replay Studios, 2009.

Woolf, Virginia, *A Room of One's Own*. eBooks@Adelaide, University of Adelaide, 2015, https://ebooks.adelaide.edu.au/w/woolf/virginia/w91r/.

8

VIOLENCE AND OPPRESSION

Introduction

In November 2009, as Activision was releasing *Call of Duty: Modern Warfare 2*, the satirical news website *The Onion* posted a fake news report on the development of *Call of Duty: Modern Warfare 3*. The anchorman expresses excitement over what developers "say will be the most true to life military game ever, created with the majority of gameplay spent hauling equipment and filling out paperwork." The report goes on to provide further details of the game's "real-life military action," promising that "gamers will stand guard outside a photo-realistic warehouse for hours, dig 10-foot deep holes in the immaculately rendered sand, and sit around complaining about how bad the cell phone reception is." A member of the development team explains that she is "at the stage right now where you get homesick and you go out into the desert and just sort of stare at nothing." At this point a sniper shoots her character and the screen goes red as she falls to the ground. "I was just standing there and I got shot in the back and now I guess the game's over," she sighs. The report closes with the anchorman excitedly declaring that the Wii version of the game "will come packaged with a 17-pound controller shaped like an m-249 machine gun that you must carry at all times but cannot fire without explicit orders."

What makes the report so funny is that, in showing how dull a videogame would be that simulated the actual experiences of American soldiers in Iraq, it highlights how unrealistic popular combat first-person shooters (FPSs) are. Unlike game series such as *Call of Duty, Medal of Honor*, and *Sniper Elite*, *The Onion*'s fictitious *Call of Duty* game has the protagonist doing the types of mundane, menial, or bureaucratic tasks that really fill up the days of soldiers deployed in war zones. Moreover, when action does occur in the game, it is often sudden, unexpected, and fatal. For the designer who lost her soldier to a sniper in the desert, there was no action until the single shot that ended the game. Finally, when the player's character dies the scene does not reset so that the player can try to survive through repeated replays. Rather, the game ends along with the character's life.

The Onion's lampoon of one of the most popular FPSs raises a couple of important themes in this chapter. One is the extent to which developers misrepresent reality in order to transform what are often some of the least pleasant moments in a person's life into a source of entertainment and pleasure in the virtual world. For there is no denying that violence sells videogames, but only because it isn't real. People who have really encountered serious violence often emerge traumatized. Moreover, as The Onion clearly demonstrates, the life of a combat soldier involves very little glory, and plenty of boredom. Since boredom is anathema to a videogame's success, virtual worlds eliminate the vast majority of downtime between the exciting, yet less-than-terrifying, moments of action.

If one restraint on videogames' depiction of violence is playability, another is social (and sometimes legal) acceptance of dealing frankly with inhumane behavior in the past. For decades critics of videogames have raised alarms about the level of violence that they simulate. Various studies have attempted to demonstrate that playing violent videogames makes players more likely to commit violent acts in reality. Yet a consensus hasn't emerged. When it comes to historical videogames, however, developers face a problem of equal importance: whether to ignore or play down past atrocities on the one hand, or risk indulging players' racism and sadism on the other. Which type of violent acts are acceptable to portray differs among videogames, and often depends on the target audience of the game and the laws of the country in which it lives.

In order to examine videogames' portrayals of past violence, this chapter first discusses what historians and other scholars have written on the topic. It then examines the portrayal of combat and collateral damage. Finally, it deals with games' portrayals of more systemic forms of violence: slavery and genocide. In all these cases videogame designers must compromise with reality. The question is how much.

Historical scholarship on violence and oppression

As long as people have studied history, violence has been a major theme in how they perceived the past. Most cultures' foundational texts, whether ancient epics or religious scriptures, highlight military conflicts, heroic deaths, and martyrdom. Herodotus's fifth-century-BCE history focused on the Greco-Persian Wars. A generation later, Thucydides' magnum opus was the Peloponnesian Wars. One of the core foundational stories of monotheism is the Exodus, involving slavery, and the pharaoh's attempt to destroy migrating Hebrews with his chariots. Christianity begins with one of the most brutal forms of execution and the Bhagavad Gita occurs on a battlefield. Violence is dramatic and creates the tension necessary to draw readers' and players' interest. If people perceive acts of violence and oppression as turning points in their history, they will naturally focus on those events. It's not surprising, therefore, that much historical scholarship has focused on violence. Some of the most popular histories written in the twentieth century focus on war, whether Barbara Tuchman's *Guns of August* (about the origins of World War I) or Winston Churchill's memoir, *The Second World War*.

Two of the most influential political ideologies of the twentieth century drew on nineteenth-century interpretations of ideas that at least appeared to focus on oppression and violence. One, communism, drew on Marx's belief that the driving force in history is the economic haves' oppression of the have-nots. As we have seen in earlier chapters Marx's dialectic has history going through a series of phases in which these have-nots violently overthrow the haves and take their place. Another ideology, fascism, drew on Darwin's theory of natural selection. Extending this principle to human society, fascists saw competition between nations as a manifestation of the supposed struggle for existence between ethnic groups. The resulting assumption that a nation must expand or die helps to explain the tendency of fascist states to launch wars of conquest against their neighbors.

As historians focused increasingly on history from the "bottom up," they emphasized ways in which institutions had oppressed people, sometimes even as they purported to preserve "liberty." Historians examined supposedly heroic episodes in their countries' pasts with greater cynicism. One of the most famous of these revisionists was Howard Zinn, whose *A People's History of the United States* was assigned in many high school and college classes and read widely outside academe. Reflecting the growing sentiment among specialists in US history, Zinn's book was nevertheless a dramatic departure from the typical glorification of America's past that appeared in most high-school textbooks. From Zinn's perspective Christopher Columbus was not the visionary navigator who "discovered" the New World, but a war criminal who began the process of European devastation of indigenous American societies. The Founding Fathers were not creators of a free society, but a wealthy elite who manipulated poorer whites in an effort to preserve power and maintain slavery. Pioneers "settling" the West were actually stealing it from Mexicans and Native Americans while they effectively perpetrated genocide. The United States fought World War II not so much against fascism as to secure its own markets and influence around the world. And the US government adopted civil rights legislation after the war in order to strengthen its influence among newly independent former European colonies in Africa and Asia. Many historians criticized the book for taking a simplistic approach to American history, framing it entirely in terms of class struggle. Ironically, Zinn also received criticism for not paying enough attention to the lives of ordinary people, focusing instead too much on violent conflict.

However, Zinn's book was important because it highlighted to the general public many issues that historians had already been raising over the previous two decades. Indeed, much of the historical profession on either side of the Atlantic was, by the mid- to late twentieth century, moving away from glorifying their countries' pasts toward frank acknowledgement of past transgressions. The process was slow and uneven, but it continues to this day. The work of historians continues to spill over into public debate, as groups who were victims of past oppression and violence demand that monuments honoring their oppressors come down.

While the United States has struggled with its history of slavery, forced removal of Native Americans, and oppression of African-Americans even after emancipation, other countries have confronted (or failed to confront) similar unpleasant truths about their pasts. Turkey officially refuses to acknowledge the massacres the Ottoman Empire perpetrated against Armenians during World War I, and Japan has been reluctant to apologize to Korea for its sexual enslavement of "comfort women" during World War II. Most recently, Poland's government passed a law making it a crime to assert that Poles were partially responsible for carrying out the Nazi Holocaust; this in the face of widespread scholarly opinion to the contrary.

Indeed, as the most widespread and murderous conflict in world history, World War II has long caused deep unease among the general population when historians have dug under the heroic rhetoric surrounding it. For decades after the war, French authorities encouraged the myth of a large-scale resistance to Nazi rule against a small minority of French citizens who collaborated. Historians have turned this equation on its head, swelling the number of collaborators and pointing out that the relatively much smaller number of resisters were mainly communists, whom the United States and Britain tried to prevent gaining power after the war ended. The German approach has been to acknowledge Nazi crimes openly, but to distinguish between Nazis and Germans. In this interpretation of the past, Nazis appear as a gang of ideological extremists who hijacked the government and forced honest, peaceful ordinary Germans to participate in their evil schemes of world domination and genocide. Once again historians overturned such convenient distinctions between good Germans and bad Germans, demonstrating the roots of Nazism in German culture (and Western society generally) and Hitler's popularity with Germans until Germany started losing the war.

Recent scholarship has also shown the ways in which the United States and Britain served as models for Nazi behavior. Hitler admired Britain's ability to rule a vast empire of supposedly inferior races, and his concept of *Lebensraum* (living space) for German settlers in Russia drew on America's Manifest Destiny, which argued that European Americans were entitled to occupy Native American lands in the West. Moreover, Nazis based the Nuremberg Laws (1934), separating out Jews from the rest of the German population and making them second-class citizens, on the legal codes of southern US states that discriminated against people of color. Most historians have been underscoring the universality of violence. In this view of the past, the Nazis are one of the most extreme examples of racist and tribalist inhumanity, but by no means the only one. Their ideology arose from prevailing racist and anti-semitic views in early twentieth-century Western societies, and Nazi atrocities merely ramped up similar behavior elsewhere. Reflecting this analysis of Nazism's place in history, Mark Mazower describes the movement's goals as "a nightmarish revelation of the destructive potential in European civilization – turning imperialism on its head and treating Europeans as Africans" (Mazower xiii).

This universality of violence can lead to pessimism. Students of history are sometimes disappointed to discover that the heroes they learned about growing up weren't so heroic after all, and the progress that they thought their recent ancestors had achieved wasn't so permanent or nobly motivated as they may have believed. Nevertheless, although some historians might dispute Martin Luther King's assertion that "the arc of the moral universe is long, but it bends toward justice,"[1] few would wish to live far in the past. Not only was disease more rampant, but violence was more common. Brutal executions, torture, beatings, slavery, censorship, and suppression of people based on religion, race, gender, and sexual orientation, have all become less acceptable than they were just a lifetime ago. In fact, psychologist Steven Pinker argues that "violence has declined over long stretches of time, and today we may be living in the most peaceable era in our species' existence" (Pinker xxi). Even the world wars and savage persecutions of Nazi and Communist regimes do not alter his assertion since, he argues, when adjusted for population the average human being was less likely to die violently in the twentieth century than in most of its predecessors. In terms of the number of people killed as a percentage of the population involved, for instance, Pinker ranks World War II as the ninth-worst conflict in history, well behind China's eighth-century An Lushan Revolt and the thirteenth-century Mongol conquests, which rank first and second, respectively.

The past, therefore, appears to have been more violent than the present, in spite of today's daily diet of depressing news focusing on murders, mass shootings, bloody wars, and impoverished refugees. The question for the remainder of this chapter is how videogames portray that violence and whether they do so consistently. The answers to these questions depend on the genre of the game, the period of history, the country of the designers, and the game's primary audience. The rest of this chapter explores the limitations of videogames across genres as they deal with various aspects of violence and oppression.

Combat and the treatment of civilians

The opening example of this chapter highlighted the lack of realism in videogames portraying combat. Apart from the obvious difference that players' lives are not actually in jeopardy, several other features of most FPSs make the experience playing them significantly different from actual combat. Media analyst Holger Pötzsch has identified four "filters predisposing players' experiences and performances" in first- or third-person shooter (F/TPS) games: violence, consequence, character, and conflict:

First, the violence and consequence filters limit the types of violence that the player witnesses or engages in and the exposure of players to the negative and inhumane consequences of their characters' actions. Most F/TPS games usually rule out death by friendly fire. For instance, if in *Call of Duty: World War II* the player shoots at a comrade, the screen freezes with the message "Friendly fire will not be tolerated," and the player must go back to the most recent save point in the game. But in reality, friendly fire is an ever-present issue in the chaos of combat. The American War Library estimates that 21 percent of American military casualties in World War II resulted from friendly fire ("Friendly Fire Notebook").

Perhaps even more important is the treatment of civilian deaths:

> If civilian deaths are presented, their fates are disconnected from player involvement and usually presented as the consequence of the opponents' actions and decision. The only violence that is enabled is strictly battle related and targeted at opposing soldiers or paramilitary forces this way excluding such documented war-related abuses as rape, the killing of children, or the unintended targeting of noncombatants with heavy weapons.
>
> *(Pötzsch 160)*

Here again *Call of Duty: World War II* is true to form. The protagonist and the American soldiers with whom he fights kill no civilians themselves. Rather, they witness the results of German atrocities, the bodies of civilians hanging from trees and the victims of a Nazi concentration camp. While Nazi atrocities are well documented and outnumbered those of the United States both in scope and intent, even the most well-intentioned American soldiers could hardly avoid killing civilians as they fought through the villages and towns of northern France and western Germany. Moreover, Allied air forces during the final years of World War II deliberately dropped incendiary bombs on populated areas of Germany in an effort to demoralize the population. Even many of their more targeted bombardments from shell guns and bombers aiming at German installations within France inevitably killed French civilians. Regarding these casualties, *Call of Duty: World War II* is silent. Finally, although American authorities prosecuted and convicted some of their soldiers for raping civilians, many cases went unpunished (Lilly). However, *Call of Duty: World War II*'s American soldiers act honorably toward the women they encounter.

Indeed, as media studies scholar Debra Ramsay points out, "In [*Call of Duty:*] *World at War*, the spaces of war are entirely devoid of civilians, and the damage of war is evident only on the environment or on the bodies of soldiers"(108). This, she grants, is partly a result of the "technological difficulties and expense" at the time of production of including non-combatant variables in the artificial intelligence (AI). Subsequent technological advances made the incorporation of these elements easier in later games. Yet, as *Call of Duty: World War II* demonstrates, the focus on the war front as an arena for combat between warriors has limited such efforts in the F/TPS genre. Ramsay suggests that this reluctance to mix home front and war front in the World War II setting arises in American videogames from the American experience of the war, in which the fighting occurred overseas and the major effects at home were industrial expansion and full employment rather than death and destruction. American popular memory often perceives the Pacific islands, for which the United States struggled in hard-fought battles against Japan, as devoid of civilians. Yet 95,000 civilians died during the American conquest of Okinawa (Dower 45). As it follows an American serviceman through the Pacific Theater, *World at War* manages to ignore these unpleasant consequences of combat. The absence of civilians is even more jarring in the ruined urban landscapes of the games' Eastern Front segments, in which the player assumes the role of a Russian soldier liberating his homeland from German occupation and going on to participate in the capture of Berlin. The Soviet Union suffered over 26 million deaths during World War II, most of them civilian. Having witnessed the devastation and murder that German occupation had visited on their own country, Soviet troops entering Germany visited upon its inhabitants what historian William Hitchcock describes as a "tidal wave of rape, beatings, wanton violence, looting, destruction, murder" (132). Reflecting the hate that German occupation engendered among Soviet troops, the playable character's mentor exhorts him to "show no mercy" and "kill them all." In the context of the game, however, these instructions apply only to German soldiers, since civilians are nowhere to be found.

So far, we have examined the short-term consequences of war that F/TPS games usually ignore. However, they pay even less attention to the long-term consequences, such as famine, disease, poverty, and the traumatization of the population. Even such an obvious effect as post-traumatic stress disorder (PTSD) rarely shows up in these games. A notable exception is the beginning scene of *Battlefield 1*, in which the African-American protagonist of the game's first single-player segment awakes in his bed at home from a nightmare of the horrors he had witnessed during World War I. Even *Battlefield 1*, however, only describes the war in terms of its combatants. The divide between home front and war front remains secure.

A contrast to the prevailing absence of consequences to civilians in F/TPS games is apparent in the survival strategy game *This War of Mine*. Developed by Warsaw-based 11 bit studios, and inspired by the siege of Sarajevo in the 1990s Bosnian War, this game puts the player in charge of twelve characters trying to survive the siege amid shortages of food, medicine, and the basic amenities of modern life – all the while threatened with death from snipers or even other civilians competing for the same resources. Although fighting does occur in the game, most of it is foraging and bartering amid the depressing background of a ruined modern city. Decisions the player makes for each character determines who lives and who dies. The consequences of war are all around the player. Of course, *This War of Mine* isn't an F/TPS game, and it's unlikely to appeal to many fans of *Call of Duty*. Nevertheless, it shows what aspects of war most F/TPS games leave out, and why. Declaring that "*This War of Mine* starts off feeling like the most depressing variation of *The Sims* ever," *Kotaku* reviewer Evan Narcisse nevertheless praises the game for its realism and unconventional perspective.

A third-person shooter that does deal with war's consequences for civilians and the protagonist, albeit in a setting contemporary to the time of its release, is Berlin-based Yager Development's *Spec Ops: The Line*. Published in 2012, this game begins with an unusual backstory. The worst series of sandstorms on record hits the city of Dubai in the United Arab Emirates. The Emirates' leaders flee, abandoning the population to the chaos of the city's collapsed infrastructure. Caught in the sandstorm is the US 33rd Infantry Battalion returning home from Afghanistan. Its commander, Colonel John Konrad, who is suffering from PTSD, volunteers the 33rd to help in relief efforts. However, after receiving orders to abandon the city, Konrad instead declares martial law. Some members of the 33rd commit atrocities while others attempt, but fail, to dislodge the deranged colonel and his rogue forces. In an attempt to control the situation, the CIA sends a black ops team, which organizes local militias to fight the renegade battalion. The result is a ceasefire guaranteeing the safety of a caravan evacuating the civilian population from Dubai. However, the caravan never shows up and the sandstorm continues to block radio signals and satellite surveillance. American intelligence does receive a broken message from Konrad indicating that the evacuation has failed and the death toll is high. US authorities decide to send in a three-man reconnaissance Delta Force to locate survivors and arrange their rescue. This is where the game begins, as the player assumes the role of team leader Captain Martin Walker, who served with Konrad in Afghanistan and greatly admired the man.

So far in the narrative it is worth observing that, although both the protagonist and antagonist in this game are American, its authors are not. The design team's location in Germany, a country that lost its last major conflict while earning a reputation for unparalleled acts of evil, probably contributed to the unusual presentation of the game's characters. At the outset, the story doesn't present a simple dichotomy of good American soldiers fighting against some evil, foreign other. The indigenous Arab inhabitants are not terrorists. Rather, they form a backdrop, and a remarkably invisible one, to a conflict between good Americans and bad ones. There is an orientalist aspect to this setting, with white men fighting each other over the fate of non-white populations. However, this awkward feature is not what makes the game stand out. Rather, it's Walker's own descent into madness as the mission continues and expands beyond one of simple reconnaissance. The initially anonymous enemies shooting at the team turn out to be rogue members of the 33rd, and as Walker's options narrow, he resorts to ever greater and more questionable acts of violence to complete the mission successfully. Players have little to no choice in these decisions and must take virtual ownership of orders whose ethical basis becomes increasingly dubious. Most disturbing is Walker's decision to order an air strike, using the chemical agent white phosphorus, on a position held by the 33rd. This strike silences the guns that threaten Walker's team. Calling in air strikes is a common device in many F/TPS games. It happens frequently in the *Call of Duty* series. However, in contrast to other F/TPS games, *Spec Ops* reveals the devastating results of the air strike as the

Delta team traverses the target area in its aftermath. Not only do they (and the player) encounter horribly burned and dying American soldiers against whom Walker had called the attack. They also witness gut-wrenching scenes of dead and dying civilians, the "collateral damage" of this decision. Particularly poignant are the disfigured corpses of a mother holding her child. Walker's reaction is to blame Konrad for creating the circumstances that forced him to call the air strike. The power of *Spec Ops* is its depiction not only of the physical consequences of war on soldiers and civilians, but also the psychological costs, which reshape the protagonist's character negatively during the course of the game.

Britain introduced white phosphorus into warfare during World War I and many countries have used it since. The United States and Britain dropped it and other incendiary bombs on German and Japanese neighborhoods during World War II and used it to support their troops in combat. Yet F/TPSs set during World War II don't focus on the human cost of using these weapons. *Call of Duty* doesn't present its players with the consequences for civilians of Allied actions. By filtering such scenes out of their games, designers of the most popular F/TPSs perpetuate the perception, commonly held in Britain and the United States, of World War II as a "good war," without complicating or questionable behavior on the part of these two countries. Whitewashing Western Allied behavior allows players to feel good, and probably boosts sales for doing so. However, it does a disservice to our understanding of the complexities of war. One can acknowledge the evils of the Axis agenda and behavior, while still recognizing excesses on the part of the Western Alliance. *Call of Duty* and similar games prefer to avoid such self-examination.

Pötzsch applies his four filters to F/TPSs, but some of them could also work with strategy games. On the one hand, these games by their very nature tend to spare the player from witnessing the immediate human consequences of war, since they don't immerse the player in a simulation of combat at the personal level. On the other hand, because many strategy games cover much longer stretches of history than their F/TPS counterparts, they sometimes explore the long-term economic and political consequences of war in ways that are difficult to do in the more limited timelines of F/TPSs. Two examples, one from ancient warfare and the other from modern, illustrate this point. Both involve the fate of cities under attack.

The ancient example comes from *Rome: Total War*.[2] Like many strategy games, *Rome* encourages abstract thinking. Soldiers and civilians alike become statistics in calculating the most efficient path to victory. For instance, upon conquering a city, players have three choices. The first is to occupy the city. In this case, the population stays in place and pays tribute to the player's faction. This works best in provinces near to the player's capital that share the same culture as the player's faction. Since the city's population and wealth remain largely intact, conquering players gain very little money in the short run from exercising this option. However, players don't need to spend much repairing the city or building up the population through migration from their home territories. The problem with this most merciful option arises when the city doesn't belong to a player's home culture, because the inhabitants of the conquered city are more likely to rebel in the future. The second choice, to enslave the inhabitants, addresses the last problem. In this case, players sell the inhabitants as slaves, dispersing the population across the empire. Doing so brings in more immediate cash, but requires more time to rebuild the city's economy. However, with most of the original inhabitants gone, there is less chance of the city rebelling. There is, of course, a greater chance of rebellion elsewhere. However, since the enslaved inhabitants disperse, it's not as great as it would be if the inhabitants remained in place. The third choice is to exterminate the population. This option yields the most cash immediately and makes the city very unlikely to rebel, since almost all the potential rebels are dead. However, it requires the greatest investment in time and money rebuilding the city and replenishing the population from the player's existing territories ("Exterminate/Enslave/Occupy?").

From a purely strategic perspective, the choice depends on how immediately a player needs cash (presumably more of it in the middle of a larger war), and the likelihood of rebellion if the population remains in place (depending on the similarity of its culture to the player's faction). Moreover, enslaving or exterminating the populations of cities increases the fear a faction instills in enemy cities they approach, making them more likely to switch sides without a fight. A track record of exterminating cities that resist accelerates this process quicker than one of only enslaving the population.

Such calculations doubtless weighed on the minds of commanders in the ancient world, and may have affected their reputations both at home and among potential enemies. A common practice in the ancient Mediterranean was to offer cities terms of surrender and occupy them peacefully if they agreed. However, if they resisted, the invading power would lay siege to them. If the city fell to the siege, the conqueror would do with the population as he wished. This often involved a period of looting, rape, and massacre, the extent of which depended upon the commander of the invading force. The conquering commander might sell surviving inhabitants into slavery, enriching himself and those under his command. If a commander wanted to set an example and sow fear among the populations of enemy cities, he might lean more heavily on the side of massacre. For instance, after successfully besieging Tyre in 332 BCE, Alexander the Great crucified all the surviving men of military age and enslaved all the women and children. *Rome: Total War* reflects these practices with a box that pops up after the player decides to exterminate the population. It declares, "Resistance is Futile," a reference to the unstoppable Borg of the rebooted 1990s *Star Trek* series. Underneath it observes: "Harsh times demand harsh measures." Above is a road lined with the condemned dying on crosses (see Image 8.1).

From an ethical perspective, however, these choices illustrate a dilemma of playing the role of a historical conquering power. Few people today would condone crucifying and enslaving one's enemies after a military victory. Yet in order to be true to history, the player of an ancient Mediterranean faction

IMAGE 8.1 *Rome: Total War*, pop-up screen resulting from decision to massacre inhabitants. Images from *Total War* videogames developed by Creative Games and published by SEGA; published with kind permission of SEGA.

should be willing to do so. This is simply the way military leaders behaved at the time. *Rome: Total War* provides the player several incentives to commit what today would be considered war crimes. One might argue that in doing so, it encourages violent thinking among players. Whether or not this is the case, presenting the choice to be brutal, with all its advantages, also encourages players to understand the attitudes of the age.

Over the last few hundred years, international agreements have increasingly condemned the type of behavior that was commonplace in the ancient world. It is no longer acceptable to rape, enslave, and massacre conquered civilian populations. Although this behavior has continued with depressing frequency, leaders rarely approve openly of their forces perpetrating such acts. Debates today usually occur over the appropriate targeting of installations supporting enemy war efforts when doing so endangers civilians working in those installations or living nearby. The term "collateral damage," used to describe destruction of property and people as a side effect of war, arose in the context of "total war" in the twentieth century. As countries industrialized, so their armed forces came to rely on the ability of these industries to supply them with modern weaponry. When armed forces shelled or bombed these cities, they often killed civilians, either because they worked in the munitions factories or because their explosives missed the mark and fell on nearby houses. The bombarding side considered these losses acceptable, as long as the targets of the explosives were installations supporting the war effort.

During a total war, however, the entire population and economy mobilizes to support the war. Among the belligerent powers during World War II, almost everything anybody did related to the war effort. This led Germany to justify the Blitz, bombing British cities, simply because they were cities. Later in the war, Britain and America adopted a similar policy against Germany, raining destruction on its cities. Similar practices continued in the proxy wars that the Soviet Union and the United States fought against one another in the developing world during the second half of the twentieth century. The main argument distinguishing this behavior from Alexander the Great's is that civilians were only the target inasmuch as they participated in the war effort. Some critics consider this a distinction without a difference.

No weapons conflate the distinction between soldier and civilian more than nuclear weapons. When the United States dropped atom bombs on Hiroshima and Nagasaki, they wiped out the centers of those cities, each in a single explosion. Although both cities were arguably military targets, America's leaders knew well that the vast majority of dead from these attacks would be civilians. What they did not fully appreciate before the attacks was the environmental damage that nuclear weapons would create, poisoning the water and the soil, and killing survivors through cancer years after the war had ended. So terrifying is the destructive power of nuclear weapons that they have never been used in combat since.

Like its predecessors, *Civilization VI* attempts to simulate the effects as well as the strategic considerations relating to nuclear war. Once a faction has researched enough technology late in the game and acquired access to uranium, it is possible to build nuclear bombs. There are two types: "nuclear devices" (fission bombs, such as those dropped on Japan) and "thermonuclear devices" (fusion-fission bombs, which formed the arsenal of the superpowers for most of the Cold War and continue to do so today). Nuclear devices have a blast radius of one hex, and thermonuclear devices of two (see Image 8.2). Depending on other advances, either planes or missiles can deliver these weapons to their targets. Detonating a nuclear weapon destroys all citizens and units (whether working or military) occupying any hexes within the blast radius. It has the effect of pillaging any buildings in the radius too. It also reduces the city's defenses and health level to zero. Moreover, the entire blast area remains contaminated for ten turns for nuclear and twenty turns for thermonuclear devices. During this period, no production can occur in any affected tile, and any unit ending its turn there suffers fifty damage points per turn. However, it's possible to clean the contamination sooner with a builder or military engineer. These are the physical effects. They bring pros and cons to weigh against one another when using nuclear weapons. On the one hand, players can easily conquer an enemy city in the wake of a nuclear attack, if they have deployed forces nearby. On the other hand, doing so is risky for any units ending their turns in a contaminated hex ("Nuclear Weapons (Civ6)").

The public relations consequences of using nuclear weapons, however, are almost entirely negative. In the *Rise and Fall* expansion for *Civilization VI*, using nuclear weapons first in a war is likely to trigger a coalition of non-allied powers against the user. Furthermore, using nuclear weapons greatly increases

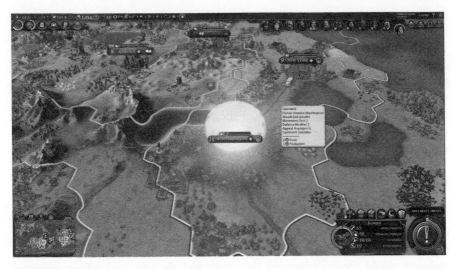

IMAGE 8.2 *Sid Meier's Civilization VI*, nuclear attack. Licensed Asset Courtesy of Firaxis Games, Inc. and 2K Games, Inc.

war weariness among the user's population, leading to decreased productivity and possible rebellion. This feature assumes that a faction's inhabitants are less likely to regard their war as just if their leaders use nuclear weapons. On the other hand, certain social policies and the fascist form of government can mitigate these effects. *Civilization VI* therefore provides obvious military incentives, but serious diplomatic and domestic disincentives to launching a nuclear war. Indeed, *Civilization VI* recognizes diminishing tolerance of wars of aggression among different historical eras. There is no penalty for declaring war on one's enemy in the Ancient Era. However, as one progresses through the Classical, Medieval, and Renaissance eras and beyond, the diplomatic consequences of declaring war without a good reason (*casus belli*) become so great that to do so late in the game is likely to bring the rest of the world into the war on the side of one's enemy. The *Total War* series also imposes severe penalties for going to war without a *casus belli* in games set during the Middle Ages and after. Both design teams therefore recognize changing attitudes toward war during the course of history and attempt to simulate its growing constraints on gameplay.

Slavery and genocide

Serious Games Interactive is a Danish Company dedicated to developing videogames that allow "students to interact and engage with educational content leading to more motivated students that learn more." Its series *Playing History* targets primary school children to "gain the opportunity to take part in history, within a living breathing world," to enable them "to learn about historic events that they cannot alter – instead, they witness how the historic events altered history as a whole" (*Children & Young*). So far, the series visits three settings: the Black Death, the slave trade, and the Vikings. The games contain aids that teachers can use to discuss the settings in coordination with students playing them. The entire series is in cartoon format with characters depicted with exaggerated features – particularly large heads and eyes – as is common in cartoons. The contexts, however, are serious, involving oppression, violence, and death.

This attempt to combine a childlike artistic format with such serious content contributed to controversy in 2015 over the series' second title *The Slave Trade*. The game centers on Tim, an enslaved African boy serving the captain of a slave ship. The game involves steering the ship on its mission to the west coast of Africa, loading slaves on the ship, then navigating the middle passage to the Americas. The game also involves the player, through Tim, helping the captain bargain down the price of enslaved children. The slave-loading scene involves stacking slaves on board a ship in a manner reminiscent of the game *Tetris*. (Visit www.pcgamer.com/slave-tetris-cut-from-playing-history-2slave-trade-after-backlashfor a screenshot.) Then follows a scene in the hold during the middle passage, in which slaves discuss what will happen to them. The view is from above and the player can clearly see their feces littering the floorboards below. One of the slaves expresses optimism that they are heading to a better life. Another fears they will be eaten. As the game progresses the slaves describe their suffering, from scurvy, confinement, and beatings. At one point, the captain has the twenty-five sickest slaves thrown overboard, albeit off-screen. When Tim and his sister reach the Caribbean, they, along with several other Africans, manage to escape, albeit an ocean away from home.

A side feature of the game is the many anachronistic items that Tim can locate (for extra points) through his "chrono goggles," bulky green goggles that he usually wears across his forehead. When he puts them over his eyes he sees items that don't belong in the eighteenth century. One of these, visible near the game's end, is a white Ku Klux Klan hood. Highlighting the hood causes a screen to pop up briefly, explaining the Klan's role in oppressing African-Americans after emancipation and warning the player to avoid the hoods. This launches a PacMan-like mini-game in which the head of Dabo, a fellow captive, chases around the screen bumping into hoods, eliminating them.

Critics accused the game of being insensitive and even racist. High-school physics teacher Frank Nosches tweeted: "the whole concept of making it a game – it trivializes the atrocity of slavery. There are some topics that are just off limits" (*CEO Chalks Up Outrage*). Writing for *Gamasutra*, sociologist Katherine Cross argued that slavery could be the topic of a game, but not the way that *Playing History* presents it. One possibility she suggests for dealing with such topics is through dissonance. Her article didn't mention it, but a potential example of dissonance exists in *Bioshock Infinite*'s supposed utopia of Columbia, which in fact masks a racist eugenicist society. The clash between the bright exterior and the grim underlying reality serves quite consciously to highlight the latter. Cross argues, however, that *Playing History* is not dissonant, but incoherent:

> It mixed a serious topic with a sunny atmosphere and gamey elements that trivialized that topic rather than illuminated it. The Tetris minigame, further, has the stunning side effect of rendering the player complicit in creating one of the signature atrocities of the slave trade: heinously over-crowded ships. All as a smiling sea dragon looks on.
>
> *(Cross)*

Serious Games CEO Simon Egenlfeldt-Nielsen rebutted these arguments with a few points that deserve examination. First, he pointed out that those claiming that slavery is too sensitive a topic for videogames might as well argue the same for using it as the subject of books and films. There is some truth to this, but Egenfeldt-Nielsen ignores games' participatory nature. In *Playing History*, the player stacks the virtual slaves, rather than simply watching it occur on screen. To charges that the slave *Tetris* sequence was insensitive, Egenfeldt-Nielsen eventually edited the half-minute mini-game out of the game. However, he did so under duress, arguing:

> I definitely agree it is insensitive and gruesome. It has to be like this to show what was done to load slave ships. People treated human beings as pieces that just had to fitting [*sic*] into the cargo. The reactions people have to this game is something they will never forget, and they will remember just how inhumane [the] slave trade was.
>
> *(Egenfeldt-Nielsen)*

It's true that slave traders stacked people in ships in a manner remarkably similar to the process in *Tetris*. However, this argument speaks to a deeper concern: does playing as unethical actors cause players to empathize with their characters and acquire the same unethical attitudes themselves? Although numerous studies have investigated whether taking on the role of a violent character in videogames leads to violence in players, the results have been contradictory and inconclusive. Just as stage and film actors can play evil characters, so presumably can gamers. Finally, noting that most of the criticism came from the United States, Egenfeldt-Nielsen attributed the uproar to differences between Americans and Europeans in their tolerance of unpleasant subjects. He may be onto something here, but not in the way that he framed it. For as this section argues, there are taboos on both sides of the Atlantic regarding what historical atrocities are permissible for videogames to portray. However, the taboos differ, reflecting the divergent histories and social contexts of the societies in which the games are developed.

The controversy over *Playing History 2: Slave Trade* highlights the public relations dilemmas that developers face when they try to create games covering historical periods characterized by massive violence, particularly when it was targeted against specific ethnic groups. On the one hand, to cover the period while ignoring the atrocities risks whitewashing the past, the suffering of the victims, and the effects that past oppression has today. On the other hand, any attempt to include past atrocities runs the risk of perpetuating the dehumanization of oppressed ethnic groups by enabling a player to oppress them again virtually. Two of the most sensitive historical episodes to haunt modern societies are the early modern Atlantic slave trade and the Nazi Holocaust. However, both episodes form part of practices going much further back in time, of slavery on the one hand and genocide on the other. The remainder of this section examines videogames' treatments of slavery and genocide – particularly how they differ depending on the game's historical setting, intended audience, and development team.

As the previous section demonstrates, videogames don't shy away from slavery and massacre in the ancient world. Similar choices to those in *Rome: Total War* are also available in *Medieval II: Total War* and *Total War: Rome II*. Other strategy games dealing with the ancient world also incorporate slavery. In the *Hegemony* series, whose titles focus on ancient Greece and Rome, captured soldiers' uniforms morph into slaves' loincloths onscreen, after which the players can either deploy the former warriors to work or execute them if they present a strategic liability. However, two aspects of classical Mediterranean slavery distinguish it from early modern Atlantic slavery. First, race was not an issue. As Philip of Macedon conquers Greece in *Hegemony Gold: Philip of Macedon*, the slaves he acquires are Greek and look no different from their conquerors. Even in the Roman Empire, which encompassed much ethnic diversity, no physical feature, such as skin color, distinguished slave populations from free ones. Second, ancient slavery occurred so long ago that no one alive today can be certain whether or not they are descended from slaves of ancient times.

The situation regarding the enslavement of Africans to serve in the Americas is dramatically different. First, because Africans constituted the overwhelming majority of slaves in the Americas and Europeans the overwhelming majority of free people, the former's status was as a slave race, recognizable instantly by their physical features. Second, because this system of slavery ended less than 200 years ago, it continues to have a profound effect on modern societies. The emancipation of African slaves did not mean that Europeans were willing to treat them as equals. Slavery had left American descendants of Africans penniless and powerless, and many American descendants of Europeans attempted to keep them that way through discriminatory laws and practices. Meanwhile European countries occupied Africa, exploiting its resources, distorting its societies, and relegating its people to second-class citizenship in their homelands. White and black populations in the Americas, Europe, and Africa continue to have dramatically different interpretations of why white people continue on average to hold greater wealth and power than black people. White Europeans and white Americans have the luxury of viewing their histories as a succession of struggles and accomplishments of white people with little reference to the role that the oppression of people of color played in achieving these goals. By contrast, people of color are much more likely to be conscious of past oppression and aware of its continuance today. In other words, the history of African enslavement in the Americas is not just about history. It's also about current politics and society.

For similar reasons, genocide becomes more problematic to portray in games the more recently it occurred. In the United States and Australia, white settlers, aided by diseases, annihilated whole ethnic groups among the original inhabitants. For instance, British settlers in Tasmania adopted a policy of shooting native Tasmanians on sight. The last Tasmanian died in 1877. The success of English-speaking settlers at subduing or eliminating the original inhabitants of the lands they occupied inspired European fascists in the early twentieth century to do likewise, ultimately leading to the systematic slaughter of Jews, Romani, and various other unwanted ethnic groups.

The closer one gets to the present, the more sensitive slavery and genocide become. Therefore, game designers have trodden carefully around the issue. Individual design teams have sometimes been inconsistent in their willingness to allow players to perpetrate virtually the type of atrocities and oppression that occurred during the periods their games portray. A much-criticized example is *Sid Meier's Colonization* (1994) and its successor *Sid Meier's Civilization IV: Colonization* (2008). These standalone strategy spinoffs from the *Civilization* series give players the option of playing Dutch, English, French, or Spanish colonists settling the New World. Their task is to establish settlements and build up their economies and militia to the point at which they can declare independence from their motherland and successfully repel an attempt to subdue their rebellion. The size and weaponry of the militia depend on the economic base supporting it. Players can build up their economies by trading with Indian villages or destroying them, and encouraging European immigrants to farm plantations around the settlement and serve as artisans within it. Native Americans can also assimilate into European settlements. However, the game doesn't allow players to play an Indian faction, and Indian villages are incapable of growing into productive settlements on their own (see Image 8.3).

While *Colonization* is content with treating interactions with indigenous Americans exclusively from a white-settler perspective, its treatment of slavery is nothing short of bizarre. Simply put, in this game, which focuses on the development of the colonial New World economy, slavery doesn't exist. *Colonization* portrays an Atlantic economy better described as a golden line than a Golden Triangle, and it develops plantations without slaves. *Empire: Total War* displays a similar contrast between its treatment of indigenous Americans and enslaved Africans. Colonizing the Caribbean or North America requires defeating the native population. Yet the game abstracts the slave trade, never mentioning it by name. The game depicts it instead by encouraging players to send ships to

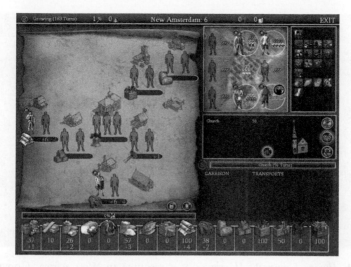

IMAGE 8.3 *Sid Meier's Civilization IV: Colonization*, settlement. Licensed Asset Courtesy of Firaxis Games, Inc. and 2K Games, Inc.

African ports. Once established there, gold coins rise from these ships indicating revenue – from what, the game never explains.

By contrast, the *Europa Universalis* series has always acknowledged the presence of both genocide and slavery in its depiction of the early modern world. The game rates targets for colonization according to the size and "aggressiveness" of their native populations, and in order to establish a settlement, colonizing powers must often deploy armies to reduce their numbers. The slaughter is not always total, but subsequent conversion of the population and its assimilation into the conquering faction's "core" culture indicate the destruction of the indigenous culture. *Europa Universalis* depicts slaves as a resource for production and trade, just as it does coffee or cotton. Playable factions establishing colonies in Africa will see shackles, or Africans in shackles depending on the edition, who represent the major export commodity of the region (see Image 8.4). Where playable African kingdoms exist, other factions can trade with them for slaves. *Europa Universalis*, therefore, shows slaves the way that state actors of the day saw them, as commodities rather than people. It frankly acknowledges the ethnic specificity of the slave population by only having slaves as a commodity for development and export from African locations.

What among the developers of *Colonization* and *Empire: Total War* might account for the greater reluctance to depict the enslavement of Africans than the slaughter of indigenous inhabitants? And why does the development team for *Europa Universalis* not display a similar inconsistency in how it allows players to interact with these two large and diverse populations? Developers aren't keen to discuss these issues, but social context suggests some answers. *Civilization*

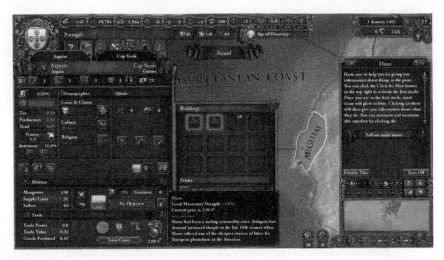

IMAGE 8.4 *Europa Universalis IV*, slaves as a resource in West Africa. Copyright © 2019 Paradox Interactive AB. www.paradoxplaza.com.

developer Firaxis is based in the United States and founded by Americans. Historians have long criticized the *Civilization* series for adhering to a triumphalist approach to history that emanates from the white American experience. Particularly as it applies to the United States, this narrative is heroic, involving settlement of a wild and hostile frontier; teleological, involving struggle for liberation from the motherland; and triumphant, involving the march toward ever greater freedom. If the designers had included a system in which players bought Africans and forced them to work on plantations with no hope of liberation, and if they had concluded the game with a war of independence that didn't free these slaves from their bondage, these features would have fit awkwardly with this dominant national narrative. Moreover, African-Americans, who currently constitute just over 12 percent of the United States' population, would likely have found a game that has the player buying enslaved Africans and forcing them to work on plantations racially offensive, as many did regarding the "slave *Tetris*" mini-game discussed above. It was probably in anticipation of these potential problems that *Colonization*'s developers decided to ignore slavery altogether. As one of the major slave-trading countries of the seventeenth and eighteenth centuries, Britain was originally responsible for the presence of enslaved Africans in what became the United States. Moreover, Britain has a significant minority community descended from enslaved Africans who worked plantations in the West Indies. Finally, the United States is a major market for Creative Assembly's games. Similar concerns, therefore, apply. By contrast, Paradox's home country, Sweden, had far less involvement in colonization or the slave trade. It also has a far smaller percentage of its population descended from enslaved Africans.

Although the United States and Britain form important markets for Paradox games, so does the European mainland, where the legacy of slavery is less pronounced. Even the African population in France originates more from direct migration from Africa than it does from French West Indian plantations.

Of course, one might argue that Paradox simply takes a franker and more accurate approach to the past than does Firaxis or Creative Assembly. Its games certainly pay greater attention to detail from the past than do those of the other two development teams. However, even Paradox draws the line at one set of atrocities: the Nazi Holocaust. The *Hearts of Iron* games simply ignore it. To be sure, Paradox has good reason for omitting history's most infamous genocide from its games. Many of its target markets in Continental Europe tightly regulate depictions of Nazi symbols and the Holocaust in order to prevent the resurgence of Nazi ideology. For instance, Germany forbids the display of the swastika for political purposes, although it allows its use in artistic works depicting the Nazi era. The problem for the videogame industry has been persuading German courts that their products constitute art. German law governing the display of Nazi symbols in videogames was, until 2018, based on a 1998 ruling of the Frankfurt High District Court regarding *Wolfenstein 3D*. This version of the *Wolfenstein* series, like all others, portrayed Nazis as the enemy, and even had the player kill Adolf Hitler. However, because the game featured many Nazi symbols, a lower court convicted the distributor of violating the law. The defendant appealed the decision, arguing that *Wolfenstein 3D* was art condemning Nazism. In upholding the lower court's decision the Frankfurt High District Court assumed that the videogame's primary audience was "children and adolescents," who, through habitual exposure to Nazi symbols, would become "used to them," making "them more vulnerable for ideological manipulation by national socialist ideas" (quoted in translation in Schwiddessen).

The ramifications of the 1998 decision have extended not only to consumers in Germany, but also to those in the rest of the world. In order to avoid major costs in reconfiguring their games for the German market, most companies simply distribute censored versions to all their customers no matter what their country's laws regarding Nazi symbols. For instance, *Call of Duty: World War II* has crosses, rather than swastikas, in white circles on red banners, even for the version distributed in the United States.

Even when they omit the swastika, however, some companies produce special versions of their games for Germany with much more extensive edits. *Wolfenstein II: The New Colossus* occurs in a dystopian world in which the Nazis won World War II. The German version changes Hitler to "Heiler" (which, awkwardly, means "healer"), and "Mein Führer" to "mein Kanzler" ("my chancellor," the constitutional office to which Hitler originally rose through the democratic process). More controversially, it omits any mention of Jews or the Holocaust. Whereas the game's global release has Nazis sending Jews to die in labor camps, its German version has "traitors" "dying in captivity." So careful were *Wolfenstein II*'s producers to avoid crossing German laws designed to prevent the fetishizing of Nazi symbols and leaders, they opened themselves to charges of whitewashing Germany's past. German newsmagazine *Der Spiegel* commentator argued that the game creates a "revisionist history, in which the historical crimes of National Socialism are hidden and their deeds marginalized" (Schott, my translation). The German board (created since the Frankfurt ruling) in charge of age-rating games heard such criticisms. In August 2018 it decided to allow Nazi symbols and historical figures when included for historical context.

In such a legal and social climate, it is hardly surprising that Paradox Interactive has avoided Nazi symbols for its global distribution and changes the identities of Germany's World War II leaders in its German version. If the makers of *Wolfenstein*, an action series in which the Nazis are always the enemy, elide the Holocaust, then Paradox will certainly do the same for *Hearts of Iron*, a strategy series in which one can play as Germany. So determined is Paradox Interactive to avoid the slightest risk of allowing its games to indulge Nazi sympathizers or serve as a simulator of genocide and other atrocities, that it forbids any posting on its discussion board regarding the omission of these features from the game. Nevertheless, for gamers located outside Central Europe, choosing to play the German faction involves playing as the Nazis, with their infamous leaders – even though the swastika isn't present (see Image 8.5).

The omission of Nazi symbols and atrocities more generally from games set in World War II raises ethical issues about how games should portray violence in the past. By not mentioning the Holocaust, videogame producers no doubt make their games less enticing to gamers eager to play out sadistic and racist fantasies. However, in doing so, developers also invite criticism that they are sanitizing the

IMAGE 8.5 *Hearts of Iron IV*, German Reich government screen. Copyright © 2019 Paradox Interactive AB. www.paradoxplaza.com.

past. A major concern when playing Germany in any grand strategy game covering the entire war is the decision to invade the Soviet Union. If the early game proceeds roughly in keeping with the past, then the German player will easily subdue the Low Countries and France. Britain will be more difficult. So the question is, why attack the Soviet Union before either conquering Britain or forcing it to make peace? From a strategic point of view, attacking Russia at all appears foolhardy, and all the more so with an undefeated Britain at Germany's rear. In order to persuade gamers playing Germany to do so, designers have to make the control of certain Soviet cities a requirement for victory. However, such rules only mask the real reason that Germany attacked the Soviet Union: Nazi racial ideology. Hitler regarded Russians as racially inferior to Germans, and their land as a legitimate target for German settlement. This belief and goal drove most of his other military actions. Similarly, even as they were losing the war, Nazi leaders diverted scarce resources to wipe out Jewish and Romani civilians, because they believed that their extermination would help to racially purify Europe. History courses that cover World War II almost always discuss these motives, yet strategy games generally avoid them. Obviously, there are strong legal, social, and business reasons to do so, but that doesn't necessarily result in a better representation of the past.

A game that involved the construction of gulags (as the Soviet player), con-centration and death camps (as the German player), or terror bombing (as either the German, British, or American players) would require some sort of measure-ment of ethical behavior to balance off against the rage that often accompanies war. While games set in World War II tend to avoid these moral dilemmas, some games in more dystopian settings have made ethics a central theme. One of the most acclaimed examples of this genre is the *Bioshock* series, which draws heavily on historical social themes in its fantastic dystopian settings. The series' first title, *Bioshock*, draws on many twentieth-century themes, from its art-deco backdrop to the combination of religious fanaticism with mechanization. Most memorable, however, are the moral choices. In its horrifying underwater setting, slugs containing superpower-endowing genetic material inhabit the bodies of young girls, called "Little Sisters." The game creates a situation in which the player may decide to "harvest" the slugs from the Little Sisters in order to gain extra powers. Doing so kills the child. It also alters the game's ending. If the player has the protagonist, Jack, refrain from killing children, then he adopts five of them and they grow up to care for him near the end of his life. If, on the other hand, Jack kills more than one of the Little Sisters, in order to harvest their enhanced DNA, he ends up becoming corrupt and power-hungry, and a danger to the rest of the world. While the game does not strictly pronounce whether the player has won or not, it makes clear its approval of the former outcome and its disapproval of the latter.

Less fantastic, but also addressing the ethics of state power, is *Papers Please* (2013). This game has the player control an immigration officer for the fictional country of Arstotska at the border crossing with its neighbor and recent enemy, Kolechia. The setting is in 1982, drawing inspiration from bureaucratic corruption in Eastern European communist regimes. The protagonist receives a demanding and constantly changing set of directives from the government, which expects him to comply or receive increasing fines for his incompetence. At the same time, however, he must pay for his family's basic needs from an inadequate salary. As he does so, he must decide whether to break the law by letting through unauthorized entrants either out of compassion (for instance, reuniting a family) or in return for bribes. The game has twenty possible endings including the death of the officer's family due to illness brought on by a poor diet, and numerous scenarios in which he is arrested for breaking the law by showing compassion or allowing "terrorists" to enter the country. In one case, he is executed. Only three endings are unambiguously happy for the protagonist ("Endings"). Critics have praised this game for its realistic portrayal of the pressures facing low-level employees of a police state, while showing the powerful incentives against behaving ethically in such situations. While *Papers Please* does not deal with the Holocaust, it evokes the bureaucratic aspects of mechanized oppression.

Although neither *Bioshock* nor *Papers Please* seeks to simulate the actual past, both games demonstrate the possibilities of confronting the player with ethical choices in historical settings. In both cases, these games' designers set out to address moral issues. However, they avoid identifying players with historical individuals or countries that have committed crimes against humanity. They therefore dodge the dilemma of either failing to mention historical atrocities or inadvertently creating "genocide simulators," possibly in violation of some countries' laws. It's hardly surprising that developers of games with actual rather than metaphorical historical settings are more reluctant to portray the brutality of the past. Particularly when the ethnic groups targeted for persecution are still around, as is the case with early modern American slavery or the genocides of World War II, developers must be careful to avoid trivializing or celebrating these crimes on the one hand, while not ignoring them on the other. Either practice fails to recognize the importance of crimes against humanity in shaping society both then and now.

Conclusion

Although critics of videogames often claim they are violent, many historical videogames refrain from depicting the level of violence that occurred in the past. Many reasons account for this restraint, but a few stand out. One is playability. Players rarely enjoy losing a game, and are unlikely to buy a game in which fighting is actually as difficult and unforgiving as it is in reality. Another reason is to allow the player to act as a consistent hero, not killing comrades through friendly fire or civilians as collateral damage – and certainly not perpetrating war crimes. Finally, videogame developers must be careful when they give players the option of playing factions (rarely do they do so for individuals) that perpetrated atrocities. This is most obvious in the case of fascism, whose symbols some countries censor. But it also applies to almost all major powers in history. Whether it was Romans conquering the Mediterranean, Europeans promoting the slave trade, or American settlers annihilating and removing the indigenous inhabitants of the United States, major powers have almost always engaged in activities that modern historians regard as morally reprehensible. The dilemma in all these cases, whether simulating combat in an action game or atrocities and oppression in a strategy game, is how much to compromise the violence of the past for the sake of playability or the social expectations and legal requirements of the target market. The reason these issues remain dilemmas is because they lack easy answers. When evaluating the historical accuracy of games as they pertain to violence, it's therefore important to consider motive. If developers omit collateral damage or past atrocities in order to glorify warfare or the past then it's fair enough to criticize the effort. If, on the other hand, developers omit certain symbols or atrocities because they fear that their inclusion may encourage people to glorify them once again, then the decision is more understandable. Nevertheless, no matter how understandable the reasons for omitting or diminishing the portrayal of historical violence, doing so compromises the presentation of the past. It may sometimes be necessary, but players should be aware that it's occurring.

Notes

1 King made this remark on several occasions. It's a paraphrase of the nineteenth-century American Transcendentalist and Unitarian abolitionist Theodore Parker.
2 I discuss *Rome: Total War* (2004) rather than *Total War: Rome II* (2013) because the latter's choices are more complex – and nuanced – but more difficult to explain. The earlier game presents the choices more starkly.

Works cited

Battlefield (game series), EA DICE, 2002–18.
Battlefield 1, EA DICE, 2016.
Bioshock, 2K Boston/2K Australia, 2007.
Bioshock (game series), Irrational Games/2K, 2007–13.
Call of Duty (game series), Infinity Ward/Sledgehammer Games/Treyarch, 2003–18.
Call of Duty: Modern Warfare 2, Infinity Ward, 2009.
Call of Duty: World at War, Treyarch, 2008.
Call of Duty: World War II, Sledgehammer Games, 2017.
CEO Chalks Up Outrage Over 'Slave Tetris' To Cultural Differences Between Europe And The U.S. https://thinkprogress.org/ceo-chalks-up-outrage-over-slave-tetris-to-cultural-differences-between-europe-and-the-u-s-9239652ebdfb/.
Children & Young – Serious Games Interactive. www.seriousgames.net/home/playful-learning/.
Churchill, Winston, *The Second World War*, 6 vols. Houghon Mifflin, 1948–53.
Cross, Katherine, "Opinion: What Can We Learn from That Tone-Deaf 'Slave Tetris' Minigame?" *Gamasutra: The Art and Business of Making Games*, 4 September 2015, /view/news/253003/Opinion_What_can_we_learn_from_that_tonedeaf_Slave_Tetris_minigame.php.
Dower, John W., *War Without Mercy: Race and Power in the Pacific War.* Pantheon, 1987.

Egenfeldt-Nielsen, Simon, "The Rationale Behind the Game Slave Trade: Playing History 2 – Slave Trade General Discussions." *Steam Community*, https://steamcommunity.com/app/386870/discussions/0/520518053448210719/?ctp=2.

Empire: Total War, Creative Assembly, 2009.

"Endings." *Papers Please Wiki*, http://papersplease.wikia.com/wiki/Endings.

Europa Universalis (game series), Paradox Development Studio, 2000–18.

"Exterminate/Enslave/Occupy New Conquered Cities?" *Total War Forums*, https://forums.totalwar.com/discussion/144152/exterminate-enslave-occupy-new-conquered-cities.

"Friendly Fire Notebook." *American War Library*, www.americanwarlibrary.com/ff/ff.htm.

Hearts of Iron (game series), Paradox Development Studio, 2002–18.

Hegemony: Philip of Macedon, Longbow Games, 2010.

Hitchcock, William I., *The Bitter Road to Freedom: A New History of the Liberation of Europe*, 1st Free Press hardcover edn. Free Press, 2008.

Lilly, J. Robert, *Taken by Force: Rape and American GIs in Europe during World War II*. Palgrave Macmillan, 2007.

Mazower, Mark, *Dark Continent: Europe's Twentieth Century*. Vintage Books, 2000.

Medal of Honor (game series), Dreamworks et al., 1999–2012.

Medieval II: Total War, Creative Assembly, 2006.

Mir, Rebecca and Owens, Trevor, "Modeling Indigenous Peoples: Unoacking Ideology in *Sid Meier's Colonization*." *Playing with the Past: Digital Games and the Simulation of History*, ed. Matthew Kapell and Andrew B. R. Elliott. Bloomsbury, 2013.

"Nuclear Weapons (Civ6)." *Civilization Wiki*, http://civilization.wikia.com/wiki/Nuclear_weapons_(Civ6).

"Ultra-Realistic Modern Warfare Game Features Awaiting Orders, Repairing Trucks." *The Onion*, www.theonion.com/ultra-realistic-modern-warfare-game-features-awaiting-o-1819594864.

Papers Please, 3909 LLC, 2013.

Pinker, Steven, *The Better Angels of Our Nature: Why Violence Has Declined*. Penguin Books, 2011.

Playing History 2 – Slave Trade, Serious Games Interactive, 2013.

Pötzsch, Holger, "Selective Realism: Filtering Experiences of War and Violence in First- and Third-Person Shooters." *Games and Culture*, vol. 12, no. 2 (March 2017), 156–78.

Ramsay, Debra, "Brutal Games: Call of Duty and the Cultural Narrative of World War II." *Cinema Journal*, vol. 54, no. 2 (Winter 2015), 94–113.

Rome: Total War, Creative Assembly, 2004.

Schott, Dominik, "Fall 'Wolfenstein II': Warum Spielehersteller Auf Nazi-Symbole Verzichten." *Spiegel Online*, 10 November 2017. www.spiegel.de/netzwelt/games/wolfenstein-ii-und-das-nazi-thema-es-muss-sich-nur-einer-trauen-a-1177427.html.

Schwiddessen, Baker and Sebastian, McKenzie, *German Attorney General: Video Game with Swastika Does Not Violate the Law; Constitutes Art | Lexology*. www.lexology.com/library/detail.aspx?g=dd44ce45-d5cf-4189-a1b6-7bcc7e31605f.

Sid Meier's Civilization IV: Colonization, Firaxis Games, 2008.

Sid Meier's Civilization VI: Rise and Fall, Firaxis Games, 2018.

Sniper Elite (game series), Rebellion Developments, 2005–17.

Spec Ops: The Line, Yager Development, 2012.

This War of Mine, 11 Bit Studios, 2014.

Total War (game series), Creative Assembly, 2000–18.

Total War: Rome 2, Creative Assembly, 2013.

Tuchman, Barbara W., *The Guns of August*. Macmillan, 1962.

Wolfenstein (game series), Muse Software et al., 1981–2017.

Wolfenstein 3D, id Software, 1992.

Wolfenstein II: The New Colossus, Machine Games, 2017.

Zinn, Howard, *A People's History of the United States*. Harper Perennial Modern Classics, 2005.

CONCLUSION

The future of the virtual past

All history is edited. It's an interpretation of the past. What distinguishes different forms of history from one another are the criteria that they use to determine what to include, what to exclude, and how to interpret. For professional historians, the historical method emphasizes an awareness of the origins of and motivations behind written and archaeological sources. It requires the author to back up assertions with evidence. By contrast, videogame developers must take into account playability and entertainment. These distinct approaches to portraying the past shape videogames in ways that are fundamentally different from historical scholarship. Game developers must work within the constraints of their medium, which requires a mathematical calculation for every decision. They must make their products fun, even if this requires knowingly distorting the past. They must also consider how to present serious issues from the past without trivializing them.

As videogames have become one of the most popular forms of entertainment, they have also become objects of criticism. This development is hardly surprising. All forms of entertainment in historical settings have come under criticism for the accuracy of their content. Many of the details that videogames get wrong result from necessary conflations of time and space in order to make games playable. These compromises with the past are similar to those made in the film industry. While it's important to note these departures from the historical record, an insistence on absolute adherence to the reality of the past would render videogames incapable of portraying it at all. This would be a shame, since it would deprive us of the unique opportunities that videogames provide us to examine the past.

These opportunities are significant and come in two major forms. One is immersion. Action and simulation games can create the partial illusion of actually being in a historical setting. The more open-world they are, the more they allow players to explore the past almost as if they were there. The current level of immersion will certainly intensify with the introduction of ever more sophisticated technology. Virtual reality glasses are in their infancy, but they show great promise. Virtual smells are under development too. Moreover, some medical technologies, such as the sense of touch in prosthetics, could eventually work in simulations as well. (Presumably, such innovations would not involve accurate simulations of shot and stab wounds!) The time may not be far off when we can surround ourselves with interactive sights, sounds, smells, and even touch from the virtual past.

The other opportunity almost unique to videogames is experimentation. Unlike novels, films, and scholarly books, videogames allow players to explore what might have occurred if circumstances had been different. Although the actual past occurred only once, and resulted from far too complex a set of contingent circumstances to be duplicated in reality, videogames can let us approximate a recreation of the past, tweaking different contingencies to appreciate how much they affected the actual outcome. Strategy games are particularly good at doing this, and the fun associated with them encourages players to become deeply engaged in issues of cause and effect that form the basis of the history discipline. Technology is not so much the obstacle to greater nuance and accuracy in these recreations as is the limits of players' abilities to manage too complex a set of variables.

If videogames are becoming technologically more sophisticated in their portrayal of the past, so they are also becoming more nuanced in their application of the scholarship behind that portrayal. Even if game designers have no formal training in history themselves, many have shown willingness to listen to those who have, in some cases hiring professional historians as advisors for their projects. Moreover, the growing ethnic and gender diversity of design teams has promoted a better appreciation of what they are leaving out. Also important has been constructive criticism from fans, many of whom have shown remarkable insight into ways that games can better simulate the past.

The result has been a marked improvement in the simulation of historical processes and the inclusion of poorly represented groups from the past in a number of major game series. Women, people of color, and people of varied sexual orientations have appeared with greater frequency in action games. For instance the *Assassin's Creed* series has gone from having women as a mere backdrop in the original game (2007) to enabling players to play as a female character throughout *Assassin's Creed: Odyssey* (2018). *Odyssey* also permits players to be involved in same-sex relationships. Regarding religion, one of the most sensitive yet integral aspects of past societies, the *Sid Meier's Civilization* series has gone from almost ignoring it in its first three releases to encouraging players to design their own belief systems in versions *V* and *VI*. Similarly, the *Europa Universalis* series has gained greater nuance regarding differences in productivity and innovation among early modern societies. Most notably, it has dropped its system of handicapping technological advancement according to supposed essential features of major cultural groups in favor of allowing players to shape their societies through responses to contingent events. In portraying environmental forces, *Crusader Kings II* has made the progress of plague more obvious in its *Reaper's Due* DLC expansion, and *Total War: Attila* models climate change in the late Roman Empire. All these developments show that game designers are applying a broader set of historical considerations to their creations than simply high politics and warfare. In this sense, their shift has reflected what occurred in the last century among professional historians.

Nevertheless, there remains plenty of scope for further improvement and innovation. All strategy games dealing with any period before the mid-twentieth century should model epidemics. All games covering long stretches of time (several centuries) should incorporate climate fluctuations. And game designers have only just begun to address issues of gender and ethnic diversity. Moreover, some aspects of history remain unexplored. Although *Anno 1404* models crop transfers, games focusing on European expansion have yet to convincingly depict the Columbian Exchange. Finally, there are aspects of history whose sensitivity have led to almost comical errors at one extreme or the other. Slavery was an integral part of the early modern world economy. Developers of games set during this period can't simply ignore it, as did *Civilization IV: Colonization*. However, they must be careful not to create awkward dissonances that appear to trivialize it, as occurred with *Playing History 2 – The Slave Trade*. It remains to be seen what effect the change in German policy on videogames' references to Nazism will have on future titles focusing on World War II. It will not remove the awkwardness of explaining (or failing to explain) the racial reasoning behind Nazi aggression. Just as it is logically impossible to model the geographical ignorance of explorers on a map of the actual world, it may be ethically impossible to have gamers play Nazi Germany and simultaneously acknowledge the central role of genocidal racism in its actions.

The shortcomings of historical videogames, however, should not cause us to dismiss the whole genre as a medium for presenting the past. The immersion and experimentation possible in videogames make them a powerful tool for generating initial interest and subsequent deep appreciation of the past. The medium's treatment of history continues to evolve generally toward greater levels of sophistication. As long as designers and players approach games with critical eyes, they can learn a great deal while having a lot of fun.

Works cited

Anno 1404, Blue Byte, 2009.
Assassin's Creed, Ubisoft Montreal, 2007.
Assassin's Creed (game series), Ubisoft, 2007–18.
Assassin's Creed: Odyssey, Ubisoft Quebec, 2018.
Playing History 2 – Slave Trade, Serious Games Interactive, 2013.
Sid Meier's Civilization (series), Firaxis, 1991–2018.
Sid Meier's Civilization IV, Firaxis, 2004.
Sid Meier's Civilization IV: Colonization, Firaxis, 2008.
Sid Meier's Civilization V, Firaxis, 2010.
Sid Meier's Civilization VI, Firaxis, 2016.

INDEX

Page numbers in *italics* refer to figures, page numbers in **bold** refer to tables.

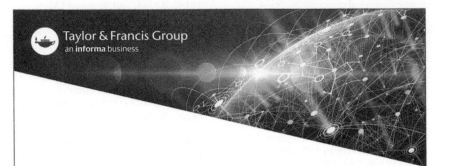

Printed and bound by CPI Group (UK) Ltd, Croydon, CR0 4YY

18/10/2024

01776222-0001